EMPLOYMENT LAW PRACTICE SERIES

General Editor: PROFESSOR JOHN McMULLEN
Partner and Head of Employment Law, Watson Burton LLP
Professor of Labour Law, University of Leeds

EMPLOYMENT ASPECTS OF BUSINESS REORGANISATIONS

EMPLOYMENT LAW PRACTICE SERIES

General Editor: Professor John McMullen
Partner and Head of Employment Law, Watson Burton LLP
Professor of Labour Law, University of Leeds

The series aims to publish books that examine important aspects of UK and
EC employment law in an analytical manner yet with practical application.
They are intended to be of use to both practioners and academics alike.

Employment Aspects of Business Reorganisations

OLIVER HYAMS

OXFORD
UNIVERSITY PRESS

OXFORD
UNIVERSITY PRESS

Great Clarendon Street, Oxford OX2 6DP

Oxford University Press is a department of the University of Oxford.
It furthers the University's objective of excellence in research, scholarship,
and education by publishing worldwide in

Oxford New York

Auckland Cape Town Dar es Salaam Hong Kong Karachi
Kuala Lumpur Madrid Melbourne Mexico City Nairobi
New Delhi Shanghai Taipei Toronto

With offices in

Argentina Austria Brazil Chile Czech Republic France Greece
Guatemala Hungary Italy Japan Poland Portugal Singapore
South Korea Switzerland Thailand Turkey Ukraine Vietnam

Oxford is a registered trade mark of Oxford University Press
in the UK and in certain other countries

Published in the United States
by Oxford University Press Inc., New York

© Oliver Hyams 2006

The moral rights of the author have been asserted
Database right Oxford University Press (maker)

Crown copyright material is reproduced under Class Licence
Number C01P0000148 with the permission of OPSI
and the Queen's Printer for Scotland

First published 2006

British Library Cataloguing in Publication Data

Data available

Library of Congress Cataloging in Publication Data

Hyams, Oliver.
Employment aspects of business reorganisations / Oliver Hyams.
p. cm.
Includes bibliographical references and index.
ISBN–13: 978–0–19–927119–1 (alk. paper)   1. Consolidation and merger of corporations—
Law and legislation—England.   2. Great Britain. Transfer of Undertakings (Protection of Employment) Regulations.
3. Corporate reorganizations—Law and legislation—England.   4. Labor laws and legislation—England.   I. Title.
KD2127.H93 2006
346.42′06626—dc22   2006029534

Typeset by RefineCatch Limited, Bungay, Suffolk
Printed in Great Britain
on acid-free paper by
Biddles Ltd, King's Lynn

ISBN 0–19–927119–4   978–0–19–927119–1

1 3 5 7 9 10 8 6 4 2

GENERAL EDITOR'S PREFACE

The restructuring of business enterprises on a national and global level is a subject of great immediacy for employment lawyers. Changes in the structure of businesses come about through a variety of causes, ranging from the contraction and disappearance of existing economic activities (and therefore jobs), the development of new kinds of economic activity through technological innovation, the opening up of new markets, and the transition to a service-led economy. The trend towards outsourcing (and, globally, offshoring) is also a phenomenon of recent times.

All of these emerging influences subject the enterprise to structural change, and, occasionally, disintegration, and the rights of workers (and their job security) consequent on this change need to be viewed in an holistic way.

Oliver Hyams has therefore brought together in a most timely fashion the various strands of employment law that are engaged upon business reorganisations. These include the new law on TUPE, contained in the Transfer of Undertakings (Protection of Employment) Regulations 2006, redundancy payments law, unfair dismissal law (including the potentially fair 'some other substantial reason for dismissal' relied upon by employers in reorganisational dismissal cases), collective information and consultation on multiple redundancies and TUPE, and the position of the employee under the individual employment relation.

Fittingly, too, the work includes coverage of the Information and Consultation of Employees Regulations 2004, especially apposite at a time when the European Commission has called for greater involvement of social partners in decisions which may lead to the restructuring of businesses (see Communication from the Commission: Restructuring and Employment: *Anticipating and Accompanying Restructuring in Order to Develop Employment: the Role of the European Union* (Brussels, 31.03.2005 COM (2005) 120 final)).

I commend this book as a single authoritative guide to the labour and employment aspects of business reorganisations.

Professor John McMullen
Leeds
July 2006

v

PREFACE

need to *tala*
in
D.sso

Key

A number of legal issues may arise in a reorganisation. A reorganisation may involve a transfer under the Transfer of Undertakings (Protection of Employment) Regulations (ie TUPE). In most reorganisations, dismissals for redundancy are likely. Alternatively, an employer may wish to change employees' terms and conditions of employment. Employees' statutory rights may be infringed in a number of ways. Employers may be under an obligation to consult representatives of the workforce, or individual employees. In addition, the common law may affect a reorganisation in a surprisingly large number of ways.

Some areas of the law which are covered in this book are likely to be unfamiliar to most readers. A good example is the part of Chapter 10 which concerns the Transnational Information and Consultation of Employees Regulations 1999. Other areas of the law are, however, likely to be familiar to most readers.

In writing the book I have attempted to state the law as succinctly but as accurately as possible. Some of the reported case law concerns what appeared to me, after a careful analysis, to be no more than interesting examples of the application of previously determined principles. Accordingly, I have not referred to all of the existing case law, although I have stated all of the principles which appear to me to be capable of being derived from the decided cases. However, in two places in particular I have described in detail some of the reported cases in order to illustrate the manner in which a somewhat nebulous test has in practice been applied. Those two tests are (1) whether there will be, or has been, a TUPE transfer; and (2) whether or not an employee has been assigned to an undertaking or part of an undertaking which has been transferred under TUPE.

I am grateful to Elisabeth Griffiths of Northumbria University, who read and commented on about a third of the text in draft form, and to Sophie Belgrove, of Devereux Chambers, who read and commented on several draft chapters. Responsibility for any errors is, naturally, mine alone.

I am grateful also to the staff of Oxford University Press for their unfailing courtesy and helpfulness, and for their forbearance. Luckily, we agreed that the book could not sensibly be finished until the new TUPE Regulations were finally published.

My wife Gill and daughters Sarah and Katy have had to be particularly forbearing, and I am grateful to them for their willingness to forgive my long absences from the family milieu.

I have attempted to state the law as it stood on 11 May 2006, although subsequent developments up to mid-August 2006 have been taken into account when making changes to the proofs of the book.

Oliver Hyams
Devereux Chambers
15 August 2006

CONTENTS—SUMMARY

CONTENTS

TABLE OF CASES

TABLE OF STATUTES AND
STATUTORY INSTRUMENTS

LIST OF ABBREVIATIONS

ARD	Acquired Rights Directive; originally 77/187/EEC, now 2001/23/EC, neither of which are entitled 'Acquired Rights Directive', but which have come to be known as such
CA	Court of Appeal
EA 2002	Employment Act 2002
EAT	Employment Appeal Tribunal
ECJ	European Court of Justice
ERA 1996	Employment Rights Act 1996
EWC	European Works Council
Harvey	*Harvey on Industrial Relations and Employment Law*, Butterworths, looseleaf; all references are to the text as published in the June 2006 CD
he	he or she
him	him or her
HL	House of Lords
ICE Regulations	Information and Consultation of Employees Regulations 2004, SI 2004/3426
McMullen	J McMullen, *Business Transfers and Employee Rights*, Butterworths, looseleaf, first published in 1998
SOSR	some other substantial reason within the meaning of section 98(1) of the ERA 1996
TICE Regulations	Transnational Information and Consultation of Employees Regulations 1999, SI 1999/3323
TULRA	Trade Union and Labour Relations (Consolidation) Act 1992
TUPE	(unless otherwise stated) the Transfer of Undertakings (Protection of Employment) Regulations 2006, SI 2006/246
TUPE 1981	the Transfer of Undertakings (Protection of Employment) Regulations 1981, SI 1981/1794
TUPE transfer	a transfer of an undertaking, business, or part of an undertaking or

business (which may also be a service provision change within the meaning of regulation 3 of TUPE)

TUPE transferee   an employer to whom there is or may be a transfer of an undertaking, business, or part of an undertaking or business under TUPE

TUPE transferor   an employer from whom there is or may be a transfer of an undertaking, business, or part of an undertaking or business under TUPE

1

INTRODUCTION AND OVERVIEW

A. Introduction

This book is concerned with the kind of issues which are likely to arise where **1.01** there is a reorganisation of an employer's business. This may occur where the employees' employer does not change, and that is the situation which is most likely to come to mind when the word 'reorganisation' is used. Yet, a business may be owned by a company which is in a group of companies, and the parent company may carry out a reorganisation by transferring some or all of the subsidiary's employees to another company within the group. That could clearly be regarded as a business reorganisation. However, it will constitute the transfer of a business or part of a business from one employer to another.[1]

In addition, it is not stretching the concept of a reorganisation to include **1.02** within its scope the situation where an employer 'outsources' (to use the current term) one or more functions. The employer is then still utilising services of the sort which were formerly provided in-house by its own employees, but is now buying those services from a third party.

---

[1] *Allen and others v Amalgamated Construction Co Ltd* C–234/98; [2000] IRLR 119, ECJ.

1

B. What Is Meant by the Word 'Business'?

1.03 It is instructive to consider what is meant by the word 'business' in this context. A business will be owned by either a person (whether legal or natural) or a group of persons (whether legal or natural). Hence the possibility, to which further reference is made below, of the transfer of a business. Groups of persons may be acting together on a number of different bases. If they are all formally bound to each other only by a contract between them, then they will be either an unincorporated association or a partnership within the meaning of the Partnership Act 1890.[2] An English or Welsh partnership is not a legal person,[3] and is in reality no more than a vehicle by means of which the partners can sue and be sued. In contrast, a Scottish partnership is a legal person.[4] The members of an unincorporated association who are jointly responsible are usually sued jointly, although a representative action is possible in some circumstances.[5] A company limited by shares or guarantee within the meaning of the Companies Acts will have legal personality. An unincorporated association may have exclusively charitable purposes, in which case the property held by the association for those purposes will be held under charitable trusts, the trustees of which will usually be several members of the association. A business may also be owned by a statutory corporation, such as a higher education corporation established under section 121 or 122 of the Education Reform Act 1988.

C. What Is Meant by 'Business Reorganisation'?

1.04 A business reorganisation may take place as a result of a reorganisation of the internal structure of a business. This is the classic example of what is normally thought of as a business reorganisation. A business reorganisation may take place as a result of a decision to cease to provide a particular service (such as catering or cleaning) in-house, by persons employed by the owner(s) of the (main) business under a contract of employment, and to begin buying the service from an external provider. This is a situation which it is now possible to say with some confidence will usually give rise to a transfer within the meaning of the Transfer of Undertakings (Protection of Employment) (TUPE) Regulations 2006.[6] If a limited company transfers one part of its organisation to another person (whether natural or legal) and that part includes, in addition to employees, property and the benefit of contracts entered into with the transferring company,

---

[2] See Partnership Act 1890, ss 1 and 2.   [3] ibid, s 4.   [4] ibid.
[5] See J Warburton, *Unincorporated Associations*, 2nd edn, 89–91.
[6] SI 2006/246. See Ch 2 below.

then there will usually be a transfer within the meaning of TUPE, or what is called below throughout this book, 'a TUPE transfer'. If, however, the control of a company limited by shares changes through the majority of the shares being acquired by a new owner, then there will be no TUPE transfer.[7]

D. The New TUPE Regulations

The publication of this book was delayed until the enactment of the replacement **1.05** of the Transfer of Undertakings (Protection of Employment) Regulations 1981[8] by the Transfer of Undertakings (Protection of Employment) Regulations 2006.[9] The original version of those regulations eventually came to be known as 'TUPE', and that usage is adopted below in relation to the 2006 version of the regulations, unless it is helpful, for the sake of clarity, to refer to the new regulations as the TUPE Regulations 2006. If the original version is referred to below, where it is helpful to do so, it is referred to as 'TUPE 1981'. The TUPE Regulations 2006 came into force on 6 April 2006,[10] and apply to transfers taking place on or after 6 April 2006.[11]

E. Legal Issues Arising Where There Is a Business Reorganisation

A number of employment law issues can arise in the situations described in **1.06** paragraph 1.01 above. They include the following issues arising from statutory provisions:

- In what circumstances can a business reorganisation be affected by TUPE?
- What are the effects of TUPE on individuals?
- What are the effects of TUPE on collective agreements and trade union rights?
- What consultation obligations arise where TUPE applies?
- Are any employees technically redundant within the meaning of section 139 of the Employment Rights Act 1996 ('ERA 1996')?
- If so, is there a need to select one or more employees from a pool?
- If so, what fetters (if any) are there on the selection of the pool?
- Can employees be required to apply for new jobs in the reorganised business?
- What constitutes suitable alternative employment?
- When can an employee refuse such alternative employment and remain entitled to a redundancy payment?

---

[7] See para 2.01 below.   [8] SI 1981/1794, as amended.   [9] SI 2006/246.
[10] See reg 1(2).   [11] See reg 21.

- What sort of trial period is an employee entitled to, and in what circumstances?
- Can an employee who takes up such suitable alternative employment nevertheless claim unfair dismissal?
- What are the remedies in principle available to an employee who is dismissed for redundancy?
- What sort of consultation (if any) is required in relation to proposed redundancies?
- What statutory provisions apply if there is a reorganisation where there is no TUPE transfer, but some employees are not redundant (ie, how can an employer rely on 'some other substantial reason' within the meaning of section 98(1)(b) of the ERA 1996)?
- To what extent does the law relating to discrimination affect a business reorganisation?

1.07 In addition, employees may have rights arising from the common law, and those need to be considered separately, albeit in the light of the potentially limiting effect of the statutory framework on common law rights as a result of the decisions of the House of Lords in *Johnson v Unisys Ltd*[12] and *Eastwood v Magnox Electric plc.*[13]

1.08 Further, individuals have rights arising under (1) the law of trusts; and (2) statutory provisions in relation to pensions. The importance of a pension to a retired employee is of course great, and a pension represents at least in part deferred pay. Business reorganisations can affect pension rights, and a short chapter of this book is devoted to legal issues arising in relation to pensions from reorganisations. That too is an area which has seen considerable change over recent years, the most recent change at the time of writing being the enactment of the Transfer of Employment (Pension Protection) Regulations 2005.[14]

1.09 Consideration is given in the following chapters to all of the issues mentioned above, except for the impact of the law of discrimination, which is outside the scope of this book.

1.10 Necessarily, what is said in this book consists of what could sensibly be described as a 'snapshot' of the law.

---

[12] [2001] UKHL 13; [2003] 1 AC 518.   [13] [2004] UKHL 35; [2005] 1 AC 503.
[14] SI 2005/649.

F. The Purpose of This Book

The aim of this book is to provide a practical guide to a number of rather **1.11** technical areas of employment law. Some parts of the law which are described in the following chapters will be familiar to most readers. However, others, including the law relating to the conditions for entitlement to a redundancy payment where there are lay-offs or there is short-time working, will rarely be familiar. The intended purpose of this book is to provide an overview of the issues which arise where a business is reorganised, as well as a succinct but reasonably comprehensive statement of the law in all relevant areas.

2

WHEN IS THERE A TUPE TRANSFER?

A. Introduction and Overview

The subject matter of this chapter is a question which has given rise to much **2.01** litigation and which is likely, even with the coming into force of the helpfully expanded definition in the TUPE Regulations 2006[1], to continue to be difficult to answer. That question is 'When is there a TUPE transfer?' It should first be said that a share sale does not give rise to a TUPE transfer. This is clear as a matter of principle, given the language of TUPE, but it was confirmed by the EAT in *Brookes v Borough Care Services Ltd*[2] that the principle applies even where the change in control of the business by share sale rather than the transfer

---

[1] SI 2006/246.   [2] [1998] ICR 1198.

of the ownership of the business occurs as a result of a desire to avoid the application of TUPE.

2.02   The TUPE Regulations 2006 effect some helpful changes to the law as it stood before 6 April 2006, under TUPE 1981. However, the TUPE Regulations 2006 will continue to need to be interpreted in the light of the ECJ's case law and UK case law concerning the question whether there has been a TUPE transfer. Accordingly, the definition in the TUPE Regulations 2006 is set out and analysed first below. In the course of the analysis, reference is made to some of the reported cases. An attempt is then made to state some further general principles to be derived from the case law, both national and European. Many of the reported cases can best be understood as concerning the application of those principles to particular facts, rather than as involving the development of those principles, and accordingly reference is made in that section of the chapter only to those cases which appear to be the best authority for the propositions stated.

2.03   Much can nevertheless be gained by considering the manner in which the principles have been applied in practice, and therefore the final section of this chapter concerns a number of cases which are illustrative of the principles. Over the years there has been a steady stream of new reported cases involving the application of the various statements of principle which have been made in the ECJ and domestic courts (but, notably, never the House of Lords[3]) concerning the circumstances in which the Acquired Rights Directive (originally 77/187/EEC, now 2001/23/EC) ('ARD') applies. This is in part because the trend of the decisions has changed significantly over time. It is also because TUPE 1981 in their original form applied to the transfer of an undertaking or part of an undertaking only if it was in the nature of a commercial venture, so that some of the early cases turned exclusively on that question.[4] Given those factors, the focus of the final section of this chapter is the current trend of the reported cases.

---

[3] The House gave permission to appeal against the decision of the Court of Appeal in *RCO Support Services Ltd v UNISON* [2002] EWCA Civ 464, [2002] ICR 751 (see [2003] ICR 89), but the case was settled and the appeal did not proceed.

[4] See eg *Woodcock v Committee for the Time Being of the Friends School, Wigton* [1987] IRLR 98, CA, and *Expro Services Ltd v Smith* [1991] ICR 577, EAT. The correctness of the decisions in those cases was in fact doubted by the Court of Appeal in *Alderson v Secretary of State for Trade and Industry* [2003] EWCA Civ 1767, [2004] ICR 512, 521, para 29.

B. The Definition of a TUPE Transfer

The main definition

A transfer within the meaning of TUPE is defined by regulation 3(1). Regula- **2.04**
tion 3(1)(a) restates the definition of a transfer in TUPE 1981. The new
definition reflects the content of the relevant provisions of the current ARD,
2001/23/EC, namely Articles 1(a) and (b). Those reflect the ECJ case law
concerning the issue. Regulation 3(1)(a) provides simply that the TUPE
Regulations 2006 apply to 'a transfer of an undertaking, business or part of an
undertaking or business situated immediately before the transfer in the United
Kingdom to another employer where there is a transfer of an economic entity
which retains its identity'.

Regulation 3(2) defines 'economic entity' for the purposes of TUPE. It means **2.05**
'an organised grouping of resources which has the objective of pursuing an
economic activity, whether or not that activity is central or ancillary'. This is
consistent with the statement of the ECJ in *Mayeur v Association Promotion de
l'Information Messine*[5] that:

> the concept of an undertaking, within the meaning of Article 1(1) of Directive
> 77/187, covers any stable economic entity, that is to say, an organised grouping of
> persons and assets facilitating the exercise of an economic activity which pursues
> a specific objective . . . Such a concept is independent of the legal status of that
> entity and the manner in which it is financed.

Nevertheless, a public undertaking, or a private undertaking which is not **2.06**
'operating for gain', may be an economic entity for the purposes of TUPE.[6]
The key is that it is 'engaged in economic activities'.[7] However, an 'administrative reorganisation of public administrative authorities or the transfer of
administrative functions between public administrative authorities is not a relevant transfer'.[8] This gives effect to the decision of the ECJ in *Henke v Gemeide
Schierke*.[9]

Service provision change

Regulation 3(1)(b) contains a new definition, which reflects the developments **2.07**
which have occurred in relation to the application of the ARD in a series of
decisions of the ECJ, to which reference is made below. Regulation 3(1)(b)
provides:

> These regulations apply to—

---

[5] C–175/99, [2000] IRLR 783, para 32.   [6] Regulation 3(4)(a).
[7] ibid.   [8] Regulation 3(5).   [9] C–298/94; [1996] ECR I–4989; [1997] ICR 746.

. . .

(b) a service provision change, that is a situation in which—

  (i) activities cease to be carried out by a person ('a client') on his own behalf and are carried out instead by another person on the client's behalf ('a contractor'),[10]

  (ii) activities cease to be carried out by a contractor on a client's behalf (whether or not those activities had previously been carried out by the client on his own behalf) and are carried out instead by another person ('a subsequent contractor') on the client's behalf, or

  (iii) activities cease to be carried out by a contractor or a subsequent contractor on a client's behalf (whether or not those activities had previously been carried out by the client on his own behalf) and are carried out instead by the client on his own behalf

and in which the conditions set out in paragraph (3) are satisfied.

2.08 Regulation 3(3) provides:

The conditions referred to in paragraph (1)(b) are that:

(a) immediately before the service provision change—

  (i) there is an organised grouping of employees[11] situated in Great Britain which has as its principal purpose the carrying out of the activities concerned on behalf of the client;

  (ii) the client intends that the activities will, following the service provision change, be carried out by the transferee other than in connection with a single specific event or task of short-term duration; and

(b) the activities concerned do not consist wholly or mainly of the supply of goods for the client's use.

2.09 It is of note that regulation 3(3) refers to 'the activities', although regulation 3(1)(b) refers to 'activities'. Accordingly, if there is a change in the activities carried out after a service provision change, then the relevant case law concerning the retention of the entity's identity will continue to be relevant.[12]

Place of work and governing law

2.10 It is irrelevant that the transfer of an undertaking, business, or part of an undertaking or business, or (as the case may be) the service provision change, is governed or effected by the law of a country or territory outside the United Kingdom ('UK').[13] It is also irrelevant that the employment of persons employed in the undertaking, business, or part transferred, or, in the case of a service provision change, persons employed in the organised grouping of employees, is governed by the law of any country or territory outside the

---

[10] The word 'contractor' as used in reg 3 of TUPE includes a subcontractor: see reg 2(1).
[11] There need be only one employee for there to be an organised grouping: see reg 2(1).
[12] See in particular paras 2.13 and 2.15 onwards below.   [13] Regulation 3(4)(b)(i).

UK.[14] In addition, there may be a transfer within the meaning of TUPE where persons employed in the undertaking, business, or part transferred (which may also be a service provision change), ordinarily work outside the UK.[15]

Is there a transfer where there is a series of transactions?

It is provided by regulation 3(6)(a) that a TUPE transfer may be effected by a series of two or more transactions. This must now be understood in the light of the ECJ's ruling in *Celtec Ltd v Astley*,[16] which is that there is a specific date when the transfer occurs: thus it cannot take place over a period, such as over a period of several months. Rather, it takes place when 'responsibility as employer for carrying on the business of the unit in question moves from the transferor to the transferee'.[17] The ruling is attractive theoretically, but it is likely to cause difficulties in practice where it is impossible to say precisely when in practical terms a transfer occurred. The facts of the case were unusual, however, and it may be that the ruling could be confined to situations in which there are secondees (as there were in *Celtec*). Alternatively, in similar circumstances, an employment tribunal could lawfully conclude that all seconded employees are deemed to have transferred under TUPE on a particular date.[18] **2.11**

The relevance of the transfer or otherwise of property

It is specifically provided by regulation 3(6) that a TUPE transfer 'may take place whether or not any property is transferred to the transferee by the transferor'. This does not mean that the absence of a transfer of property will be irrelevant in all cases.[19] **2.12**

The decision of the ECJ in *Güney-Görres v Securicor Aviation*[20] is consistent with regulation 3(6). In that case, the ECJ held that there may be a transfer of assets for the purpose of determining whether the ARD applies where the assets are owned by the buyer of a service and the assets are used first by one contractor and then by another who takes the first contractor's place. The specific holding of the ECJ was this: **2.13**

> the fact that the tangible assets are taken over by the new contractor without those assets having been transferred to him for independent commercial use does

---

[14] Regulation 3(4)(b)(ii).   [15] Regulation 3(4)(c).
[16] Case C–478/03; [2005] ICR 1409.   [17] ibid, at 1433–4, para 36.
[18] It is of interest that that is precisely what the House of Lords ruled—as far as the date of the deemed transfer was concerned (1990) contrary to the employees' initial contentions (they had contended that the transfer occurred in 1993)—in *Celtec* once the ECJ had given its ruling: see [2006] UKHL 29; [2006] ICR 992.
[19] See for example *Balfour Beatty Power Networks Ltd v Wilcox* [2006] IRLR 258, concerning the facts of which see para 2.87 onwards below.
[20] Cases C–232/04 and C–233/04; [2006] IRLR 305.

not preclude there being either a transfer of assets, or a transfer of an undertaking or business within the meaning of Directive 2001/23.[21]

Application to the transfer of ownership of a ship

2.14 The situation of the transfer of a ship was specifically excluded from the scope of TUPE 1981, by regulation 2(2) of those regulations. That provision has not been repeated in the TUPE Regulations 2006. Instead, regulation 3(7) of the latter provides:

> Where, in consequence (whether directly or indirectly) of the transfer of an undertaking, business or part of an undertaking or business which was situated immediately before the transfer in the United Kingdom, a ship within the meaning of the Merchant Shipping Act 1995 registered in the United Kingdom ceases to be so registered, these Regulations shall not affect the right conferred by section 29 of that Act (right of seamen to be discharged when ship ceases to be registered in the United Kingdom) on a seaman employed in the ship.

C. The Case Law—Some General Principles

The application of TUPE is automatic

2.15 Despite the importance of taking a purposive approach in deciding whether TUPE applied to a particular situation (the importance of which is clear from a number of cases, such as *Fairhurst Ward Abbotts Ltd v Botes Building Ltd*[22]), the application of TUPE is automatic, and the parties cannot by agreement make it apply where it does not in fact do so.[23] In addition, it is clear from the House of Lords' decision in *Secretary of State for Employment v Globe Elastic Thread Co Ltd*[24] that statutory employment rights cannot be acquired as a result of an employer's agreement that they should be.

The concept of a transfer may be regarded as a 'judicial fiction'

2.16 One comment made by a Court of Appeal judge which was informative and may be thought to be helpful is contained in the following passage from the judgment of May LJ in *ADI (UK) Ltd v Willer*:[25]

> Notwithstanding the retention in the amended article 1 of the 1977 Directive of the requirement for the transfer to result from 'a legal transfer or merger',

---

[21] *Güney-Görres v Securicor Aviation*, Cases C–232/04 and C–233/04; [2006] IRLR 305, 314, para 41. See too para 42.

[22] [2004] ICR 919, CA, concerning which see further para 2.31 onwards below.

[23] cf *Dabell v Vale Industrial Services (Nottingham) Ltd* [1988] IRLR 439, and see *Mackie v Aberdeen City Council* [2006] CSIH 36, the facts of which are described in para 2.93 onwards below.

[24] [1980] AC 506; [1979] ICR 706. See further para 4.29, n 64 below concerning the case.

[25] [2001] EWCA Civ 971; [2001] IRLR 542, para 9. May LJ repeated the passage in para 50 of his judgment in *Fairhurst Ward Abbotts Ltd v Botes Building Ltd* [2004] EWCA Civ 83; [2004] ICR 919. The facts of *ADI v Willer* are described in para 2.68 onwards below.

that requirement has been emasculated out of existence by purposive judicial interpretation. The literal words, and indeed the whole structure, of the Directive appear to require some legal relationship effecting a transfer between the transferor employer and the transferee employer, such as, for instance, might take place upon the assignment of an undertaking or the sale of a business. But the cases have eliminated the need to look for such an orthodox legal relationship. Speaking generally, the question of transfer may arise where an undertaking or business carried out by one or more employees ceases to be carried out by one employer and starts to be carried out by another employer. If the undertaking or business is 'an economic entity which retains its identity, meaning an organised grouping of resources which has the objective of pursuing an economic activity', there is or may be a transfer within the meaning of the Directive. Thus the concept of transfer is now a judicially constructed fiction derived from the purpose of the Directive and the Regulations to safeguard the rights of employees.

Question of fact, not law

It is essential to bear in mind that the question whether there has been a TUPE transfer is ultimately a question of fact for the court or tribunal to which a relevant claim is made. Thus, as long as the court or tribunal (1) directs itself properly as to the law by asking itself the right questions and neither takes into account an irrelevant factor nor fails to take into account a relevant factor; and (2) does not come to a perverse conclusion on the facts, an appellate court should decline to overturn its decision.[26] Another possible ground of appeal, but which is unlikely to be applicable in this context, is that there was no evidence for the conclusion of the first instance court or tribunal.[27] However, as the EAT commented in *Argyll Training Ltd v Sinclair*:[28] **2.17**

> As for whether there was anything here that could properly have been recognised by the tribunal as the national fact-finding body as an undertaking, a stable economic entity, the breadth of approach sanctioned by the authorities in the ECJ makes it difficult to identify error of law in particular cases.

Accordingly, it is necessary here to attempt to identify the test for determining whether there has been a TUPE transfer, and for it to be understood that many of the reported cases concerning the question whether there was in fact a TUPE transfer cannot be regarded as determinative. Many should be regarded as merely indicative of what an employment tribunal could decide. A good illustration of this proposition is the decision of the EAT in *Dudley Bower Building Services Ltd v Lowe*,[29] where the EAT declined to overturn an employment **2.18**

---

[26] cf *Lewis v Motorworld Garages Ltd* [1986] ICR 157, at 171 per Glidewell LJ, and *Thompson v SCS Consulting Ltd* [2001] IRLR 801, para 37(5), EAT.
[27] *Piggott Brothers Ltd v Jackson* [1992] ICR 85, 96, CA.
[28] [2000] IRLR 630, para 10. See paras 2.64–2.65 below for the facts of the case.
[29] [2003] ICR 843.

tribunal's decision that the provision of minor electrical work pursuant to a contract under which eight other packages of work were also provided gave rise to a TUPE transfer despite the fact that only one employee carried out that minor electrical work. Even though the employee was engaged full-time on the work, it can be seen that the approach may be seen as being contrary to the approach of the ECJ in *Süzen*, set out below,[30] although the situation may now fall within regulation 3(1)(b) of TUPE.[31]

2.19   Given that the question of whether there has been a TUPE transfer is very much a question of fact, it will be all the more important that the employment tribunal sets out its reasoning appropriately. The proper approach in this regard was emphasised by the EAT in *Balfour Beatty Power Networks Ltd v Wilcox*,[32] in the following manner:

> in any case in which a transfer of undertaking comes to be reviewed by a tribunal, we would expect that Tribunal to indicate the matters which it selects as being of particular relevance in reaching that conclusion and to indicate also those matters which might tell substantially against it if only to indicate why it is the tribunal has rejected them as important factors.

2.20   It is of interest that in that case the EAT also said this:[33]

> It seems to us that what matters in determining whether there is an undertaking is whether the test in the Directive can be said to be met or not. That is essentially a question of practicality. It is not to be defined by legal constructs other than those implicit in the Directive itself.

Can a single employee's work be an 'undertaking'?

2.21   It is theoretically possible for TUPE to apply where the work of a single employee is the subject of a contracting-out, or 'outsourcing' exercise. The ECJ so held in *Schmidt v Spar- und Leihkasse*,[34] and that ruling was applied by the Court of Appeal in *Dines v Initial Healthcare Services*.[35] The ECJ subsequently appeared to resile from that (perhaps extreme) position when it decided *Süzen v Zehnacker*.[36] In the latter case, the ECJ indicated that at least in some circumstances it may be necessary, to bring about a transfer within the meaning of the ARD, for there to be the transfer not only of the employment of one or more employees but also the transfer of significant tangible or intangible assets. It should be borne in mind that the following extracts from the judgment of the ECJ are in some respects superseded by the enact-

---

[30] Paragraphs 2.21 and 2.22.
[31] See paras 2.07 and 2.08 above.   [32] [2006] IRLR 258, para 17.
[33] ibid, para 34. See further para 2.87 onwards below for the facts of the case.
[34] C–392/92; [1994] ECR I–1311; [1995] ICR 237.   [35] [1995] ICR 11.
[36] C–13/95; [1997] ECR I–1259; [1997] ICR 662.

14

ment of regulation 3(1)(b) of the TUPE Regulations 2006, especially since regulation 2(1) provides that 'references to "organised grouping of employees" shall include a single employee'. However, they may remain relevant where it is claimed that only a very small number of employees, or one employee, has transferred under TUPE. The ECJ referred to the test which it had previously stated to be applicable, in particular in *Spijkers*,[37] namely:[38]

> In order to determine whether the conditions for the transfer of an entity are met, it is necessary to consider all the facts characterising the transaction in question, including in particular the type of undertaking or business; whether or not its tangible assets, such as buildings and movable property, are transferred; the value of its intangible assets at the time of the transfer; whether or not the majority of its employees are taken over by the new employer; whether or not its customers are transferred; the degree of similarity between the activities carried on before and after the transfer, and the period, if any, for which those activities were suspended. However, all those circumstances are merely single factors in the overall assessment which must be made and cannot therefore be considered in isolation.

The ECJ also said this in *Süzen*:   **2.22**

> 15. As observed by most of the parties who commented on this point, the mere fact that the service provided by the old and the new awardees of a contract is similar does not therefore support the conclusion that an economic entity has been transferred. An entity cannot be reduced to the activity entrusted to it. Its identity also emerges from other factors, such as its workforce; its management staff; the way in which its work is organised; its operating methods, or indeed, where appropriate, the operational resources available to it.
> 16. The mere loss of a service contract to a competitor cannot therefore by itself indicate the existence of a transfer within the meaning of Directive (77/187/E.E.C.). In those circumstances, the service undertaking previously entrusted with the contract does not, on losing a customer, thereby cease fully to exist, and a business or part of a business belonging to it cannot be considered to have been transferred to the new awardee of the contract.

A reasonably comprehensive statement of the applicable test

The most helpful and comprehensive statement of the proper test to apply   **2.23** (or, perhaps, it should be said, the proper series of tests, some of which appear to conflict with others) is to be found in the judgment of the EAT given by Lindsay J in *Cheesman v R Brewer Contracts Ltd*.[39] The passage bears repeating

---

[37] [1986] ECR 1119, 1128–1129, para 13.
[38] See para 14 of *Süzen*, at 670–671. See para 2.48 below for the facts of the case.
[39] [2001] IRLR 144, paras 9–12.

in full,[40] since it is such a helpful analysis and summary and since paraphrasing it would not be helpful. However, what has been said in several subsequent cases can be seen to have added materially to the guidance which it contains. Further, given the enactment of regulation 3(1)(b) of TUPE,[41] the passage may well come to be regarded as superseded in relation at least to situations in which there is a change in the provider of a service. The passage is as follows:

9

It is, we think, possible to discover the present state of the law for the purposes of this appeal, without any need to delve to any great depth into earlier cases, by looking only at four recent cases, all decided after the employment tribunal promulgated its decision in the case at hand. We shall need to make some passing references to some earlier cases than these four but, in large part, in so far as the earlier cases are still relevant, their conclusions are repeated in the four cases which we shall mention. The four cases are *Francisco Hernández Vidal SA v Gomez Pérez and associated cases* [1999] IRLR 132 ECJ decided on 10 December 1998; *Sánchez Hidalgo and others v Aser and one associated case* [1999] IRLR 136 ECJ, also decided on 10 December 1998 and by the same judges who decided *Vidal* [1999] IRLR 132; *ECM (Vehicle Delivery Service) Ltd v Cox* [1999] IRLR 559 CA, decided on 22 July 1999 and to which we have already referred; and *Allen and others v Amalgamated Construction Co Ltd* [2000] IRLR 119 ECJ decided on 2 December 1999.[42]

10

From those four cases we distil the following. We shall attempt, although it is not always a clear distinction, to divide considerations between those going to whether there is an undertaking and those, if there is an undertaking, going to whether it has been transferred. The paragraph numbers we give are references to the numbering in the IRLR reports of the ECJ's judgments. Thus:

(i) As to whether there is an undertaking, there needs to be found a stable economic entity whose activity is not limited to performing one specific works contract, an organised grouping of persons and of assets enabling (or facilitating) the exercise of an economic activity which pursues a specific objective—*Sánchez Hidalgo* [1999] IRLR 136 paragraph 25; *Allen* [2000] IRLR 119 paragraph 24 and *Vidal* [1999] IRLR 132 paragraph 6 (which, confusingly, places the reference to 'an economic activity' a little differently). It has been held that the reference to 'one specific

---

[40] Paragraph 11 of it at least was implicitly commended by the EAT in *Balfour Beatty Power Networks Ltd v Wilcox* [2006] IRLR 258, where, in para 18, the EAT said that the employment tribunal in that case had 'entirely appropriately addressed its task as advised by this tribunal under the presidency of Lindsay J in *Cheesman v Brewer Contracts Ltd*' and referred to paragraph 11 as having been applicable.

[41] See para 2.07 above.

[42] The ECJ's decision in *Allen* put it beyond doubt that a transfer of an economic entity from one subsidiary company to another subsidiary company in the same group will give rise to a TUPE transfer.

works contract' is to be restricted to a contract for building works—see *Argyll Training* [2000] IRLR 630, infra, EAT at paragraphs 14–19.

(ii) In order to be such an undertaking it must be sufficiently structured and autonomous but will not necessarily have significant assets, tangible or intangible—*Vidal* [1999] IRLR 132 paragraph 27; *Sánchez Hidalgo* [1999] IRLR 136 paragraph 26.

(iii) In certain sectors such as cleaning and surveillance the assets are often reduced to their most basic and the activity is essentially based on manpower—*Sánchez Hidalgo* [1999] IRLR 136 paragraph 26.

(iv) An organised grouping of wage-earners who are specifically and permanently assigned to a common task may, in the absence of other factors of production, amount to an economic entity—*Vidal* [1999] IRLR 132 paragraph 27; *Sánchez Hidalgo* [1999] IRLR 136 paragraph 26.

(v) An activity of itself is not an entity; the identity of an entity emerges from other factors such as its workforce, management staff, the way in which its work is organised, its operating methods and, where appropriate, the operational resources available to it—*Vidal* [1999] IRLR 132 paragraph 30; *Sánchez Hidalgo* [1999] IRLR 136 paragraph 30; *Allen* [2000] IRLR 119 paragraph 27.

11

As for whether there has been a transfer:

(i) As to whether there is in any relevant sense a transfer, the decisive criterion for establishing the existence of a transfer is whether the entity in question retains its identity, as indicated, inter alia, by the fact that its operation is actually continued or resumed—*Vidal* [1999] IRLR 132 paragraph 22 and the case there cited; *Spijkers v Gebroeders Benedik Abattoir CV* [1986] ECR 1119 ECJ; *Schmidt v Spar-und Leihkasse* [1994] IRLR 302 ECJ paragraph 17; *Sánchez Hidalgo* [1999] IRLR 136 paragraph 21; *Allen* [2000] IRLR 119 paragraph 23.

(ii) In a labour-intensive sector it is to be recognised that an entity is capable of maintaining its identity after it has been transferred where the new employer does not merely pursue the activity in question but also takes over a major part, in terms of their numbers and skills, of the employees specially assigned by his predecessors to that task. That follows from the fact that in certain labour-intensive sectors a group of workers engaged in the joint activity on a permanent basis may constitute an economic entity—*Sánchez Hidalgo* [1999] IRLR 136 paragraph 32.

(iii) In considering whether the conditions for existence of a transfer are met it is necessary to consider all the factors characterising the transaction in question, but each is a single factor and none is to be considered in isolation—*Vidal* [1999] IRLR 132 paragraph 29; *Sánchez Hidalgo* [1999] IRLR 136 paragraph 29; *Allen* [2000] IRLR 119 paragraph 26. However, whilst no authority so holds, it may, presumably, not be an error of law to consider 'the decisive criterion' in (i) above in isolation; that, surely, is an aspect of its being 'decisive', although, as one sees from the 'inter alia' in (i) above, 'the decisive criterion' is not itself said to depend on a single factor.

(iv) Amongst the matters thus falling for consideration are the type of undertaking, whether or not its tangible assets are transferred, the value of its intangible assets at the time of transfer, whether or not the majority of its employees are taken over by the new company, whether or not its customers are transferred, the degree of similarity between the activities carried on before and after the transfer, and the period, if any, in which they are suspended—*Sánchez Hidalgo* [1999] IRLR 136 paragraph 29; *Allen* [2000] IRLR 119 paragraph 26.

(v) In determining whether or not there has been a transfer, account has to be taken, inter alia, of the type of undertaking or business in issue, and the degree of importance to be attached to the several criteria will necessarily vary according to the activity carried on—*Vidal* [1999] IRLR 132 paragraph 31; *Sánchez Hidalgo* [1999] IRLR 136 paragraph 31; *Allen* [2000] IRLR 119 paragraph 28.

(vi) Where an economic entity is able to function without any significant tangible or intangible assets, the maintenance of its identity following the transaction being examined cannot logically depend on the transfer of such assets—*Vidal* [1999] IRLR 132 paragraph 31; *Sánchez Hidalgo* [1999] IRLR 136 paragraph 31; *Allen* [2000] IRLR 119 paragraph 28.

(vii) Even where assets are owned and are required to run the undertaking, the fact that they do not pass does not preclude a transfer—*Allen* [2000] IRLR 119 paragraph 30.

(viii) Where maintenance work is carried out by a cleaning firm and then next by the owner of the premises concerned, that mere fact does not justify the conclusion that there has been a transfer—*Vidal* [1999] IRLR 132 paragraph 35.

(ix) More broadly, the mere fact that the service provided by the old and new undertaking providing a contracted-out service or the old and new contract-holder are similar does not justify the conclusion that there has been a transfer of an economic entity between predecessor and successor—*Sánchez Hidalgo* [1999] IRLR 136 paragraph 30.

(x) The absence of any contractual link between transferor and transferee may be evidence that there has been no relevant transfer but it is certainly not conclusive as there is no need for any such direct contractual relationship: *Sánchez Hidalgo* [1999] IRLR 136 paragraphs 22 and 23.

(xi) When no employees are transferred, the reasons why that is the case can be relevant as to whether or not there was a transfer—*ECM* [1999] IRLR 559 p. 561.

(xii) The fact that the work is performed continuously with no interruption or change in the manner or performance is a normal feature of transfers of undertakings but there is no particular importance to be attached to a gap between the end of the work by one subcontractor and the start by the successor—*Allen* [2000] IRLR 119 paragraphs 32–33.

12

More generally the cases also show:

(i) The necessary factual appraisal is to be made by the national court—*ECM* [1999] IRLR 559 p. 561, 23; *Allen* [2000] IRLR 119 paragraph 28.

(ii)   The Directive applies where, following the transfer, there is a change in the natural person responsible for the carrying on of the business who, by virtue of that fact, incurs the obligation of an employer vis-à-vis the employees of the undertaking, regardless of whether or not ownership of the undertaking is transferred—*Allen* [2000] IRLR 119 paragraph 16.

(iii) The aim of the Directive is to ensure continuity of employment relationships within the economic entity irrespective of any change of ownership—*Allen* [2000] IRLR 119 paragraph 23—and our domestic law illustrates how readily the courts will adopt a purposive construction to counter avoidance—see Lord Oliver's speech in *Litster v Forth Dry Dock Co Ltd* [1989] IRLR 161 at 167.

Accordingly, and on one view slightly confusingly (as was implicitly recognised **2.24** by the EAT, at the beginning of paragraph 10 of the EAT's judgment), it is necessary to consider first whether there is an undertaking and second whether that undertaking was transferred. Yet it is sometimes necessary first to consider what has transferred before it is possible to ascertain whether what has transferred was an economic entity and therefore an undertaking.[43] Similarly, it will sometimes be necessary to consider whether there has been such a substantial change in the manner of the operation of an undertaking or part of an undertaking after a claimed TUPE transfer that there has been no such transfer.[44]

Parallel and subsequent developments in the case law

Lightways (Contractors) Ltd v Associated Holdings Ltd

Subsequent reported decisions add significantly to this analysis. In *Lightways* **2.25** *(Contractors) Ltd v Associated Holdings Ltd*,[45] to which reference was not made in *Cheesman*, the Court of Session concluded that the fact that the parties to a maintenance contract have agreed that TUPE will apply to the situation is relevant. As Lord Hamilton (with whom Lord Cullen and Lord Morrison agreed) said: 'A declared intention that TUPE will apply, made prior to the transaction by the alleged transferee, may make even easier an inference of

---

[43] See for example *Wynnwith Engineering Co Ltd v Bennett* [2002] IRLR 170, EAT, where a number of employees who took early retirement and were later re-engaged were held not to constitute an economic entity because they were not 'engaged on a common function': see paras 9 and 13 of the judgment.

[44] Although Lindsay J did not refer (and was not referred) in *Cheesman* to the case of *Porter and Nanayakkara v Queen's Medical Centre* [1993] IRLR 486, it is a useful illustration of how a change in the manner in which a service is operated after a claimed TUPE transfer will not necessarily mean that that which has occurred was not a TUPE transfer. In contrast, *Perth & Kinross Council v Donaldson* [2004] IRLR 121, EAT, is a useful illustration of how a difference in the manner of the provision of services after a claimed TUPE transfer may have the effect that there was no such transfer.

[45] [2000] IRLR 247.

transfer'.[46] However, it would not be open to an employment tribunal to decide that the alleged transferee in those circumstances was 'barred by their earlier conduct from maintaining that TUPE did not apply'.[47] Further, the parties cannot by their agreement that TUPE will apply make TUPE apply when TUPE would otherwise not have applied.[48]

Liskojarvi v Oy Liikenne

2.26 In *Liskojarvi v Oy Liikenne*,[49] the ECJ held that where a contract for the provision of a public bus service over a number of routes changed hands but no buses were transferred from the outgoing contractor to the incoming contractor, the fact that 33 of 45 employees of the outgoing contractor were taken on by the incoming contractor did not have the effect in the circumstances that there was a transfer within the meaning of the ARD. This was because the undertaking which it was alleged had transferred depended on the use of substantial assets.

RCO Support Services v UNISON

2.27 The Court of Appeal's decision in *RCO Support Services v UNISON*[50] is of interest for a number of reasons. However, many of those reasons are of diminished importance in the light of the enactment of regulation 3(1)(b) of TUPE. One aspect of the decision of the Court of Appeal remains highly relevant, however, and that is the statement of Mummery LJ (with whom Hale LJ and Pill LJ agreed) that he was

> inclined to accept the [submission that] a subjective motive of the putative transferee to avoid the application of the Directive and the 1981 Regulations is not the real point. The relevant exercise is that in *Spijkers* [1986] ECR 1119, ie objective consideration and assessment of all the facts, including the circumstances of the decision not to take on the workforce.[51]

P & O Trans European Ltd v Initial Transport Services Ltd

2.28 In contrast to the decision of the ECJ in *Oy Liikenne*, in *P & O Trans European Ltd v Initial Transport Services Ltd*,[52] applying a 'multifactorial' approach, the EAT concluded that the fact that none of the tankers used by a contractor (Initial) had transferred to P & O when Shell contracted out its delivery functions to P & O did not preclude there being a TUPE transfer to P & O of the contracts of employment of (in fact all of) the tanker drivers who had previously

---

[46] *Lightways (Contractors) Ltd v Associated Holdings Ltd* [2000] IRLR 249, para 23.
[47] ibid, para 25.
[48] See *Mackie v Aberdeen City Council* [2006] CSIH 36, the facts of which are described in para 2.93 onwards below.
[49] Case C–172/99; [2001] ECR I–754; [2002] ICR 155.
[50] [2002] EWCA Civ 464; [2002] ICR 751.   [51] ibid, para 36.
[52] [2003] IRLR 128.

worked exclusively for Shell while being employed by Initial and four administrative staff. The EAT was referred to and took into account the decision of the ECJ in *Oy Liikenne*, but, noting what had been said by the Court of Appeal in *ADI (UK) Ltd v Willer*[53] and *RCO Support Services Ltd v Unison*,[54] commented that:

> The relative significance of assets in relation to manpower and how each contributes to the performance of the particular activity will vary according to the facts of the particular case. The whole of the transaction has to be looked at in order to see whether one particular factor is decisive; that includes all the circumstances of the transaction.[55]

Since the employment tribunal had (1) 'set out the facts fully and accurately'; (2) **2.29** 'set out the appropriate tests and, even without the decision of *Oy Liikenne* before them, noted that the fact that no tangible assets were transferred was an important factor'; and (3) taken an 'impeccable' approach to 'weighing the various factors before them',[56] and since (in contrast to what happened in the *Oy Liikenne* case) the drivers (but not the four administrative staff) had been 'taken on "as if TUPE applied" ',[57] the *Oy Liikenne* case 'did not bind the tribunal to conclude that the absence of a transfer of Initial's wagons inevitably meant that no transfer had taken place'.[58]

Abler v Sodexho

In *Abler v Sodexho*,[59] the ECJ clarified the position in relation to the importance **2.30** of the transfer or otherwise of the workforce in a labour-intensive operation which nevertheless required premises and equipment to function. The case concerned a catering service provided from within a hospital for the patients and staff who were on the hospital's premises. The necessary premises, water, energy, and both 'small and large equipment' were provided by the body which was responsible for the hospital.[60] The service was contracted out, and was subsequently subjected to a competitive tender. The existing contractor lost the contract, and the incoming contractor refused to take over the outgoing contractor's stock, materials, and any of its staff. The ECJ rejected the argument of the incoming contractor that the refusal to take on the staff precluded there being a transfer. Here, the court ruled, there was an activity which was not 'based essentially on manpower', as 'Catering . . . requires a significant amount of equipment'.[61] The ECJ's judgment contains a rehearsal of previous relevant judgments of the ECJ of the sort which has become standard in cases decided

---

[53] [2001] EWCA Civ 971; [2001] IRLR 542.
[54] [2002] EWCA Civ 464; [2002] ICR 751.   [55] [2003] IRLR 128, para 40.
[56] ibid, para 41.   [57] ibid, para 42.   [58] ibid, para 43.
[59] Case C–340/01; [2004] IRLR 168.   [60] See ibid, 169, para 9.
[61] See ibid, paras 36, 37, and 43.

by it in recent years concerning the question of whether there has been a transfer within the meaning of the ARD. It can sensibly be regarded as supporting the approach taken by the Court of Appeal in *RCO Support Services Ltd v Unison*[62] and *ADI (UK) Ltd v Willer*,[63] although that approach will cease to be determinative as a result of the enactment of regulation 3(1)(b) of TUPE.

Fairhurst Ward Abbotts Ltd v Botes Building Ltd

2.31 One case which will continue to be determinative despite the enactment of that new provision is that of *Fairhurst Ward Abbotts Ltd v Botes Building Ltd*,[64] the Court of Appeal's decision in which was the subject of an unsuccessful application for leave to appeal to the House of Lords.[65] There, the Court of Appeal held that it was unnecessary for an economic entity to retain its identity after a claimed TUPE transfer for there to have been a TUPE transfer. The circumstances were that a local authority's housing repair and maintenance works were, before a competitive tendering exercise, carried out by a contractor under a single contract. The tendering exercise led to a partitioning of the authority's area into two for the purpose of the provision of housing maintenance services, and the award of a contract for each of those areas to two new contractors. The Court of Appeal held that this did not have the effect that TUPE did not apply. It was argued on behalf of one of the incoming contractors that the split of the original contract into two meant that the economic entity which had previously existed had necessarily lost its identity. Logically, that argument was correct (as was recognized by Mummery LJ[66]). However, if it had been correct, then it would have reduced the protection which, reading TUPE 1981 and the ARD purposively, might have been thought to apply in the circumstances. Mummery LJ commented that the 'approach to partial transfers' which was being urged on behalf of the incoming contractor was 'too narrow and literal'.[67] All that was necessary was that 'a part of the larger stable economic entity becomes identified for the first time as a separate economic entity on the occasion of the transfer separating a part from the whole'.[68] As he also said:[69]

> I would add that the attainment of the aim of the Acquired Rights Directive and of the 1981 Regulations, in preserving the continuity of employment relationships within an undertaking, does not require a distinction to be drawn between (a) the case where the part of the entity transferred was identifiable as a discrete part before the transfer and (b) the case where the part of the entity transferred

---

[62] [2002] EWCA Civ 464; [2002] ICR 751.
[63] [2001] EWCA Civ 971; [2001] IRLR 542, for the facts of which, see para 2.68 onwards below.
[64] [2004] EWCA Civ 83; [2004] ICR 919.   [65] See [2005] ICR 212.
[66] See [2004] ICR 919, 928, para 26.   [67] ibid, para 31.   [68] Paragraph 32.
[69] Paragraph 34.

became identifiable as a separate entity, in this case geographically, on the actual making of the transfer. On the contrary, if [counsel for the incoming contractor] is correct, the Regulations and the Directive would not apply to the case where an existing stable economic entity, in which there are employment relationships, is partitioned into separate identifiable parts for the first time on the making of the transfer, even in cases in which it is evidentially possible to trace the organisation of the work carried on after partition back into a part of the larger pre-partition stable economic entity. That result is not, in my view, consistent with the aim of the Regulations and the Directive nor is it dictated by the text and scheme of the domestic and Community legislation.

D. The Effect of Insolvency

The 'hiving down' provisions in regulation 4 of TUPE 1981 have not been rep- **2.32**
eated in the TUPE Regulations 2006. The latter in addition introduce two new sets of provisions which apply where there are certain types of insolvency proceedings afoot. They are taken from Article 5 of Directive 2001/23/EC. Unlike regulation 4 of TUPE 1981, they do not affect the manner in which a transfer may take place. Accordingly, their effects are described in Chapter 3 below.

E. Illustrative Cases

Introduction

As stated above, it is likely to be helpful to illustrate the principles which may be **2.33**
derived from the relevant case law concerning whether there has been a transfer within the meaning of the ARD, and to do so by reference to decided cases. Although the following cases are set out in chronological order, only those which appear to continue to be relevant are described. However, some of the cases are likely to be of diminished importance for cases concerning reorganisations taking place after 5 April 2006 given the enactment of regulation 3(1)(b) of the TUPE Regulations 2006. Those cases are nevertheless described either because they help to illustrate the development of the current law or because they are relevant in one or more respects despite the enactment of regulation 3(1)(b).

Decided cases

Foreningen af Arbejdsledere i Danmark v Daddy's Dance Hall[70]

The facts   In the *Daddy's Dance Hall* case, Irma Catering held a non- **2.34**
transferable lease of restaurants and bars owned by Palads Teatret. On

---

[70] Case 324/86; [1988] IRLR 315, ECJ.

28 January 1983, that lease was determined by Palads Teatret with effect from 25 February 1983. As a result of the termination of that lease, a manager employed by Irma Catering, Mr Tellerup, was dismissed on notice, the notice expiring on 30 April. Palads Teatret entered into a new lease with Daddy's Dance Hall with effect from 25 February 1983, which immediately employed the staff of Irma Catering, including Mr Tellerup. Mr Tellerup's new contract of employment differed in several respects, and he asked for a three-month trial period, under which either party could give 14 days' notice. He was then dismissed with such notice on 26 April 1983, and his trade union brought proceedings concerning the length of notice to which he was entitled, such length being affected by the question whether there had been a transfer within the meaning of the ARD.

2.35 **The decision of the ECJ** The ECJ decided (so far as relevant) that there was a transfer within the meaning of the ARD in the circumstances.

2.36 **Comment** The *Daddy's Dance Hall* case remains relevant. It was referred to in *Astle v Cheshire County Council*[71] as one of the 'most significant European authorities'. *Astle* is described below.

Dr Sophie Redmond Sophie Stichting v Bartol [72]

2.37 **The facts** The Dr Sophie Redmond foundation provided assistance to drug-dependent persons belonging to certain groups in Dutch society. The work was funded by a local authority. The authority then terminated the funding and switched it to another foundation which was also active in the area of providing assistance to persons who were dependent on drugs—the Sigma Foundation.

2.38 **The decision of the ECJ** The ECJ decided that the ARD was capable of applying to the circumstances of the case, commenting (in paragraph 31 of its judgment) that 'the unit in question' must retain its identity for there to be a transfer for the purposes of the ARD. The court also said in that paragraph:

> In order to ascertain whether or not there is such a transfer in a case such as that which is the subject of the main proceedings, it is necessary to determine, having regard to all the circumstances of fact surrounding the transaction in question, whether the functions performed are in fact carried out or resumed by the new legal person with the same activities or similar activities, *it being understood that activities of a special nature which pursue independent aims may, if necessary, be treated as a business or part of a business within the meaning of the Directive.* [Emphasis added.]

---

[71] [2005] IRLR 12, para 9, EAT.   [72] Case C–29/91; [1992] IRLR 366, ECJ.

Comment   This case led to the removal of the wording in TUPE 1981 which **2.39** confined the application of those regulations to transfers of undertakings which were in the nature of a commercial venture.[73] *Redmond* in any event remains a valuable guide to the breadth of the circumstances in which TUPE may apply.

Schmidt v Spar- Und Leihkasse[74]

The facts   In *Schmidt*, the claimant was the sole cleaner employed by one **2.40** of the branches of the defendant savings bank. The bank was renovated and enlarged, and the claimant was dismissed when that occurred. The cleaning firm which the defendant wished to take over the cleaning of the branch offered to continue the claimant's employment there at a higher monthly wage than that which she had been receiving, but she refused on the ground that on her calculation her hourly rate of pay would be lower. In her action challenging her dismissal under the German law on protection against dismissal, the court of first instance held against her. The court to which she appealed referred to the Court of Justice for a preliminary ruling two questions on the interpretation of the ARD (Directive 77/187/EEC). The questions were whether an undertaking's cleaning operations which were transferred to another undertaking could be treated as 'part of a business' and, if in principle they could, whether that was so even if before the transfer the cleaning work had been performed only by a single employee.

The decision of the ECJ   The ECJ held that where an undertaking contracted **2.41** out the responsibility for operating a service, such as cleaning, which it had previously performed itself, to another undertaking which thereby assumed the obligations of an employer towards employees assigned to those duties, that operation could come within the scope of the ARD. The ECJ held, further, that the absence of the transfer of any tangible assets was not decisive for the purpose of establishing whether there was a transfer for the purposes of the ARD. It was a relevant factor, however. The decisive criterion was, held the ECJ, whether the business retained its identity. The application of the ARD was not precluded by the fact that the activity transferred was for the transferor an ancillary activity not necessarily connected with the transferor's objects, nor by the fact that before the transfer the activity had been performed by a single employee.

Comment   *Schmidt* is the subject of strong criticism in J McMullen, *Business* **2.42** *Transfers and Employee Rights*,[75] at page 5/29, on the basis that although the

---

[73] See para 2.03 above for several of the cases which turned on that restriction.
[74] Case C–392/92; [1995] ICR 237, ECJ.
[75] 1998, Butterworths, looseleaf. The book is referred to below as 'McMullen'.

ECJ referred to *Spijkers*, the factors which were said in that case to be relevant were not set out in full and were 'certainly not applied by the court in the *Christel Schmidt* case'.

Rygaard v Strø Molle Akustik [76]

2.43 **The facts**   Mr Rygaard was employed by a firm of carpenters called Pedersen A/S ('Pederson'). Pedersen had a contract with SAS Service Partner A/S ('SAS') to build a canteen. Pedersen, in financial difficulties, subsequently wanted part of the job to be subcontracted, with the subcontract entered into between SAS and the new contractor. On 27 January 1992, Pedersen formally informed SAS of that wish. Two days later, Strø Moølle Akustic A/S ('Strø'), at the request of SAS, submitted a tender to SAS in respect of the work which Pedersen was under a contractual obligation to SAS to complete. A day later, ie on 30 January 1992, Pedersen entered into a contract with Strø under which Strø agreed to complete that part of the work. The work related to ceilings of the canteen and to joinery. Under the agreement between Pederson and Strø, Strø was obliged to reimburse Pedersen the expenditure, including wages, which Pedersen had already incurred in regard to the work which was the subject of the subcontract. The agreement also provided for the transfer of two of Pedersen's apprentices to Strø.

2.44 On the day after that agreement was entered into, Pedersen gave notice of the termination of Mr Rygaard's employment on the ground that Pedersen had been placed in liquidation and had decided to transfer to Strø part of the joinery works which Pedersen had contracted with SAS it would carry out. Mr Rygaard was given notice to 30 April and informed that with effect from 1 February 1992 he would be transferred to Strø.

2.45 Ten days later, on 10 February 1992, SAS accepted Strø's tender for the work in question. Mr Rygaard worked for Strø with no break in service, with a seamless transition from Pedersen to Strø. Pedersen, however, continued to work on the site but was declared bankrupt in March 1992. Mr Rygaard was given notice on 26 May 1992, the notice terminating on 30 June 1992. The question arose whether there had been a transfer under TUPE of Mr Rygaard's employment to Strø.

2.46 **The decision of the ECJ**   The ECJ decided[77] that

> the taking over, with a view to completing, with the consent of the awarder of the main building contract, works started by another undertaking, of two

---

[76] Case C–48/94; [1996] ICR 333, ECJ.   [77] See para 23 of the ECJ's judgment.

apprentices and an employee, together with the materials assigned to those works, does not constitute a transfer of an undertaking, business or part of a business, within the meaning of article 1(1) of Directive (77/187/E.E.C.).

Comment   It is of interest that in *Rygaard* only two cases were referred to: **2.47** those of *Spikjers* and *Schmidt*. It is also of interest that the EAT in 2000, in *Argyll Training Ltd v Sinclair*,[78] under the chairmanship of Lindsay J, the then President, commented: '*Rygaard* . . . is not an authority which readily yields up its principles, if, indeed, there are any to be found.'

Süzen v Zehnacker[79]

The facts   The claimant worked as a cleaner at a school in Germany with **2.48** which her employer had a cleaning contract. Pending the termination of that contract, the claimant was dismissed. The school subsequently awarded the cleaning contract to another cleaning company. The question which was referred to the ECJ was whether the ARD was applicable.

The decision of the ECJ   The core statements of principle made by the ECJ **2.49** are set out in paragraphs 2.21 and 2.22 above. The ECJ decided that there was in the circumstances no TUPE transfer.

Comment   The ECJ's decision in *Süzen* must now, ie in relation to situations **2.50** arising after 5 April 2006, be seen as superseded by the enactment of regulation 3(1)(b) of the TUPE Regulations 2006 as far as UK law is concerned, as must much of the case law in relation to which *Süzen* was influential. Nevertheless, there will continue to be cases affected by *Süzen* for some time to come, and in any event a number of cases in relation to which the ECJ's decision in *Süzen* was important remain relevant for reasons not related to *Süzen*. It is therefore helpful to chart the development of the case law after *Süzen*.

In McMullen, at page 5/37, the following is said: 'The upheaval initially caused **2.51** by the *Süzen* case can not be underestimated.' However, after *Süzen* was decided, there was a softening of the approach of the ECJ. Further, and in any event, the ECJ did not say in *Süzen* that it was necessary for there to be a transfer of any employees for there to have been a transfer of an undertaking or part of an undertaking within the meaning of the ARD. The ECJ specifically applied (in paragraph 17 of its judgment) its earlier ruling in *Schmidt*. Thus, *Süzen* did not require a different approach from that taken before the case was decided. There were nevertheless several cases which indicated a change of approach for the time being, including the following case.

---

[78] [2000] IRLR 630, para 12. See further para 2.64 onwards below.
[79] C–13/95 [1997]; ECR I–1259; [1997] ICR 662, ECJ.

Betts v Brintel Helicopters [80]

2.52   **The facts**   The claimants in *Betts* were employed by the first defendant, a company providing helicopter services from its three mainland bases under contracts with an oil company, to transfer men and goods to and from oil rigs in a sector of the North Sea from its base at Beccles. When the contracts expired, on 30 June 1995, the Beccles contract was awarded to the second defendant (KLM), which did not take over any of the existing staff or equipment and operated from a different helicopter base. Some Beccles staff were redeployed by the first defendant, but the claimants were dismissed. They sought a declaration that as from 1 July 1995 they became employees of the second defendant on the ground that there had been a transfer of an undertaking within the meaning of TUPE 1981. The judge granted the declaration on the basis that the first defendant's operation at Beccles prior to 30 June 1995 was an undertaking for the purposes of regulation 3(1) of TUPE 1981 and that, as the second defendant continued to perform the same service or activity, there was a transfer of that undertaking. The second defendant appealed against that ruling.

2.53   **The decision of the Court of Appeal**   The Court of Appeal allowed the appeal. Relying on and purporting to apply *Süzen*, the court held that (1) an 'undertaking' within the meaning of TUPE 1981 comprised a stable economic entity and not merely the performance of a service or activity; (2) the decisive criterion for determining that there had been a transfer of such an undertaking was that the economic entity retained its identity in the hands of the transferee; (3) there could be no transfer, on the termination of one fixed-term contract for services and the commencement of another such contract to provide essentially similar services, unless there was a concomitant transfer of significant assets or taking over by the new employer of a major part of the workforce; and that (4) consequently, while the first defendant's operation at Beccles had constituted an 'undertaking', consisting of helicopters, infrastructure, staff, and a contractual right to land on oil rigs and use the facilities, even if the right to land on the oil rigs had been transferred to the second defendant, transfer of only such a limited part of the original undertaking could not amount to the transfer of the 'undertaking' such that it retained its identity in the hands of the second defendant. Thus, held the court, there had been no transfer of an undertaking for the purposes of TUPE 1981.

2.54   The Court of Appeal (in fact Kennedy LJ, who gave the only reasoned judgment, with which Auld LJ and Sir Roger Parker agreed) commented that

---

[80] [1997] ICR 792, CA.

the decision in *Süzen* . . . does represent a shift of emphasis, or at least a clarification of the law, and . . . some of the reasoning of earlier decisions, if not the decisions themselves, may have to be reconsidered. With the benefit of the judgment in *Süzen*, which was not available to the trial judge, I am satisfied that the proper approach to this case is to consider first the nature of Brintel's Beccles operation. For the reasons I have given I accept that there was an undertaking or an economic entity. I turn then to the second question, namely, whether that undertaking was transferred so that it retained its identity in the hands of K.L.M. In my judgment the answer to that question is now clear, namely, that there was no such transfer.

Comment   This was surely the high-water mark in recent UK jurisprudence **2.55** in relation to the question of whether there has been a TUPE transfer. As Mummery LJ subsequently said in *ECM (Vehicle Delivery Service) Ltd v Cox*,[81] 'the importance of *Süzen* has . . . been overstated'.

Vidal SA v Gomez Perez[82]

The facts   *Vidal* concerned three cases in which cleaning work was done by **2.56** one company for another company under a contract which was then terminated. Following that termination, in each case the company to which the cleaning work was provided started doing the work 'in-house'; in other words it engaged its own employees to do the work. The question in each case was whether this could constitute a transfer within the meaning of the ARD.

The decision of the ECJ   The ECJ held, expressly applying *Süzen*,[83] that **2.57** the ARD

> must be capable of applying where, as in these cases before the national courts, an undertaking which used to have recourse to another undertaking for the cleaning of its premises or part of them decides to terminate its contract with that other undertaking and in future to carry out that work itself.[84]

The ECJ reiterated the need for there to be 'a stable economic entity whose **2.58** activity is not limited to performing one specific works contract (case C–48/94 *Rygaard* . . ., paragraph 20)', and that the term 'entity' 'refers to an organised grouping of persons and of assets enabling an economic activity which pursues a specific objective to be exercised (*Süzen* . . ., paragraph 13)'. Nevertheless, the ECJ said:[85]

> Whilst such an entity must be sufficiently structured and autonomous, it will not necessarily have significant assets, tangible or intangible. Indeed, in certain sectors, such as cleaning, these assets are often reduced to their most basic and the

---

[81] [1999] ICR 1162, 1168. The full passage is set out below.
[82] Cases C–127/96, C–229/96, and C–74/97; [1999] IRLR 132, ECJ.
[83] See paras 24 and 26 of the judgment.   [84] ibid, para 25.   [85] ibid, para 27.

activity is essentially based on manpower. Thus, an organised grouping of wage earners who are specifically and permanently assigned to a common task may, in the absence of other factors of production, amount to an economic entity.

2.59 **Comment** The ECJ, in a decision handed down on the same day, *Hidalgo*,[86] came to the same conclusion in relation to the situation in which a public body buys a service such as a home help service or a surveillance (ie security) service and then awards a new contract for that service to a different service provider.

ECM (Vehicle Delivery Service) Ltd v Cox[87]

2.60 **The facts** The claimants in *ECM v Cox* were drivers and yardmen who had been employed by a company by the name of Axial Ltd in relation to the delivery pursuant to a contract between Axial and VAG Ltd of Audi and Volkswagen cars on transporters from Grimsby docks to local delivery centres and dealers in different parts of the UK. In 1993, Axial lost the contract to ECM, which decided not to employ any of Axial's employees in view of an intention expressed by representatives of the employees to initiate proceedings for unfair dismissal in respect of employees who were not taken on by ECM. The employees claimed that they had been unfairly dismissed, contrary to regulation 8(1) of TUPE 1981 (now regulation 7(1) of the TUPE Regulations 2006). The industrial tribunal which decided the claims upheld them, finding that if there had been no contract with VAG then the employees would have had no jobs and that there was a discrete economic entity which was transferred from Axial to ECM and which retained its identity following the transfer. ECM appealed to the EAT, which dismissed the appeal. ECM then appealed to the Court of Appeal.

2.61 **The decision of the Court of Appeal** The Court of Appeal dismissed the appeal, holding that the industrial tribunal had been entitled to have regard to the reason why the employees had not been employed by ECM. Mummery LJ gave the only reasoned judgment, and Laws and Henry LJJ agreed with him. The passage in which Mummery LJ set out his essential reasoning bears repeating in full.[88]

> In my judgment, it is clear that, but for the argument about the scope and effect of the later decision in *Süzen*, there would be no possible ground of appeal in this case. ECM's case has to be that *Süzen* makes all the difference. It does not in this case. The importance of *Süzen* has, I think, been overstated. The ruling in *Süzen* should be seen in its proper context.

---

[86] Cases C–173/96 and C–247/96; [1999] IRLR 136.   [87] [1999] ICR 1162, CA.
[88] [1999] ICR 1168–1169.

(1) The Court of Justice has not overruled its previous interpretative rulings in cases such as *Spijkers* and *Schmidt*. This is clear not only from the citation of those cases in the judgment in *Süzen*, but also from their continued prominence in the reasoning of the Court of Justice in its post-*Süzen* decision in *Sánchez Hidalgo v. Asociación de Servicios Aser* (Case C–173/96) [1999] I.R.L.R. 136.

(2) It is still the case that it is for the national court to make the 'necessary factual appraisal' in order to decide whether there is a transfer in the light of the criteria laid down by the Court of Justice.

(3) It is still the case that those criteria involve consideration of 'all the facts characterising the transaction in question,' as identified in *Spijkers*, at para. 13 of the judgment of the Court of Justice, in order to determine whether the under-taking has continued and retained its identity in different hands. The employment tribunal carried out a full factual appraisal, applied the correct criteria and concluded that, despite changes in the organisation of the operation for the delivery of cars under the VAG contract, there was a continuation in the hands of ECM of the existence of the discrete economic entity previously carried on by Axial.

(4) The importance of *Süzen* [1997] I.C.R. 662 is that the Court of Justice identified limits to the application of the Acquired Rights Directive. On the one hand, it affirmed that: (a) 'The decisive criterion for establishing the existence of a transfer within the meaning of the Directive is whether the entity in question retains its identity, as indicated inter alia by the fact that its operation is actually continued . . .' (p. 670, para. 10); (b) the absence of a direct contractual link or relationship between the transferor and the transferee is not conclusive against a transfer (paras. 12 and 13); (c) consideration of all the facts characterising the transaction in question is necessary (pp. 670–671, para. 14).

(5) On the other hand, it set limits by indicating that: (a) 'the mere fact that the service provided by the old and the new awardees of a contract is similar does not therefore support the conclusion that an economic entity has been transferred.' Other factors are important—the workforce, the management staff, its operating methods and its operational resources (p. 671, para. 15); (b) 'The mere loss of a service contract to a competitor cannot therefore by itself indicate the existence of a transfer within the meaning of [the] Directive . . . In those circumstances, the service undertaking previously entrusted with the contract does not, on losing a customer, thereby cease fully to exist, and a business or part of a business belonging to it cannot be considered to have been transferred to the new awardee of the contract' (p. 671, para. 16); (c) the question whether the majority of the employees are taken over by the new employer to enable him to carry on the activities of the undertaking on a regular basis is a factual circumstance to be taken into account, as well as the similarity of the pre and post transfer activities and the type of undertaking concerned, e.g., in labour intensive sectors (p. 672, paras. 20 and 21).

(6) This case is unaffected by the limits indicated in *Süzen*. It is not a case (like *Süzen*) of the loss of a contract with one customer being asserted to amount to a transfer of an undertaking. It is not a case like *Betts v. Brintel Helicopters Ltd*

[1997] I.C.R. 792 of the loss of a contract for one location being asserted to be a transfer of an undertaking. It is not a case of a transfer depending *merely* on a comparison of the similarity of the activities of Axial and ECM after the loss of the VAG contract by Axial. The transfer was established by the employment tribunal looking at all the relevant facts and concluding that this undertaking was based on the VAG contract and that it continued in different hands, even though no employees of Axial were appointed by ECM. The tribunal was entitled to have regard, as a relevant circumstance, to the reason why those employees were not appointed by ECM. The Court of Justice has not decided in *Süzen* or in any other case that this is an irrelevant circumstance or that the failure of the transferee to appoint any of the former employees of the transferor points conclusively against a transfer.

2.62 **Comment** McMullen comments[89] that 'It is not entirely clear why . . . the case is different from *Ayse Süzen*', and that the latter case 'should have . . . affected the analysis of both the EAT and the Court of Appeal'. However, as noted by McMullen,[90] a 'deciding factor' was that the Court of Appeal decided that it was lawful for an industrial (now employment) tribunal to take into account the motive of a claimed TUPE transferee in refusing to take on employees of a claimed transferor. Applying the requisite purposive approach to the interpretation of TUPE, it would be odd if that were irrelevant. If employees of a claimed transferor are not employed by a transferee merely because the transferee wants to avoid the application of TUPE, then that surely may properly be a decisive factor, *Süzen* notwithstanding.

2.63 The Court of Appeal's decision in *ECM v Cox* influenced the decisions of the Court of Appeal in *ADI (UK) Ltd v Willer*[91] and *RCO Support Services v UNISON*.[92] The facts of *ADI v Willer* are described below, because they give the background to a statement of principle made by May LJ to which attention is drawn below (the facts being likely to be rather less important in the future given the coming into force of regulation 3(1)(b) of the TUPE Regulations 2006). The facts of *RCO Support Services v UNISON* are not described because of the enactment of regulation 3(1)(b).

Argyll Training Ltd v Sinclair[93]

2.64 **The facts** The claimant was employed by Business & Employment Skills Training Ltd ('BEST') to arrange the placement of trainees with employers in the Argyll area. BEST employed the claimant to do this because it had entered into a contract with a company by the name of Argyll & The Islands Enterprise

---

[89] Paragraph 173, on p 5/51A.   [90] ibid, para 173.1.
[91] [2001] EWCA Civ 971, [2001] IRLR 542.
[92] [2002] EWCA Civ 464, [2002] ICR 751.   [93] [2000] IRLR 630, EAT.

Ltd ('AIE') for the provision by BEST of training to local enterprise companies in the Argyll area. BEST also provided in-house training to trainees. The claimant was the only employee of BEST who arranged placements of trainees with employers in the area. BEST was paid by reference to a formula which related to the number of trainees on its books at any given time.

2.65 AIE then terminated the contract with BEST and engaged another company, Argyll Training Ltd ('ATL'), to provide training services in place of BEST. The latter therefore gave notice to the claimant on the basis that she was redundant. ATL took over 21 of 32 placement trainees who had been on BEST's books and who remained with a training provider after ATL became responsible for the provision of training services. The claimant made claims in employment tribunal proceedings against both AIE and ATL. An employment tribunal decided that there was a TUPE transfer from BEST to AIE and then from AIE to ATL. ATL appealed on the basis that there was in the circumstances no stable economic entity which could properly be said to have been an undertaking. AIE appealed against the finding that there had been a transfer to it.

2.66 **The decision of the EAT**   The EAT dismissed the appeal of ATL, holding that it was open to the employment tribunal to find that there had been a transfer of an undertaking here. However, allowing the appeal of AIE, the EAT decided that there was no transfer to AIE, since there was 'no question of any relevant activity on BEST's part having been continued or resumed by AIE'.[94]

2.67 **Comment**   Apart from the general statements which are referred to above in this chapter[95] and the unusual and illustrative facts of the case, the case is of particular interest because of the ruling that there was no room for a transfer in stages from one contractor providing services to the buyer of the services and then on to a new contractor. It was said in *Dines v Initial Healthcare Services Ltd*[96] by Neill LJ, with whose judgment Henry LJ and Sir Christopher Slade agreed, that there was in that case a two-stage transfer of the sort which the EAT in *Argyll Training Ltd v Sinclair* rejected on the facts. There is no material difference between the facts of both cases, but it is suggested here that the approach of the EAT in *Argyll Training Ltd v Sinclair* was right. It appears that the statement of Neill LJ was obiter, but in any event it appears also not to have been the subject of argument. In none of the cases decided by the ECJ has it been said that there is a two-stage transfer, and the approach taken by the ECJ in those cases is rather more consistent with the decision of the EAT in *Argyll*

---

[94] ibid, para 30.   [95] See paras 2.17 and 2.47 above.   [96] [1995] ICR 11, 24.

Training Ltd v Sinclair than with that of the Court of Appeal in *Dines v Initial Healthcare Services Ltd.*[97]

ADI (UK) Ltd v Willer[98]

2.68 **The facts** A shopping centre operator (Hillier Parker) employed its own staff in relation to the security of the centre. The staff used a CCTV centre in the shopping centre's premises, and a control room and clocking system. Hillier Parker then contracted with ADI that ADI would provide security services in place of Hillier Parker's employees. The existing employees of Hillier Parker transferred to ADI. ADI, with the agreement of Hillier Parker, then terminated the contract, and Hillier Parker entered into a contract with a new security services provider, Firm Security Group ('FSG') for the provision of security services at the shopping centre.

2.69 A representative of FSG met the nine former Hillier Parker employees who were then employed by ADI at the shopping centre. The representative made it clear that FSG considered that overtime would not normally be necessary after FSG had taken over responsibility for the provision of security services at the shopping centre, and asked the employees to fill in a form in order to comply with FSG's vetting procedure. The employees objected to this, and declined to say that they would become employed by FSG. They did not fill in the vetting forms. FSG then wrote to them, informing them that none of them would be offered a position at the Darwin Centre and suggesting that they talked to their company 'to clarify your future employment status with on the termination of the Darwin Centre contract'[sic].[99] FSG then took over responsibility for the provision of security services at the shopping centre, and employed new staff. The employees claimed that they had been unfairly dismissed.

2.70 An employment tribunal found, by a majority, that there had not been a TUPE transfer. This was on the basis that the contract for the provision of security services for a specific customer was not an economic entity, and that in any event there had been no transfer because neither assets nor staff had been taken on by FSG. ADI appealed to the EAT, which decided that although the employment tribunal had been wrong to decide that there was not an economic entity which could have transferred, it was open to the employment tribunal to conclude in the circumstances that there was no transfer of that entity. This was because of the absence of the transfer of a major part of the alleged transferor's

---

[97] In *Whitehouse v C A Blatchford Ltd* [2000] ICR 542, where the Court of Appeal's attention was drawn to this aspect of the decision in *Dines*, at 551, Buxton LJ mentioned that fact, and said: 'I do not think that this question affects our consideration of this case.'
[98] [2001] EWCA Civ 971, [2001] IRLR 542, CA.   [99] See ibid, para 2.

workforce. ADI appealed to the Court of Appeal, arguing that there had been a TUPE transfer.

The decision of the Court of Appeal   The Court of Appeal (by a majority) **2.71** upheld the appeal and remitted the appeal to a differently constituted employment tribunal. This was because the employment tribunal had not (in the Court of Appeal's judgment) made a specific finding whether or not FSG deliberately did not take on the nine employees of ADI who were employed at the shopping centre in order to avoid the application of TUPE.

Comment   One general comment made by May LJ is set out in paragraph 2.16 **2.72** above. He made another comment of a more specific nature concerning the manner in which the question whether there has been a TUPE transfer should be approached, which will continue to be valuable while cases concerning transfers which occurred before regulation 3(1)(b) of the TUPE Regulations 2006 applied remain undetermined. In paragraph 36 of his judgment, May LJ said this:

> In my judgment, Mr Randall was correct to accept that there would have been a transfer in the present case for the purpose of the 1981 Regulations if the nine security officers had been taken on by Firm Security Group, and that there would also be a transfer if the reason why they were not taken on was in order to avoid the application of the Regulations. More generally, it seems to me that if, as in the present case, the economic entity is labour intensive such that, applying *Süzen* [1997] IRLR 255, there is no transfer if the workforce is not taken on, but there would be if they were, there will be a transfer if, although the workforce is not taken on, it is established that the reason or principal reason for this was in order to avoid the application of the Regulations. I take this form of expression from para. 8 of the 1981 Regulations, recognising that it is used there in a slightly different context. I do not accept Mr Jeans's submission that there should be a positive burden on the person arguing against the transfer to establish the reason for not taking on the workforce, failing which a transfer should be found. Nor do I consider that the reason or principal reason for not taking on the employees has to be limited to an economic, technical or organisational reason entailing changes in the workforce of the transferee, failing which a transfer will be found. There may, depending on the facts, be other possibilities.

Lord Justice Simon Brown's dissent was strongly worded. In paragraphs 78–79 **2.73** he said this:

> 78
>
> *ECM* [1999] IRLR 559 clearly represents the highwater mark of the appellants' argument in reliance upon English authority: as I observed at the outset of this judgment, the Court of Appeal there appeared to conclude that an incoming contractor cannot avoid the Directive and TUPE simply by choosing not to take on any of the previous contractor's workforce. I would, however, make

four comments upon it. First, Mummery LJ's ultimate conclusion is couched in apparently limited terms:

'The tribunal was entitled to have regard, as a relevant circumstance, to the reason why those employees [of the previous contractor] were not appointed by the *ECM* [1999] IRLR 559 [the incoming contractor].'

79

Secondly, even that limited conclusion I find impossible, for the reasons already given, to reconcile with the ruling ECJ jurisprudence.

2.74 However, as noted above, the case of *Abler v Sodexho*[100] can sensibly be regarded as having provided a firm foundation in the case law of the ECJ for the approach taken by the majority in *ADI v Willer*.

Astle v Cheshire County Council [101]

2.75 **The facts** In 1994, Cheshire County Council outsourced its architectural services to a contractor, Kennedy and Donkin. All the relevant council staff transferred to Kennedy and Donkin under TUPE. The council was unhappy with Kennedy and Donkin's performance and, in 1999, the contract was awarded to SGI. There was a TUPE transfer of staff from Kennedy and Donkin to SGI. This included 65 of the council's original staff.

2.76 At this time, the architectural services required by the council fell into two general categories: capital and planned maintenance projects ('CPM') and cyclical and response maintenance ('CRM'). In addition, a help desk was operated by SGI to deal with inquiries, and was manned by two SGI employees.

2.77 The council was of the view that SGI's performance was affected by what was regarded as below par performance by some of the original council staff. At the end of 2001, the council therefore decided to engage a panel of consultants to provide the services rather than a single contractor to deal with the council's projects. SGI's contract came to an end with effect from 31 March 2002. There was a gap in time between the date when the SGI contract ceased and the date when the panel took up the projects, and during that period the council carried out some minor activities of an architectural nature. The help desk was transferred to a company called HBM.

2.78 None of SGI's staff were taken on by the council. The staff claimed that there had been a TUPE transfer and that they should be treated as employed by the council. Their view was supported by SGI.

2.79 In respect of CRM, the employment tribunal found that 'all the functions of both types of maintenance are still carried out, or need to be carried out, but

---

[100] Case C–340/01; [2004] IRLR 168. See para 2.30 above.   [101] [2005] IRLR 12, EAT.

they are clearly performed in a substantially different way'. As to CPM, the tribunal noted that the work had been transferred to external consultants. The small amount of work done by the council on projects prior to the consultants becoming active did not amount to carrying on the operation of the business performed by SGI. The tribunal concluded that the business of the provision of architectural services by SGI did not transfer to the council under TUPE.

The employment tribunal noted that 'where no employees are transferred, the reason why that is the case can be relevant as to whether there has been a TUPE transfer'. It asked itself whether the reason, or principal reason, the council selected a 'market economy' was 'to thwart TUPE'. It concluded that the council did not want a significant number of staff who were employed by SGI to continue to be responsible for carrying out architectural services for the council, either as employees or indirect labour, so that it was concerned to avoid a TUPE transfer. The tribunal accepted the council's contention, however, that it had genuinely decided that the 'market economy' was the best method of delivering those services. The tribunal decided that 'The reason therefore the council did not accept the workforce back was not to defeat TUPE, but because it had given the responsibility of carrying out the provision of architectural services to a panel of consultants; thus the council did not require a workforce to operate the business.' **2.80**

The employment tribunal said that it would have found that the transfer of the help desk was a TUPE transfer, but that it had not been asked to consider that question. On appeal, it was accepted that this was a misunderstanding and that there was a TUPE transfer of the help desk. **2.81**

The employees and SGI appealed to the EAT against the decision that there had been no relevant transfer to the council. They argued that the employment tribunal had erred in failing to find that the purpose of what occurred was to thwart the application of TUPE and that the case should have been regarded as a TUPE transfer in the light of the decision of the Court of Appeal in *ECM (Vehicle Delivery) Service v Cox*. They argued that the correct question should have been 'Was the reason or principal reason the council did not take on the workforce to thwart TUPE?', rather than 'Was the reason, or principal reason, the council selected a market economy to thwart TUPE?' **2.82**

The decision of the EAT The EAT declined to overturn the decision of the employment tribunal. All parties concerned accepted that 'apart from the impact of the *ECM* point, the tribunal's [conclusion that the business which was carried on by the new providers was "so materially different that there was neither continuity nor retention of identity"] could not be **2.83**

challenged'.[102] The EAT dismissed the appeal because the employment tribunal was entitled to find that because the reason or principal reason for the business reorganisation was not to avoid the application of TUPE, the desire to avoid the application of TUPE was irrelevant. This ruling was based on the passage from the judgment of May LJ in *ADI v Willer* set out in paragraph 2.72 above.

2.84 The EAT's ruling in this regard was set out simply in paragraph 21 of its judgment:

> 21.1 If it is not the reason or principal reason of the transferee to avoid the application of TUPE, then the question is not relevant and does not arise.
>
> 21.2 If it is, then it is a relevant factor to take into account in the *Spijkers* exercise, and may be decisive.

2.85 Comment It could be said that the ruling of the EAT in this case involved treating the judgment of May LJ in *ADI v Willer* as if it were a statute and then interpreting it otherwise than purposively. Even then, paragraph 36 of the judgment of May LJ in that case does not compel the conclusion (of the EAT in *Astle*) that the desire to avoid the application of TUPE must be the principal or only reason for the employer's actions before it can be taken into account. That conclusion is, furthermore, apparently at odds with the statement of Mummery LJ in *RCO Support Services Ltd v UNISON* which is set out in paragraph 2.27 above (to which, it has to be said, the EAT specifically referred in *Astle*).

2.86 In any event, there seems to be no particularly good reason for ignoring the fact that an employer has deliberately sought to avoid the application of TUPE unless the employer has structured its reorganisation solely or mainly with a view to avoiding the application of TUPE. Nevertheless, it is difficult to see how that factor should be taken into account in any event, ie whether or not it was potentially decisive. Presumably, given the purpose of the ARD, namely to safeguard employees' rights, an employment tribunal should see what the position would have been if the employer's intention had not been to avoid the application of TUPE.

Balfour Beatty Power Networks Ltd v Wilcox[103]

2.87 The facts Western Power Distribution contracted with Hyder plc for a number of street lighting services. Each contract was operated by Hyder as a separate entity with a contract supervisor and foreman, with separate administration and dedicated employees. There was a jointing contract which involved services to join electrical cables one to another, and a contract known as 'RASP' relating

---

[102] *Astle v Cheshire County Council* [2005] IRLR 12, EAT, para 14.
[103] [2006] IRLR 258, EAT.

to aerial supply. Hyder unsuccessfully bid for the renewal of the contracts. At the end of 2001, the jointing contract was awarded to Balfour Beatty and the RASP contract was awarded to Interserve Industrial Services ('Interserve'). Neither of the new contractors treated the change as falling within TUPE. Before the new contracts took effect, 23 employees were assigned by Hyder to the jointing contract. Of those 23, 17 were found work within Hyder after the new contracts took effect. The claimants were employees of Hyder who were not taken on by the new contractors. They instituted employment tribunal proceedings.

The employment tribunal directed itself in accordance with the decision of the EAT in *Cheesman v Brewer*. Having done so, it held in both cases that there was an economic entity capable of being transferred and that that entity retained its identity after the transfer. In the case of the jointing contract, the employment tribunal found that the claimants did not transfer because of 'Balfour Beatty's attempt to avoid the TUPE Regulations' and that there would have been a TUPE transfer if the workforce had been taken on. In the case of the RASP contract, the tribunal found that the majority of the workers assigned to the contract did become employed by Interserve, and that the reason why labourers did not transfer was 'connected with the attempt to avoid the TUPE Regulations applying'. **2.88**

Both employers appealed to the EAT. It was argued on their behalf, among other things, that the employment tribunal had erred in characterising each of the economic entities it purported to find as being 'labour intensive', in that equipment and plant was 'significantly necessary'[104] for the operations. It was also contended that the employment tribunal had wrongly focused upon the fact that material and plant was leased as lessening the significance of the fact that there had been no transfer of plant and materials from Hyder to either Balfour Beatty or Interserve. It was submitted that because of the significance of that plant in the context of the undertakings, there could be no transfer without a transfer of such material and plant. It was also argued that the employment tribunal had not had proper regard, in assessing whether there had been a transfer, to the number of employees who had transferred. In addition, it was argued that the jointing contract did not constitute a stable economic entity because it was 'defeasible' since 'the work was, in effect, capable of collapsing at short notice and (being dependent as it was upon a single contract), thus fell foul of the principles expressed in the *Rygaard* case'.[105] **2.89**

The decision of the EAT The EAT dismissed the appeal in so far as it related to the RASP contract, but allowed it in relation to the jointing contract. This **2.90**

---

[104] See ibid, para 8.   [105] See para 33.

was because the employment tribunal had failed, when considering whether there was a TUPE transfer in relation to the jointing contract, to decide whether the fact that 17 of the 23 employees did not transfer meant that the alleged transferee had not taken on 'a major part of the workforce'.[106] The 'defeasibility' argument was rejected on the following basis:[107]

> If it were right that those working for Balfour Beatty under a contract such as this, no matter how long they had worked for Balfour Beatty, nor how carefully they were organised and structured, nor how long they might expect, even if they could not demand, to be employed further, did not constitute collectively an undertaking, then any change of employer to which those employees were subject, would not itself be subject to the transfer of undertaking regulations. If X Co succeeded over a weekend to the business of Balfour Beatty, there would [be] no transfer of an undertaking upon this analysis because the core underlying contract did not provide the necessary stability. We think that the factual circumstances are so far removed from those which operated in the *Rygaard* case that not only would that defeat the purpose of the regulations as we understand them to be, but it makes no practical sense. Moreover, as the lay members would have wished to point out, it would have significant consequences for the avoidance of the transfer regulations because such an approach would encourage would-be employers who wished to avoid any TUPE consequences to ensure that contracts were 'defeasible' even if the expectation of the parties was that they would be honoured in a practical way.

2.91 The other arguments of the appellants were all rejected. The argument concerning the leasing of equipment was rejected since it did not seem to the EAT to be

> a matter of such critical importance that that equipment or those leases are not transferred over to the would-be transferee if the transferee himself or itself similarly leases identical equipment. Each is choosing to ensure that the operation continues with equipment owned in each case by a third party and not by the proprietor of the undertaking. Instead of the equipment being a capital asset, it is something which is paid for out of revenue. The lay members, in particular, see this as being a case in which it could not be said that assets of a business had not been transferred since leased goods cannot be described easily as assets and the essential aspect of such a transaction is that, as a matter of practicality, similar items are used after as before the transfer and obtained for that purpose. Accordingly, we think that the tribunal were entitled to take account of the fact that the equipment here was leased rather than owned and to bring that into the balance in making the overall factual assessment it did.[108]

2.92 **Comment** The EAT was able to sidestep, in paragraph 50 of its judgment, the question of the relevance of the motive of the alleged transferee of the

---

[106] See para 45.   [107] See para 34.   [108] Paragraph 40.

contracts of employment of the employees who, when they worked for Hyder, worked on the RASP contract. That question will remain relevant in cases other than situations to which regulation 3(1)(b) of the TUPE Regulations 2006 applies. Given the coming into force of that provision, however, this case will be of diminished importance in the future.

Mackie v Aberdeen City Council [109]

The facts   The claimant in *Mackie v Aberdeen City Council* started to do work   **2.93** for the council when she worked for a company called Smartex Ltd. Smartex had agreed to subcontract with other suppliers to deliver to the council an 'operational smart card system which would be used by the [council], at least initially, for the cash-free payment of meals by school-children and as a bus pass by senior citizens'.[110] Smartex was based in Cambridge, but the claimant was to work at the council's premises in Aberdeen. She was the only employee of Smartex who worked there. She worked on the development and production of the smart cards. She was also responsible for training and supervising an employee of the council in connection with the production of the cards.

Towards the end of the period covered by the contract between Smartex and the   **2.94** council, the council offered the claimant the job of finance and administrative officer. The work was to consist of the administration of the smart card scheme. The claimant accepted the offer. She was given a letter from the council stating that there was in the circumstances a TUPE transfer of her employment from Smartex to the council. The employee subsequently fell ill, and the question arose whether there had in fact been a transfer under TUPE 1981 of her employment. An employment tribunal decided that there had not been such a transfer. This was because it was 'not satisfied that any economic entity subsisted which could be the subject of transfer'.[111] This was because:[112]

> The contract with Smartex was a 'one-off' matter for the production of a smart card and once that had been delivered the business was at an end. There was, in short, nothing left to transfer. Further, [the employment tribunal] found that even if there was such an entity, it had not been transferred since the business had not retained its identity, to use the characterisation of the essential criterion set out in the case of *Spijkers* [1986] ECR 1119 @1128. A distinction was drawn by [the employment tribunal] between the stage of development of the card to get it 'up and running', and the subsequent period of the operation of the scheme.

---

[109]   EATS/0095/04; the judgment is available on the EAT's website, <www.employmentappeals. gov.uk>. The Court of Session dismissed an appeal against the EAT's judgment. The Court of Session's judgment is available at <www.scotcourts.co.uk>. The case reference is [2006] CSIH 36.
[110]   See para 14 of the EAT's judgment.   [111]   See para 19 of the EAT's judgment.
[112]   ibid.

2.95 On appeal to the EAT, it was argued among other things that the employment tribunal had 'erred in failing to have due regard to the fact that, in the letter sent to the claimant by the respondents confirming her employment with them, it was stated that the transfer was a TUPE transfer'.[113]

2.96 **The decision of the EAT**   The EAT rejected the appeal, holding[114] among other things that the case of *Lightways (Contractors) Ltd v Associated Holdings Ltd*[115] was not 'authority for the proposition that a party's statement that TUPE applies to the transfer is almost conclusive of the issue', and that the employment tribunal had been entitled in the circumstances to regard the statement that TUPE applied as 'not even amounting to there having been a clear intention on the part of the [council] that the transfer be a TUPE one'.

2.97 **Comment**   The outcome of the case would probably not have been affected by regulation 3(1)(b) of the TUPE Regulations 2006. The case illustrates the unimportance of the parties' understanding as to the applicability or otherwise of TUPE. That unimportance was also illustrated, but with a different effect (which assisted the employees) in *Senior Heat Treatment Ltd v Bell*.[116]

---

[113] See para 22 of the EAT's judgment.
[114] See para 32 of the EAT's judgment.
[115] [2000] IRLR 247, EAT, concerning which, see para 2.25 above.
[116] [1997] IRLR 614, EAT. See para 3.35 below for the effect of the EAT's decision in that case.

3

THE PROTECTION GIVEN TO INDIVIDUALS BY TUPE

A. An Overview of What Transfers Under TUPE

The contracts of employment of all relevant employees and all relevant powers **3.01** and liabilities arising under those contracts are transferred by TUPE from the transferor to the transferee.[1] This is the broad effect of regulation 4 of TUPE. Its precise effects are described below, after the following paragraphs, which describe the test for determining which employees' contracts transfer by virtue of TUPE. The need to consider the latter question first arises from the fact that there may be a TUPE transfer which gives rise to the transfer of no contracts of employment. This is at first sight surprising, but there may be an undertaking or part of an undertaking which is transferred from one employer to another, to which undertaking or part of an undertaking no employees are 'assigned'. This

---

[1] The terms 'employees' and 'contract of employment' are defined in unexceptionable terms by reg 2(1) of TUPE.

would occur where a number of employees are shared equally by various parts of the transferor's operations, all of which parts are then transferred to different employers. If no employees are assigned to the undertaking or part of an undertaking which is transferred, then TUPE will not have the effect of transferring any liabilities. This is because such liabilities are transferred only in relation to particular employees.

3.02 This does not mean that an employer could not contravene TUPE in some way where no contracts of employment are transferred by TUPE. This is because the employer might in those circumstances for example breach the obligation to inform and (where relevant) consult appropriate representatives under regulation 13 of TUPE.

B. Whose Contracts of Employment Are Transferred by TUPE?

Introduction

3.03 Only the contracts of employment of some employees of a TUPE transferor are transferred by TUPE to the transferee. Those are the contracts of employees who are 'assigned' to the undertaking, business, or part of an undertaking or business which is transferred under TUPE. This word does not appear in the ARD, and it did not appear in TUPE 1981. It does, however, appear in regulation 4(1) of the TUPE Regulations 2006. It is defined partially by regulation 2(1) of those regulations, which provides that it 'means assigned other than on a temporary basis'.

Assignment

3.04 The word 'assigned' first appeared in the context of a transfer within the meaning of the ARD when the ECJ decided in *Botzen v Rotterdamsche Droogdok Maatschappij BV*[2] that the test for determining whether an employee's contract of employment is transferred under the ARD is whether the employee was 'assigned' to the business, undertaking, or part of a business or undertaking which has transferred, an 'employment relationship [being] essentially characterised by the link existing between the employee and the part of the undertaking or business to which he is assigned to carry out his duties'.[3] Thus:[4]

> the only decisive criterion regarding the transfer of employees' rights and obligations is whether or not a transfer takes place of the department to which they

---

[2] [1985] ECR 591; [1986] 2 CMLR 50.
[3] [1985] ECR 519, 528, para 15.   [4] ibid, para 14.

were assigned and which formed the organisational framework within which their employment relationship took effect.

Further, the mere fact that an employee who was not employed in the trans- **3.05** ferred part of an undertaking performed 'certain duties which involved the use of assets assigned to the part transferred' will not mean that the employee was assigned to the part which was transferred.[5] Similarly, an employee, 'who, whilst being employed in an administrative department of the undertaking which has not itself been transferred, carried out certain duties for the benefit of the part transferred', will not be regarded as having been assigned to the transferred part.[6]

The manner in which that test is to be applied has been considered in a number **3.06** of subsequent decisions of the EAT. These include *Sunley Turriff Holdings Ltd v Thomson*,[7] *Duncan Webb Offset (Maidstone) Ltd v Cooper*,[8] *Buchanon-Smith v Schleicher*,[9] and *Securicor Guarding Services Ltd v Fraser Security Services Ltd*.[10] In addition, the Court of Appeal considered the matter in *Gale v Northern General Hospital NHS Trust*[11] and *CPL Distribution Ltd v Todd*.[12] The relevant facts of all of those cases are instructive, given the difficulty in practice of applying the test of 'assignment', and accordingly those facts are described below.[13] In addition, several principles can be derived with confidence from those cases. One is that there is no need for a particular minimum percentage of an employee's time to be spent in a part of an undertaking for the employee to be assigned to it. Another is that the contract of employment is not determinative as to the part of an employer's business to which an employee is assigned: it is 'not the only matter for consideration'.[14]

Further, as a result of the decision of the Court of Appeal in *Fairhurst Ward* **3.07** *Abbotts Ltd v Botes Building Ltd*,[15] a person who is on sick leave at the time of a TUPE transfer of a part of a business or undertaking but who would otherwise have been employed in that part, is assigned for the purposes of TUPE to that part. As a matter of principle, the same must be true of an employee who is taking a period of sabbatical leave at the time of the transfer. Moreover, as a result of the decision of the EAT in *G4S Justice Services (UK) Ltd v Anstey*,[16] it is

---

[5] ibid, para 16.   [6] ibid.   [7] [1995] IRLR 184.   [8] [1995] IRLR 633.
[9] [1996] ICR 613. It is suggested in J McMullen, *Business Transfers and Employee Rights*, 1998, 3rd edn, Butterworths, looseleaf ('McMullen'), at para 6[48] that there was in that case a 'perhaps over-enthusiastic application of the approach to assignment'. It is hard to disagree with that assessment.
[10] [1996] IRLR 552.   [11] [1994] IRLR 292.
[12] [2002] EWCA Civ 1481; [2003] IRLR 28.   [13] In para 3.09 onwards.
[14] *Duncan Webb Offset (Maidstone) Ltd v Cooper* [1995] IRLR 633, para 17.
[15] [2004] EWCA Civ 83; [2004] ICR 919.   [16] [2006] IRLR 588.

clear that an employee who has been dismissed for gross misconduct, who has appealed against that dismissal, whose appeal has not been determined at the time of the transfer, and who would, if that dismissal had not occurred, have been regarded as assigned to an undertaking which is transferred under TUPE, is to be regarded as assigned to that undertaking for the purposes of TUPE.

3.08   In this context, as in relation to the question whether there has been a TUPE transfer, as long as an employment tribunal asks itself the right questions, takes into account relevant factors, does not take into account irrelevant factors, and does not come to a perverse conclusion on the facts, an appeal should stand little chance of success.[17] Nevertheless, as with the question whether there has been a TUPE transfer, it is helpful to give some examples of the decided cases to illustrate the manner in which an employment tribunal might properly approach the question of assignment.

Illustrations of the application of the word 'assigned'

Sunley Turriff Holdings Ltd v Thomson[18]

3.09   **The facts**   In *Sunley Turriff Holdings Ltd v Thomson*, the claimant was the company secretary and chief accountant of Lilley Construction Ltd ('LC') and of Lilley Construction (Scotland) Ltd ('LC(S)'). His contract of employment was with LC, but part of his work included work in relation to LC(S). Receivers were appointed for both companies on 8 January 1993. The claimant continued to work, assisting the receivers. The business of LC(S) was sold to Sunley Turriff Holdings Ltd ('Sunley') with effect from 18 January. The agreement was made in the name of the receivers of LC(S).

3.10   It was conceded that there was a transfer of an undertaking from LC(S) to Sunley and that the transfer included part of the undertaking of LC, consisting of its work in Scotland. A substantial part of the work which the claimant actually did was concerned with the part of the undertaking of LC which was transferred. However, his name was not included on the schedule of employees transferred to Sunley. Following the sale, he sought an explanation from the receivers as to why he was not being transferred. The reply he received was in these terms: 'Your contract of employment remains with LC Ltd and I only act as agent of the company and do not and will not adopt your contract of employment', although funds would be made available for his work during the receivership. The claimant continued to work on behalf of the receivers until he

---

[17] Although this is clear as a matter of principle, it is stated or indicated in a number of places in the reported cases, such as in paras 40 and 41 of the judgment of Dyson LJ in *CPL Distribution Ltd v Todd* [2002] EWCA Civ 1481; [2003] IRLR 28.

[18] [1995] IRLR 184, EAT.

was made redundant by them on 12 March. He claimed that the transferee had unfairly dismissed him, claiming that, by virtue of TUPE 1981, he was employed in the part of the undertaking which had been transferred. An industrial tribunal held that the claimant was employed in that part of the undertaking which had been sold by the receivers. The tribunal said that 'to see what had truly been transferred in the present case, it was necessary to take the exceptional step of lifting the veil of incorporation'. LC(S) was 'nothing more than a shell company'. Irrespective of what on paper the receivers purported to sell to Sunley, the reality of the situation was, in the opinion of the tribunal, that the purchase by Sunley was of all Scottish contracts in the name of LC and LC(S), together with employees engaged in that part of the business transferred.

3.11 Sunley appealed to the EAT, arguing among other things that 'there was no basis in authority or principle for the Industrial Tribunal's decision to apply the principle of "lifting the veil" in the circumstances of this case'.

3.12 **The decision of the EAT** The EAT dismissed the appeal, for the following reasons:[19]

> In the present case, it may well be that, even on the narrow test proposed by the employers in *Arie Botzen*, supra, the proper view would be that the first respondent [ie the claimant] was, as the respondents submitted, employed exclusively or almost exclusively in connection with the part of the undertaking which was transferred. However, even if that is not the case, it seems to us to be clear that, before the transfer, the first respondent was assigned to the part of the undertaking which was transferred, in accordance with the test laid down in *Botzen*.

3.13 **Comment** The EAT did not answer the question whether lifting the veil of incorporation was or was not inappropriate. However, it is surely right that the reality of the position is what matters, and not technicalities of company law, at least in this context, albeit that a sale of shares does not give rise to a TUPE transfer.[20] The next case to which reference is made below might be thought to contain some support for this proposition.

Duncan Webb Offset (Maidstone) Ltd v Cooper[21]

3.14 **The facts** *Duncan Webb Offset (Maidstone) Ltd v Cooper* concerned claims brought by three former employees of Passmore International Ltd ('Passmore') or one or more of its subsidiaries in the printing industry. These subsidiaries included Passmore Web Offset (Maidstone) ('Maidstone'), and companies in Basildon and St Albans. On 21 March 1994, the business of Maidstone, then in

---

[19] See para 13.   [20] See para 2.01 above.   [21] [1995] IRLR 633, EAT.

receivership, was transferred to Duncan Web Offset ('Duncan'). The employees in question were Mr Cooper, Mr Bateman, and Mrs Russell. They were not taken on by Duncan. They initiated industrial tribunal proceedings. It was necessary for the tribunal to determine whether they were employed in or assigned to the Maidstone undertaking at the time of the transfer.

3.15 Mr Cooper was purchasing manager for the group. He was located at Maidstone's offices and involved in the daily business of that company. After the Basildon company had been acquired, he initially spent a considerable amount of time there, but then reverted to his former work pattern. After the appointment of receivers in early 1993, he was based in Maidstone, doing work for Maidstone. The receivers ran Maidstone and Basildon as separate businesses.

3.16 Mr Bateman worked for a group company in St Albans. When that company closed down in August 1993, he became head of human resources at Maidstone. He carried out that function for both Maidstone and Basildon, but about 80 per cent of his time was spent at Maidstone. After the receivers were appointed, he spent all of his time at Maidstone. Both Mr Cooper and Mr Bateman for 'administrative convenience' were paid by Passmore.

3.17 Mrs Russell, whose last post was acting computer manager, spent about one day a week at Basildon. For the rest of her time she was based at Maidstone. This continued after the receivers were appointed.

3.18 In the sale agreement for the transfer of Maidstone's business to Duncan, those employees to be transferred were identified in a schedule. The names of the three employees in question were included, but were then crossed through.

3.19 Directing itself in accordance with the test put forward in *Gale v Northern General Hospital Trust*,[22] the industrial tribunal found that the employees were employed by Maidstone and that they were assigned to Maidstone. Any duties carried out for other companies in the group were as employees of Maidstone. Therefore, held the tribunal, the employees were employed by the transferor in the undertaking which was transferred under TUPE 1981. Duncan appealed to the EAT against that ruling.

3.20 **The decision of the EAT** The EAT dismissed the appeal, holding that the industrial tribunal had correctly found that the claimants were employed in the undertaking transferred, namely the business of Maidstone, notwithstanding that their contracts of employment with Maidstone required them to work in other parts of the Passmore group and not just for Maidstone.

---

[22] [1994] IRLR 292, concerning which see further para 3.29 below.

The EAT commented[23] that 'It would take some persuasive evidence to suggest **3.21** that an employee was not assigned to the business of his employer, where the whole of his employer's only business was transferred', and that 'such evidence would have to have shown, at the very least, that the bulk of the employees' time and responsibilities were devoted to other entities within the group'. In the present case, 'the facts were wholly against that suggestion'.

Comment The fact that the employer's only business is transferred is not **3.22** determinative in this context. The question is where the employee was assigned to work, and the EAT recognized, in paragraph 17, that

> the contract of employment test is not the only matter for consideration. In other words, an employee might be employed by one company but be assigned to the business of another. Again, tribunals will keep in mind the purpose of Directive 77/187 and the need to avoid complicated corporate structures from getting in the way of a result which gives effect to that purpose.

This might be thought to justify the proposition that it would be possible **3.23** to pierce the corporate veil. However, it is probably not a sufficiently clear statement to justify doing so. In *Michael Peters Ltd v (1) Farnfield and (2) Michael Peters Group plc*,[24] it was argued on behalf of the appellant to the EAT that the industrial tribunal had been wrong to 'pierce the corporate veil'. The EAT accepted the appellant's submissions, but did not go so far as to say that it would be wrong to pierce the corporate veil.[25] Since it did not need to do so, and the reasoning of the EAT was a little opaque (including that 'we find that four of the group's UK subsidiary companies possessed transfer status'[26]), the question may be regarded as undecided by the EAT's decision in that case also. Ultimately, the question of assignment must be one of fact, to be approached on a proper basis.

Buchanon-Smith v Schleicher[27]

The facts In *Buchanon-Smith v Schleicher*, the claimant was employed by **3.24** Tarnator Ltd. Tarnator carried on business both selling and servicing shredding machinery. On 11 February 1993, Tarnator sold the servicing part of the business to Schleicher Ltd, and on 12 February 1993 the sales side of the business stopped trading. The claimant, who had been employed by Tarnator both in selling small machinery and in organising the service department, commenced employment with Schleicher. However, she was dismissed from that employment on 29 September 1993. She made a claim to an industrial tribunal, claiming a redundancy payment. The tribunal held that, although

---

[23] [1995] IRLR 633, para 21.   [24] [1995] IRLR 190, para 15.
[25] ibid, para 17.   [26] Paragraph 18.   [27] [1996] ICR 613, EAT.

there had been a transfer of an identifiable part of Tarnator's business, namely the servicing department, the claimant had not been employed in that part but had been involved in all aspects of Tarnator's business, so that she was not assigned to the part of the business which transferred to Schleicher. Accordingly, held the tribunal, she did not have sufficient continuity of service with Schleicher to entitle her to a redundancy payment. She appealed to the EAT.

3.25 **The decision of the EAT** The EAT overturned the industrial tribunal's decision. The matter was not remitted. The EAT came to the conclusion on the facts as found by the industrial tribunal that the claimant had been assigned to the undertaking which was transferred.

3.26 **Comment** The EAT relied quite heavily on the fact that the sales part of the business of Tarnator ceased to trade on the date of the transfer.[28] However, that surely cannot be relevant to the question of where the claimant was assigned before the transfer.

Securicor Guarding Services Ltd v Fraser Security Services Ltd [29]

3.27 **The facts** In *Securicor Guarding Services Ltd v Fraser Security Services Ltd*, two employees were employed by Securicor as static guards at Datamatic Ltd's premises in Caerphilly. Their contracts of employment contained a mobility clause which allowed Securicor to require them to work at any of Securicor's branches. One employee started his employment with Securicor in 1984 and was based in Newport from then onwards throughout his employment with Securicor, but from May 1992 he worked solely at the Datamatic site. The other employee was based in Cardiff for the whole of his period of employment with Securicor from 1988 onwards, and throughout that period he worked only at the Datamatic site. Datamatic subjected the guarding contract to a competitive tender in 1994, and Fraser Security Services ('Fraser') won the tender. Fraser denied that TUPE applied, and intended to pay less per hour than Securicor had paid the two employees. As a result of the lower rate of pay on offer, the two employees refused to be employed by Fraser. They were not moved to another site by Securicor because Securicor had no equivalent jobs available for them. Five days after Fraser took over the contract, however, Securicor employed the two employees as casual workers. They initiated industrial tribunal proceedings. An industrial tribunal decided, among other things, that the employees were not assigned to the activities at the Datamatic site because of the mobility clause in their contracts of employment. The tribunal held that the employees were instead assigned to the

---

[28] See [1996] ICR 613, 623.   [29] [1996] IRLR 552, EAT.

Newport and Cardiff bases, respectively. Securicor appealed to the EAT against that ruling.

The decision of the EAT The EAT, applying the earlier decision of the Court   **3.28**
of Appeal in *Gale v Northern General Hospital NHS Trust*[30] and contrasting
the situation with the circumstances of *Gale*, allowed the appeal. In the words
of the EAT, the two employees 'were static guards, assigned solely to [the
Datamatic] site unless and until transferred to another site or sites'.[31]

Comment The facts of *Gale* were quite different from those of this case, as   **3.29**
can be seen from the following passage of the judgment of the EAT in this case:

> 23
>
> In *Gale* [1994] IRLR 292, the applicant was a student nurse. His contract
> provided that his employment was for a course in registered general nurse
> training in the Sheffield School of Nursing. He was required to undertake clinical
> nurse training within the Sheffield Health District.
>
> 24
>
> The issue before the industrial tribunal on his complaint of unfair dismissal was
> whether he was employed to work solely at the Northern General Hospital
> immediately before the date on which it assumed trust status in order to show a
> sufficient qualifying period of continuous employment.
>
> 25
>
> In the course of the judgment of the Court given by Sir Thomas Bingham MR he
> considered the question of transfer under the EEC Business Transfers Directive.
> He concluded that at the relevant time the applicant had not been assigned to the
> part transferred, namely the hospital. He was not a member of the permanent
> staff of the hospital, part of its 'human stock', he was somebody who, at the
> behest of the health authority, was completing his training there.
>
> 26
>
> The factual distinctions between that case and the instant case are immediately
> apparent. Here, the employees were Securicor's 'human stock' at the Datamatic
> site. It may have been otherwise had they been 'casuals', filling in from time to
> time at the site. They were not.

CPL Distribution Ltd v Todd[32]

The facts The claimant in *CPL Distribution Ltd v Todd* was one of nine   **3.30**
former employees of CPL Distribution Ltd ('CPL') who made claims to an
employment tribunal in connection with their dismissals. The British Coal
Corporation gave free solid fuel, known as 'concessionary coal', to former
employees in six regions of the country. In 1995, CPL entered into a contract

---

[30] [1994] IRLR 292; see further the next paragraph in the text below.
[31] [1996] IRLR 552, at para 26.   [32] [2002] EWCA Civ 1481; [2003] IRLR 28, CA.

for the supply and distribution of that concessionary coal on behalf of British Coal in five of the six regions. In 1999, Gateway Fuels Ltd ('Gateway') won a tender for a new contract. The contract was to supply all of the six regions. The claimant was employed as a personal assistant ('PA') to a Mr Brennan, who was in 1997 the manager of CPL's concessionary coal distribution business. He was later given additional duties as business acquisitions manager.

3.31   The claimant worked as Mr Brennan's PA wherever he was himself assigned. However, the majority of her typing work in 1999 was related to the concessionary coal contract. A number of employees, the claimant included, were not taken on by Gateway when it took over the supply and distribution of the concessionary coal. Mr Brennan remained employed by CPL as business acquisitions manager, but he was told that the role did not justify the employment of a PA. The affected employees, the claimant included, brought proceedings before an employment tribunal, seeking a determination as to whether there was a TUPE transfer of part of an undertaking in the circumstances, and, if so, whether they were employed in the part transferred. The employment tribunal decided that the claimant was 'effectively assigned to Mr Brennan (whatever role he happened to be doing) rather than to the concessionary coal contract itself'.[33] CPL appealed to the EAT against that decision. The EAT dismissed the appeal. CPL then appealed to the Court of Appeal, arguing that the employment tribunal, having stated the correct test, did not apply it.

3.32   **The decision of the Court of Appeal**   The Court of Appeal dismissed the appeal. All three members of the court were critical of the reasoning of the employment tribunal, but concluded that, on a fair reading of the latter's decision, its conclusion was that since Mr Brennan was not assigned to the concessionary coal contract, the claimant was not so assigned. All three members criticised the statement that the claimant was 'effectively assigned to Mr Brennan (whatever role he happened to be doing) rather than to the concessionary coal contract itself'.[34]

3.33   **Comment**   The appeal necessarily amounted to a perversity challenge, or a challenge that there was no evidence to support the conclusion of the tribunal. Such a challenge is notoriously difficult to make successfully.

Non-transfer of contract of employment of an employee who objects

3.34   In *Katsikas v Constantinidis*,[35] the ECJ ruled that it was open to an employee to object to a transfer under the ARD and that, as a result of such objection, the

---

[33]   *CPL Distribution Ltd v Todd* [2002] EWCA Civ 1481; [2003] IRLR 28, CA, para 8.
[34]   See paras 19, 32, and 39.
[35]   Case C–132/91; [1992] ECR I–6577; [1993] IRLR 179.

employee's employment would not transfer to the transferee. The alternative to such a conclusion would have been odd in modern conditions, since an employee can always resign at any time without penalty other than the theoretical possibility of paying damages for breach of contract. In the UK, there was already provision in regulation 5(5) of TUPE 1981 protecting employees who resigned because of a change in their working conditions which was substantially to their detriment, and it was never suggested that an employee could not simply resign in the event of a transfer to an employer whom he did not like. Nevertheless, in response to the ECJ's ruling in *Katsikas*, the UK Government enacted regulation 5(4A) and (4B) of TUPE 1981, the substance of which is re-enacted as regulation 4(7) and (8) of TUPE, which is subject to regulation 4(9) and (10) of TUPE.[36] Their effect is that if an employee informs the transferor or the transferee that he objects to becoming employed by the transferee, then the employee's employment is neither transferred to the transferee nor treated as having been terminated by the transferor and is instead treated as having been terminated by the transfer, unless the transfer involves or would involve a substantial change in working conditions to the employee's detriment. The objection must be 'conveyed to either the transferor or the transferee', but there is no need for 'any particular method' by which the objection is conveyed.[37] Further,

> it could be either by word or deed, or both, and each case must be looked at on its own facts to determine whether there was a sufficient state of mind to amount to a refusal on the part of the employee to consent to the transfer, and that that state of mind was in fact brought to the attention of either the transferor or the transferee. Furthermore, it must be so brought to their attention before the date of the transfer because, under reg. 5(4B) [now regulation 4(8)], the transfer itself automatically terminates the contract. Accordingly, if the terms of reg. 5(4A) [now regulation 4(7)] are not satisfied in fact, there is an automatic transfer on the appropriate date.[38]

3.35   Regulation 4(7) and (8) might be thought to have the effect that there is no half-way house between (1) the automatic transfer of the contract of employment of an employee who is assigned to the part of an undertaking which is transferred; and (2) the situation in which the employee's contract of employment is terminated by the transfer and the employee is treated as not having been dismissed by the transferor for any purpose. However, that is not so. It is possible for an employee validly to opt out of the protection of TUPE by freely deciding not to transfer under TUPE. This possibility was indicated

---

[36] See para 3.36 below for the effect of reg 4(9) and (10).
[37] *Hay v George Hanson (Building Contractors) Ltd* [1996] IRLR 427, para 10, EAT.
[38] ibid. The Employment Lawyers Association publication, *ela Briefing*, Vol 12, No 7, August 2005 contains an illuminating article by J Baker on objections to transferring under TUPE.

by the ECJ in *Berg and Busschers v Besselsen*[39] and was enunciated by the ECJ in *Katsikas*.[40] It is true that in the latter case the ECJ said that it was open to a member state to provide that in such a case the contract of employment or employment relationship must be regarded as terminated either by the employee or the employer, and that the Member State may also provide that the contract or relationship should be maintained with the transferor.[41] However, it is suggested here that this does not mean that an employee could not, in full knowledge of his right to transfer under TUPE, agree with the transferor that he will remain in the employment of the transferor. It is true that regulation 18 of TUPE precludes contracting-out of the protection of TUPE except in limited circumstances, none of which apply to this situation,[42] but it is suggested that this cannot mean that an employee could not validly agree before a TUPE transfer that, shortly before the transfer, the employee will be redeployed to another part of the transferor's organisation. It would be different if the transferee refuses to employ the employee.[43] The situation would also be different if the employer and the employee are unaware of the effect of the application of TUPE and agree that the employee is not to transfer and is to be paid a redundancy payment: in that situation, the employee's contract of employment would nevertheless transfer to the transferee.[44]

3.36 Further, if a TUPE transfer involves or would involve a substantial and detrimental change in an employee's terms and conditions of employment within the meaning of what is now regulation 4(9) of TUPE, then, subject to regulation 9,[45] the employee is entitled to treat his contract of employment as having been terminated by the transferor or (as the case may be) the transferee, notwithstanding what is now regulation 4(7) and (8).[46] Regulation 4(9) is not a straight re-enactment of regulation 5(5) of TUPE 1981, and involves a considerable change to the law as determined by the Court of Appeal in *Rossiter v Pendragon plc*,[47] where the Court of Appeal ruled that an employee could claim unfair 'constructive' dismissal under regulation 5(5) only where his contract of employment was repudiated or fundamentally breached (ie where the test in section 95(1)(c) of the ERA 1996 was satisfied and the employee

---

[39] Case 144/87; [1988] ECR 2559; [1990] ICR 396, para 12, final sentence.
[40] [1993] IRLR 179, para 34.   [41] See ibid, para 36.
[42] See para 3.48 onwards below.
[43] See eg *Rotsart de Hertaing v J Benoidt* Case C–305/94; [1996] ECR I–5927; [1997] IRLR 127, ECJ.
[44] *Senior Heat Treatment Ltd v Bell* [1997] IRLR 614.
[45] See para 3.48 onwards below for the effect of reg 9.
[46] See *Humphreys v University of Oxford* [2000] ICR 405 concerning a deemed dismissal by a transferor in such circumstances.
[47] [2002] EWCA Civ 745, [2002] ICR 1063.

accordingly had the 'ordinary' right to claim 'constructive' unfair dismissal[48]), and not where there was 'a substantial change . . . made in his working conditions to his detriment' which did not amount to a fundamental breach or repudiation of his contract of employment. Now, as a result of regulation 4(9), an employee can claim unfair dismissal where 'a relevant transfer involves or would involve a substantial change in working conditions to the material detriment of a person whose contract of employment is or would be transferred under [regulation 4(1)]',[49] even if the change is not a breach of contract of any sort. This right is 'without prejudice to any right of an employee arising apart from these Regulations to terminate his contract of employment without notice in acceptance of a repudiatory breach of contract by his employer'.[50] However, an employee who treats himself as 'constructively' dismissed pursuant to regulation 4(9) (and only regulation 4(9)) is not entitled to damages for loss of wages 'in respect of a notice period which the employee has failed to work'.[51]

C. The Effect of TUPE on Affected Employees

The general effect

The contract of employment

Where there is a TUPE transfer, except in certain cases of insolvency,[52] the   **3.37** contract of employment of an employee who is employed by the transferor and who is, immediately before the transfer, assigned (other than on a temporary basis) to the organised grouping of resources or employees that is subject to the transfer is transferred to the transferee, unless regulation 4(7) applies.[53] As a result of regulation 4(3), the same is true of the contract of employment of a person who would have been so employed 'if he had not been dismissed in the circumstances described in regulation 7(1), including, where the transfer is effected by a series of two or more transactions, a person so employed and assigned or who would have been so employed and assigned immediately before

---

[48] Concerning which, see further para 5.33 below.

[49] It will be noted that there is no repetition in reg 4(9) of a reference to the identity of the transferee, whereas reg 5(5) of TUPE 1981 concluded: 'but no such right shall arise by reason only that, under [what is now reg 4(1)], the identify of his employer changes unless the employee shows that, in all the circumstances, the change is a significant change and is to his detriment'.

[50] Regulation 4(11), which applies to reg 4(1), (7), and (8) as well as to reg 4(9).

[51] Regulation 4(10).   [52] See reg 8(7) of TUPE, concerning which, see para 3.52 below.

[53] See reg 4(1) of TUPE and the definition of 'assigned' in reg 2(1). See para 3.34 above regarding the effect of reg 4(7). There is no need for an employee to know the identity of the transferee for reg 4(1) to apply: *Secretary of State for Trade and Industry v Cook* [1997] ICR 288, EAT, declining to follow *Photostatic Copiers (Southern) Ltd v Okuda* [1995] IRLR 11, EAT.

any of those transactions'.[54] Regulation 4(3) was evidently enacted with the intention of giving effect to the decision of the House of Lords in *Litster v Forth Dry Dock & Engineering Co Ltd*.[55] Accordingly, it should not be read as having the effect that the contract of employment is transferred. This is the effect of the later decision of the House of Lords in *Wilson v St Helens Borough Council*,[56] where the House decided that an unfair dismissal in breach of what is now regulation 7(1) is valid or effective, although liability to meet the claim and to pay any compensation in relation to the dismissal passes to the TUPE transferee.[57]

3.38 The contract of employment of an employee who was employed in (or, more accurately, assigned to) a business or undertaking or part of such immediately before a TUPE transfer is often said to be novated, but that term is not used in TUPE. Rather, regulation 4(1) provides that the contract 'shall have effect after the transfer as if originally made between the [employee] and the transferee', and regulation 4(2) provides that, subject to regulations 4(6),[58] 8,[59] and 15(9),[60] (a) all of the transferor's 'rights, powers, duties, and liabilities under or in connection with' the contract which is transferred 'shall be transferred by virtue of this regulation to the transferee', and (b) 'any act or omission before the transfer is completed, of or in relation to the transferor in respect of that contract or a person assigned to that organised grouping of resources or employees, shall be deemed to have been an act or omission of or in relation to the transferee'.[61] Thus if there is a series of transfers under TUPE of an employee's contract of employment, anything done by any transferor in respect of the contract or the employee is deemed to have been done by the transferee.

The effect of collective agreements and agreements with the workforce generally

3.39 In *Whent v T Cartledge Ltd*,[62] the EAT held that changes to pay and conditions of employees whose contracts of employment incorporated a collective

---

[54] Regulation 4(3). See para 3.57 below onwards concerning the effect of reg 7(1).

[55] [1989] ICR 341. That that was the intention of the Government is clear from the statement to that effect made on page 24 of the final consultation document published in March 2005 (with the reference URN 05/926) before the TUPE Regulations 2006 were laid before Parliament. In *Litster*, the House of Lords, approaching the situation purposively, overturned the decision of the Court of Appeal in *Secretary of State for Employment v Spence* [1986] ICR 651. There, the Court of Appeal had interpreted the words 'immediately before' in reg 5(3) of TUPE 1981 literally so that they did not apply to persons who had been unfairly dismissed in breach of what is now reg 7(1) of the TUPE Regulations 2006.

[56] [1998] ICR 1141.   [57] See further para 3.44 below regarding reg 4(3).

[58] Regulation 4(6) provides that reg 4(2) 'shall not transfer or otherwise affect the liability of any person to be prosecuted for, convicted of and sentenced for any offence'.

[59] See para 3.48 below concerning reg 8.

[60] Concerning which, see paras 7.43 and 7.46 below.   [61] See further para 3.56 below.

[62] [1997] IRLR 153.

agreement were altered in accordance with changes made to the collective agreement after the transfer under TUPE of the employees' contracts of employment, even though the transferee had by then de-recognised the relevant trade union. The EAT commented that it would be open to the transferee by negotiation to avoid that result.[63] However, that comment cannot now be taken to be good law, given (1) the decision of the House of Lords in *Wilson v St Helens Borough Council,*[64] and (2) the enactment of the effect of that case in regulations 9 and 18 of TUPE (regulation 9 being new, and regulation 18 being an amended re-enactment of regulation 12 of TUPE 1981).[65] The decision in *Whent* is nevertheless now of dubious status, given the decision of the ECJ in *Werhof v Freeway Traffic Systems Gmbh.*[66] There, the ECJ held that a transferee is not obliged to comply with a collective agreement to which the transferee is not a party.

3.40 The decision in *Werhof* means that the decision of the Court of Appeal in *Glendale Managed Services v Graham*[67] is also suspect. There, the Court of Appeal came to a similar conclusion to that of the EAT in *Whent.* The relevant contracts of employment there included an express term that pay would 'normally be in accordance with' the National Joint Council ('NJC') rates. The Court of Appeal held that the employment tribunal had been right to decide that the transferee was obliged to pay the increased NJC rates. This was because, the court held, there was an implied term to the effect that the transferee would give notice that there was to be a departure from that normal situation if such a departure was to occur, and such notice had not been given.

3.41 In contrast, the decision in *Unicorn Consultancy Services Ltd v Westbrook*[68] is unaffected by *Werhof.* In *Westbrook*, the EAT ruled that employees' rights to profit-related pay ('PRP') transferred under what is now regulation 4(2)(a), even though (1) there might in other cases be some practical difficulties in relation to the determination of the amounts payable; and (2) there was some uncertainty about the liability to pay income tax on the PRP. The decision in *Westbrook* is not affected by the decision of the ECJ in *Werhof* because the latter concerned a collective agreement, and the decision in *Westbrook* concerned a scheme which applied directly to individual employees.

---

[63] [1997] IRLR 153, para 16.   [64] [1998] ICR 1141.
[65] See paras 3.48–3.50 below regarding reg 9 and para 3.65 onwards below regarding reg 18.
[66] Case C–499/04; [2006] IRLR 400.
[67] [2003] Civ 773; [2003] IRLR 465. Mention should, for the sake of completeness, be made here of *Akinclose v Gateshead Metropolitan Borough Council* [2005] IRLR 79, where the EAT distinguished *Whent* on the facts.
[68] [2000] IRLR 80.

3.42   In *MITIE Management Services v French*,[69] the EAT held that an employment tribunal had been wrong to conclude that transferred employees had the right to benefit from the transferor's profit-sharing scheme under which the transferor company had given its employees either a cash payment or shares in the transferor. Nevertheless, applying a purposive and pragmatic approach, the EAT held that the transferee was under an obligation to provide an equivalent or comparable scheme: 'the entitlement of the transferred employees in a case such as this . . . is to participation in a scheme of substantial equivalence but one which is free from unjust, absurd or impossible features'.[70] This decision is also not affected by the decision of the ECJ in *Werhof.*

The effect of restrictive covenants

3.43   Just as an employee's contractual rights transfer under TUPE, with the rights adapted as necessary to apply to the changed circumstances resulting from the transfer, so do restrictive covenants. This was expressly held in *Morris Angel & Son Ltd v Hollande*,[71] where the Court of Appeal enforced a restrictive covenant purposively.

The effect of a dismissal which is in breach of regulation 7(1)

3.44   If (a) an employee who is employed by a transferor and is assigned to the organised grouping of resources or employees that is subject to a TUPE transfer is dismissed before the transfer; and (b) the dismissal is unfair because it is contrary to regulation 7(1),[72] ie because the sole or principal reason for the dismissal is the transfer itself or 'a reason connected with the transfer that is not an economic, technical or organisational reason entailing changes in the workforce', then regulation 4(1) and (2) apply to that employee's contract of employment.[73] If the transfer is effected by a series of two or more transactions, then regulation 4(1) and (2) apply to such an employee who is unfairly dismissed for that reason, as applied in relation to any of those transactions.[74] As stated above, this does not mean that the employee's contract of employment is novated in these circumstances. Rather, the dismissal is valid, but the liability to meet a claim of unfair dismissal and to pay any compensation for such a dismissal passes to the transferee.[75]

Liability to pay interim relief

3.45   However, liability to pay an employee where an order for interim relief is made under section 163(6) of TULRA (which applies where the employee claims

---

[69] [2002] ICR 1395.   [70] ibid, para 16.   [71] [1993] ICR 71.
[72] See para 3.57 below onwards concerning the effect of reg 7(1).   [73] TUPE, reg 4(3).
[74] ibid.   [75] See para 3.37 above.

that he has been dismissed unfairly by reason of section 152 of that Act), does not transfer under regulation 4(2).[76]

Variations to the contract of employment

The general rule

Any purported variation to a contract of employment which is, or will   **3.46** be, transferred by regulation 4(1), is, unless it is permitted by regulation 9 (concerning which see the next section below) void if the sole or principal reason for the variation is either the TUPE transfer itself or a reason connected with the transfer that is not an economic, technical, or organisational reason entailing changes in the workforce.[77] Such a contract of employment may nevertheless be varied if the sole or principal reason for the variation is unconnected with the transfer or is 'a reason connected with the transfer that is not an economic, technical or organisational reason entailing changes in the workforce'.[78]

Certain variations are permitted by regulation 9 of TUPE, which applies only   **3.47** where the transferor is insolvent.

The effect of insolvency

As a result of regulation 8 of TUPE, the existence at the time of a TUPE   **3.48** transfer of insolvency proceedings as defined by regulation 8(6), ie 'insolvency proceedings which have been opened in relation to the transferor not with a view to the liquidation of the assets of the transferor and which are under the supervision of an insolvency practitioner',[79] has two main effects. One is that the Secretary of State's liability (1) under Chapter VI of Part XI of the ERA 1996 to make redundancy payments; and (2) under Part XII of the ERA 1996 to make certain other payments relating to an insolvent employer's employees applies to any employees of the insolvent transferor who have not been dismissed or who have been dismissed before the transfer in the circumstance that regulation 7(1) makes the dismissal unfair.[80] A related effect of this is that regulation 4 of TUPE does not operate to transfer to a TUPE transferee liability for the sums so payable by the Secretary of State to the relevant

---

[76] *Dowling v M E Ilic Haulage* [2004] ICR 1176, EAT.

[77] TUPE, reg 4(4). This enacts one major effect of *Wilson v St Helens Borough Council* [1998] ICR 1141, HL. The normal age of retirement may change after a transfer without contravening the protection provided by reg 4(4): see *Cross v British Airways plc* [2006] EWCA Civ 549; The Times, 5 June 2006.

[78] Regulation 4(5). See further para 3.65 onwards below.

[79] The expression 'insolvency practitioner' is defined by reg 2(1) of TUPE for the purposes of TUPE to have the meaning given to that expression by Pt XIII of the Insolvency Act 1986.

[80] See reg 8(2)–(4) of TUPE. See para 3.57 below for the effect of reg 7(1).

employee(s).[81] The other main effect of the insolvency proceedings referred to in regulation 8(6) of TUPE is that regulation 9(1) of TUPE permits the transferor or the transferee (or an insolvency practitioner) and 'appropriate representatives of assigned employees' to agree to 'permitted variations'.[82]

3.49 The definition of 'appropriate representatives' for this purpose is in regulation 9(2). If the 'assigned employees' (meaning 'those employees assigned to the organised grouping of resources or employees that is the subject of a relevant transfer'[83]) are of a description in respect of which an independent trade union is recognised by their employer, then the appropriate representatives are representatives of that trade union.[84] In any other case, the appropriate representatives are either (1) employee representatives who were appointed or elected by the 'assigned employees (whether they make the appointment or election alone or with others)' otherwise than for the purposes of regulation 9 who '(having regard to the purposes for, and the method by which they were appointed or elected) have authority from those employees to agree permitted variations to contracts of employment on their behalf'; or (2) employee representatives elected by assigned employees (whether they make the appointment or election alone or with others) for 'these particular purposes' (ie presumably the purposes of regulation 9), in an election which satisfied requirements identical to those contained in regulation 14 of TUPE apart from those in regulation 14(1)(d).[85]

3.50 A 'permitted variation' for this purpose is a variation to the contract of employment of an assigned employee the sole or principal reason for which is the transfer itself or a reason connected with the transfer that is not an economic, technical, or organisational reason entailing changes in the workforce, and which (ie the variation) is 'designed to safeguard employment opportunities by ensuring the survival of the undertaking, business or part of the undertaking or business that is the subject of the relevant transfer'.[86] Where the appropriate representatives are not representatives of an independent trade union, the agreement recording the permitted variation must be in writing and signed by each of the representatives who have made it or, where that is not reasonably practicable, by a duly authorised agent of that representative, and the employer must, before the agreement is made available for signature, provide all of the employees to whom it is intended to apply on the date on which it is intended to come into effect with copies of the text of the agreement

---

[81] Regulation 8(5).
[82] Regulation 9(1) applies where there are 'relevant insolvency proceedings', and reg 9(7) provides that such proceedings are as defined by reg 8(6).
[83] Regulation 9(7).   [84] Regulation 9(2)(a).
[85] Regulation 9(2)(b); as to reg 14, see paras 7.12 and 7.13 below.   [86] See reg 9(7).

and 'such guidance as those employees might reasonably require in order to understand it fully'.[87] Presumably for the avoidance of doubt, regulation 9(6) provides that a permitted variation takes effect as a 'term or condition' of the assigned employee's contract of employment, 'in place, where relevant, of any term or condition which it varies'.

It should be noted that, apart from the differences described in the three preceding paragraphs above, insolvency of the sort described by regulation 8(6) does not affect the transfer of liabilities to a TUPE transferee. Thus, for example, liability to meet a claim of unfair dismissal will nevertheless pass to a TUPE transferee, as will a liability to pay notice or redundancy pay which is greater than as provided for by 'the relevant statutory schemes'.[88]   **3.51**

In contrast, regulations 4 and 7 of TUPE do not apply to a transfer 'where the transferor is the subject of bankruptcy proceedings or any analogous proceedings which have been instituted with a view to the liquidation of the assets of the transferor and are under the supervision of an insolvency practitioner'.[89] This exception is in effect a simple transposition of Article 5(1) of Directive 2001/23/EC. Whether a particular insolvency procedure is within this exception will fall to be determined by reference to *D'Urso v Ercole Marelli Elettromeccanica Generale SpA*[90] and subsequent cases, including *Jules Dethier Équipement SA v Dassy*.[91] Thus 'in deciding whether Directive (77/187/E.E.C) applies to the transfer of an undertaking subject to an administrative or judicial procedure, the determining factor to be taken into consideration is the purpose of the procedure in question'.[92]   **3.52**

Pension rights

Pension rights under a transferor's occupational pension scheme (within the meaning of the Pension Schemes Act 1993) are specifically excluded by regulation 10(1) of TUPE from the operation of regulation 4 of TUPE. However, regulation 10(2) provides that for the purposes of regulation 10(1), 'any provisions of an occupational pension scheme which do not relate to benefits for old age, invalidity or survivors shall not be treated as being part of the scheme'. The combined effect of the decisions of the ECJ in *Beckmann v Dynamco Whicheloe Macfarlane Ltd*[93] and *Martin v South Bank University*[94] is that pension rights within the meaning of regulation 10(2) include rights which are contingent on   **3.53**

---

[87] Regulation 9(5).   [88] This is to be inferred from reg 8(5), read with reg 4(1) and (2).
[89] ibid, reg 8(7). See reg 2(1) for the definition of an 'insolvency practitioner'.
[90] Case C–362/89; [1992] IRLR 136, ECJ.
[91] Case C–319/94; [1998] ICR 541.   [92] ibid, 560, para 25.
[93] Case C–164/00; [2003] ICR 50.   [94] Case C–04/01; [2004] ICR 1234.

dismissal by reason of redundancy or the grant of early retirement by agreement with the employer. Thus those rights which are so contingent do transfer under TUPE.

3.54 It is now provided in regulation 10(3) that an employee may not claim that the transferee has breached his contract of employment or 'constructively' dismissed him (ie within the meaning of section 95(1)(c) of the ERA 1996) as a result of a 'loss or reduction in his rights under an occupational pension scheme in consequence of the transfer, save insofar as the alleged breach of contract or dismissal (as the case may be) occurred prior to the date on which these Regulations took effect'. However, against this must be set the effect of the Transfer of Employment (Pension Protection) Regulations 2005,[95] to which further reference is made in Chapter 9 below.

3.55 For the sake of completeness, mention is made here of the decision of the House of Lords in *Preston v Wolverhampton Healthcare NHS Trust (No 3)*.[96] There, the House of Lords ruled that, in relation to a claim for equal pension rights on the basis that there has been discrimination on the ground of sex, time begins to run on the date of a TUPE transfer.[97]

Other rights and liabilities

3.56 Rights and liabilities not arising under the contract of employment are transferred by regulation 4(2)(b) of TUPE.[98] Such liabilities include liabilities in negligence for personal injury[99] and liability for a failure properly to consult under what is now regulation 13 of TUPE.[100] The latter situation is after 5 April 2006 superseded by regulation 15(9) of TUPE, which provides that the transferor and the transferee are in that situation jointly and severally liable.[101] Where a transferor had employer's liability insurance which covered a personal injury liability which transfers, the benefit of that insurance cover is transferred by regulation 4(2)(b).[102] Where a transferor was at the relevant time as a result of section 3(1)(a), (b), or (c) of the Employers' Liability (Compulsory Insurance)

---

[95] SI 2005/649.   [96] [2006] UKHL 13; [2006] ICR 606.

[97] See further para 9.10 below.

[98] See para 3.38 above. One exception which is not mentioned in TUPE is that liability to pay income tax and national insurance contributions in respect of net pay already paid at the time of transfer does not transfer under TUPE: see reg 102 of the Income Tax (Pay As You Earn) Regulations 2003, SI 2003/2682.

[99] See *Martin v Lancashire County Council* [2001] ICR 197, CA.

[100] See *Alamo Group (Europe) Ltd v Tucker* [2003] ICR 829. The EAT sitting in London there declined to follow the decision of the EAT sitting in Scotland in *Transport & General Workers' Union v McKinnon, J R Haulage Ltd* [2001] ICR 1281.

[101] See paras 7.43 and 7.46 below.

[102] *Martin v Lancashire County Council* [2001] ICR 197, CA.

Act 1969 not required to have or (as the case may be) was exempted from the requirement to have such insurance,[103] the transferor and transferee are in relation to transfers which occurred on or after 6 April 2006 jointly and severally liable in respect of the relevant liability 'in so far as such liability relates to the employee's employment with the transferor'.[104]

Protection from unfair dismissal

Overview

If an employee is dismissed (whether expressly or 'constructively'[105]), either   **3.57**
before or after a TUPE transfer, and the sole or principal reason for the dismissal is either the transfer itself or 'a reason connected with the transfer that is not an economic, technical or organisational reason entailing changes in the workforce', then the dismissal is automatically unfair within the meaning of Part X of the ERA 1996.[106] This is so whether or not the employee is employed in the organised grouping of resources or employees which has been, or is to be, transferred.[107] There is no need for the dismissal to be connected with the specific transfer which eventuates. It need only be connected with 'a transfer'.[108] For this purpose there is no limit on the distance in time between a dismissal and the transfer which is to occur or has occurred, although the further away in time a dismissal is from the transfer, as a matter of practical reality, the more difficult it will be to satisfy an employment tribunal that the reason for the dismissal was 'a reason connected with the transfer'.[109]

The protection afforded to an affected employee by way of a right to claim   **3.58**
unfair dismissal does not apply unless the employee satisfies the conditions for

---

[103] See Sch 2 to the Employers' Liability (Compulsory Insurance) Regulations 1998, SI 1998/2573, as amended, for the employers exempted by s 3(1)(c) of the 1969 Act from the requirement to effect insurance.

[104] See reg 17(2) of TUPE, read with reg 21(1).

[105] This therefore includes the situation where the employer imposes a fundamental change to an employee's terms and conditions of employment; see further para 5.33 below.

[106] TUPE, reg 7(1).   [107] Regulation 7(4).

[108] See the decision of the EAT in *Morris v John Grose Group Ltd* [1998] ICR 655, preferring the decision of the EAT in *Harrison Bowden Ltd v Bowden* [1994] ICR 186 to that of the EAT in *Ibex Trading Co Ltd v Walton* [1994] ICR 907. McMullen comments in para 8[49] on page 8/13E that there is not in reality a conflict between the latter two cases, since 'the EAT in the *Ibex Trading* case itself contemplated that it was not *always* obligatory for an actual transferee to be identified' (emphasis in original).

[109] cf the situation of the employees in *British Fuels Ltd v Baxendale* [1998] ICR 1141, as described by Lord Slynn at 1165. An example of an appellate case in which a dismissal which occurred two years after a transfer was held to have been properly found to have been for a reason connected with the transfer is that of *Taylor v Connex South Eastern Ltd*, EAT/12434/99 (the text of which is available on the EAT's website), where, in para 26, Judge Wilkie QC on behalf of the EAT said this: 'The mere passage of time without anything happening does not in itself, constitute a weakening to the point of dissolution of the chain of causation.'

the right to claim unfair dismissal referred to in section 94(2) of the ERA 1996 (such as a year's continuous employment).[110] Nor does it apply to an employee if the employee's right to claim unfair dismissal is excluded by or under (1) any other provision of the ERA 1996; (2) any provision of the Employment Tribunals Act 1996, or (3) any provision of the Trade Union and Labour Relations (Consolidation) Act 1992.[111] Nor does it apply to an employee whose dismissal is required by reason of the application of section 5 of the Aliens Restriction (Amendment) Act 1919 to his employment.[112]

3.59 Where the sole or principal reason for the dismissal is a reason connected with the transfer and that reason is an economic, technical, or organisational reason entailing changes in the workforce ('ETOR') of either the transferor or the transferee before or after a relevant transfer, then the dismissal is not automatically unfair.[113] Further, the reason for the dismissal is then deemed to have been either (1) redundancy, where the definition in section 139 of the ERA 1996 is satisfied; or (2) where that is not so, for a 'substantial reason of a kind such as to justify the dismissal of an employee holding the position which that employee held', ie 'some other substantial reason' within the meaning of section 98(1)(b) of the ERA 1996.[114] Accordingly, in those circumstances the dismissal will be fair as long as the test in section 98(4) of the ERA 1996 is satisfied, namely that the dismissal fell within the range of reasonable responses of a reasonable employer. The need to comply with the procedures in Schedule 2 to the Employment Act 2002 ('EA 2002') should not be forgotten. Thus if there is an express dismissal (ie a dismissal within the meaning of section 95(1)(a) or (b) of the ERA 1996), then, subject to the exceptions referred to in the following sentence below, the employer will be obliged to comply with the relevant disciplinary and dismissal procedure ('DDP') in Part 1 of Schedule 2.[115] The relevant exceptions are set out in regulation 4 of the Employment Act 2002 (Dispute Resolution) Regulations 2004. These include that (1) all of the employees of the description or category to which the dismissed employee belongs have been dismissed and offered new terms to take effect either before or on the termination of the original contracts of employment; or (2) 'the dismissal is one of a number of dismissals in respect of which the duty in section 188 of the 1992 Act (duty of employer to consult representatives when proposing to dismiss as redundant a certain number of employees) applies'. A failure by the employer to follow the relevant DDP will make the

---

[110] Regulation 7(6).   [111] Regulation 7(6).   [112] Regulation 7(5).

[113] Regulation 7(2) and (3)(a). It is for the employer to establish the existence of an ETOR: *Gateway Hotels Ltd v Stewart* [1988] IRLR 287, para 14, EAT.

[114] Regulation 7(2) and (3)(b).

[115] See reg 3(1) of the Employment Act 2002 (Dispute Resolution) Regulations 2004, SI 2004/752, read with reg 2(1) of those regulations.

dismissal automatically unfair,[116] although the compensation payable for the dismissal will not necessarily be substantial.[117]

A dismissal which is in breach of regulation 7(1) is effective even though the **3.60** liability to meet the claim of unfair dismissal transfers to the transferee under regulation 4(3).[118]

What is an 'economic, technical or organisational reason entailing changes in the workforce'?

A dismissal which is effected merely in order to obtain a better price for a **3.61** business is not for an ETOR.[119] However, if a contract for the provision of services requires a reduction in the number of employees who are employed in or in connection with the provision of those services, then the dismissal of the 'surplus' employees will (according to the decision of the Court of Appeal in *Whitehouse v C A Blatchford Ltd*[120]) be for an ETOR. The situation has now been overtaken to an extent by the enactment of regulation 7(3)(b) of the TUPE Regulations 2006, which provides in relation to a dismissal for an ETOR that

> without prejudice to the application of section 98(4) of the 1996 Act (test of fair dismissal), the dismissal shall, for the purposes of section 98(1) and 135 of that Act (reason for dismissal), be regarded as having been for redundancy where section 98(2)(c) of that Act applies, or otherwise for a substantial reason of a kind such as to justify the dismissal of an employee holding the position which that employee held.[121]

Helpful guidance as to the appropriate approach to take in determining the **3.62** reason for a dismissal where there is a TUPE transfer was given by the EAT in *Thompson v SCS Consulting Ltd*,[122] where the EAT stated that where the sole or principal reason for a dismissal appears to have been the transfer or a reason connected with it but an ETOR is alleged by the employer, then the employment tribunal must make a finding of fact as to the reason for the dismissal. If the dismissal was for an ETOR, then regulation 7(1) is excluded. In making

---

[116] ERA 1996, s 98A(1).   [117] See para 5.55 below.

[118] See *Wilson v St Helens Borough Council* [1998] ICR 1141, HL.

[119] *Wheeler v Patel* [1987] ICR 631, the effect of which was approved by Buxton LJ in *Whitehouse v C A Blatchford Ltd* [2000] ICR 542 at 554.

[120] ibid, 554–5.

[121] This provision replaces reg 8(2)(b) of TUPE 1981, which did not refer to redundancy as a reason which was capable of falling within what is now reg 7(2) of the TUPE Regulations 2006. Rather, reference was made in reg 8(2)(b) of TUPE 1981 only to SOSR. It was decided by the Court of Appeal in *Warner v Adnet Ltd* [1998] ICR 1056 that redundancy was an SOSR within the meaning of reg 8(2) of TUPE 1981. Regulation 7(3)(b) of the TUPE Regulations 2006 supersedes that aspect of the Court of Appeal's decision as far as transfers after 5 April 2006 are concerned.

[122] [2001] IRLR 801, paras 36 and 37.

that finding of fact the tribunal must 'consider whether the reason was connected with the future conduct of the business as a going concern', and in doing so may take into account 'whether there was any collusion between transferor and transferee and whether the transferor or those acting on its behalf had any funds to carry on the business or any business at the time of the decision to dismiss'. Finally, an appellate tribunal 'should only interfere with such a factual decision if the tribunal erred in law by applying the wrong test, by considering an irrelevant factor, by failing to consider a relevant factor or by reaching a perverse decision'.

3.63 A dismissal in the form of the imposition by the employer of new financial and related terms and conditions of employment on employees who are protected by regulation 7(1) of TUPE (whether by giving notice and offering new terms, or simply imposing the terms and thereby giving the employees a right to claim that they have been 'constructively' dismissed, ie dismissed within the meaning of section 95(1)(c) of the ERA 1996) is not for an ETOR.[123] However, a complete change in the duties of an employee may be an ETOR.[124]

3.64 A transferee will not be able to rely on an ETOR where the transferor dismissed the employee before the transfer, in the belief that the employee was not protected by TUPE.[125]

Restriction on contracting-out of the protection afforded by TUPE

3.65 Employees are protected by regulation 18 of TUPE from improper pressure being brought to bear on them by transferors or transferees. Regulation 18 provides:

> Section 203 of the 1996 Act (restrictions on contracting out) shall apply in relation to these Regulations as if they were contained in that Act, save for that section shall not apply in so far as these Regulations provide for an agreement (whether a contract of employment or not) to exclude or limit the operation of these Regulations.

3.66 This provision, read with regulation 4(4) and (5),[126] reflects the ruling of the ECJ in *Foreningen af Arbejdsledere i Danmark v Daddy's Dance Hall A/S*[127] as applied by the House of Lords in *Wilson v St Helens Borough Council*[128] and the ECJ's decision in *Martin v South Bank University*.[129] In the latter, the ECJ said:[130]

---

[123] *Delabole Slate Ltd v Berriman* [1985] ICR 546, CA; *Martin v South Bank University*, Case C–04/01; [2004] ICR 1234, ECJ, concerning which see paras 3.66–3.67 below.
[124] *Crawford v Swinton Insurance Brokers Ltd* [1990] ICR 85, EAT.
[125] *BSG Property Services v Tuck* [1996] IRLR 134.
[126] Concerning which, see para 3.46 above.
[127] Case 324/86; [1988] ECR 739; [1988] IRLR 315.
[128] [1998] ICR 1141.   [129] Case C–04/01; [2004] ICR 1234.   [130] ibid, 1259.

41

However, the Directive [ie Directive 77/187/EEC] is intended to achieve only partial harmonisation, essentially by extending the protection guaranteed to workers independently by the laws of the individual member states to cover the case where an undertaking is transferred. It is not intended to establish a uniform level of protection throughout the Community on the basis of common criteria. Thus the Directive can be relied on only to ensure that the employee is protected in his relations with the transferee to the same extent as he was in his relations with the transferor under the legal rules of the member state concerned (*Daddy's Dance Hall*, at p 754, para 16).

42

Consequently, in so far as national law allows the employment relationship to be altered in a manner unfavourable to employees in situations other than the transfer of an undertaking, such an alternative is not precluded merely because the undertaking has been transferred in the meantime and the agreement has therefore been made with the new employer. Since by virtue of article 3(1) of the Directive [which is so far as relevant in the same terms as Article 3(1) of Directive 2001/23/EC] the transferee is subrogated to the transferor's rights and obligations under the employment relationship, that relationship may be altered with regard to the transferee to the same extent as it could have been with regard to the transferor, provided that the transfer of the undertaking itself may never constitute the reason for that amendment (*Daddy's Dance Hall*, at pp 754–755, para 17).

Nevertheless, as the ECJ also held in *Martin*, achieving the harmonisation of **3.67** terms of employment after a TUPE transfer will be connected to the transfer, and the transfer will itself at least normally be 'the reason' for any detrimental change to the transferred employees' contractual rights.[131]

If, however, there is a TUPE transfer from the private sector to the public **3.68** sector, then, according to the decision of the ECJ in *Boor v Ministre de la Fonction Publique*,[132] if the contractual terms of employees who are employed in the public sector are fixed by law, an employee's forced agreement to the new (public sector) terms will not be invalidated by regulation 18. As J McMullen suggests in *Business Transfers and Employee Rights*,[133] this decision 'sits rather oddly' with the previous ECJ authorities, and it 'remains . . . to be seen whether this is a *sui generis* case confined to the particular public sector context where there is a conflict between a transferring employee's pay rate and national scales previously laid down by legislation, or whether, alternatively, it displays a weakening of the court's approach on contract changes by reason of the transfer'.

---

[131] ibid, paras 44 and 45.   [132] Case C–425/02; [2005] IRLR 61.
[133] 3rd edn, 1998, looseleaf, Butterworths, para 9[108].

3.69 It is of interest that the EAT under the chairmanship of Elias J held in *Solectron Scotland Ltd v Roper*[134] that the predecessor to what is now regulation 18 of the TUPE Regulations 2006 (regulation 12 of TUPE 1981, which was in rather different terms to those of regulation 18) did not preclude an employee whose contract of employment was transferred under TUPE and who was subsequently dismissed from compromising a claim for an enhanced redundancy payment which it was alleged was a contractual entitlement of the transferor's employees.[135] Regulation 18 of the TUPE Regulations 2006, it seems clear, also does not prohibit such an agreement.

---

[134] [2004] IRLR 4.

[135] In *Solectron* the fact that the employee had been dismissed was determinative: see *Solectron Scotland Ltd v Roper* [2004] IRLR 4, para 44.

4

THE LAW OF REDUNDANCY

A. Introduction

If an employer 'outsources' some of its work, and there is not a TUPE transfer, **4.01** then it is highly likely that one or more employees will be redundant within the meaning of the ERA 1996.[1] The law of redundancy, in so far as it relates to an individual employee,[2] is relevant in relation to two questions. One is whether the

---

[1] See eg *Bromby & Hoare Ltd v Evans* [1972] ICR 113, NIRC, and *Scarth v Economic Forestry Ltd* [1973] ICR 322, NIRC.

[2] The definition of 'redundancy' is different for the purposes of the law relating to collective consultation: see para 6.02 below.

employee is entitled to a redundancy payment. The other is whether the employee was dismissed for a potentially fair reason. In the following paragraphs, the definition of redundancy and related questions are considered first. Questions relating to entitlement to a redundancy payment are then considered. The issues which arise where an employee claims unfair dismissal and the employer claims that the reason for the dismissal was redundancy are described in Chapter 5 below.

B. Amount of a Redundancy Payment

4.02 A redundancy payment is calculated in the same way as a basic award within the meaning of section 119 of the ERA 1996.[3] The manner in which a basic award is calculated is stated in paragraphs 5.50 and 5.51 below. The current maximum for a statutory redundancy payment or a basic award is £8,700 (ie 30 times £290).

C. The Definition of 'Redundancy'

4.03 The definition of redundancy in section 139(1) of the ERA 1996 is relevant both for the purpose of determining entitlement to a redundancy payment and for the purposes of the law of unfair dismissal.[4] It is this:

> For the purposes of this Act an employee who is dismissed shall be taken to be dismissed by reason of redundancy if the dismissal is wholly or mainly attributable to—
>
> (a) the fact that his employer has ceased or intends to cease—
>
> > (i) to carry on the business for the purposes of which the employee was employed by him, or
> > (ii) to carry on that business in the place where the employee was so employed, or
>
> (b) the fact that the requirements of that business—
>
> > (i) for employees to carry out work of a particular kind, or
> > (ii) for employees to carry out work of a particular kind in the place where the employee was employed by the employer,
>
> have ceased or diminished or are expected to cease or diminish.[5]

---

[3] See ERA 1996, s 162.

[4] But note the exception that the 'disappearing dismissal' provided for by s 138 of the ERA 1996, described in para 4.22 below, does not apply for the purposes of the law of unfair dismissal: *Hempell v W H Smith & Sons Ltd* [1986] ICR 365, approved by the Court of Appeal in *Jones v Governing Body of Burdett Coutts School* [1999] ICR 38, 43.

[5] The requirements of the employer may cease or diminish only temporarily: s 139(6). For the effect of this provision where an employee is engaged under a series of fixed-term contracts, see eg *Pfaffinger v City of Liverpool Community College* [1997] ICR 142, EAT.

Case law concerning the definition in section 139(1)

Some welcome clarity

The seemingly simple definition in section 139(1)[6] has generated much case **4.04**
law. From the point of view of exposition, it is fortunate that, in *Murray v Foyle
Meats Ltd*,[7] the House of Lords fully and firmly approved the analysis of the
EAT (Judge Peter Clark presiding) in *Burrell v Safeway Stores Ltd*,[8] where a
number of difficult issues arising from that case law were clarified.

One proposition which was therefore put beyond doubt was that, in applying **4.05**
the test in section 139(1)(b), the question is whether the employer's requirements for employees to do work of a particular kind have ceased or diminished, not whether there is work of that sort to be done.[9] The general
approach is to ask: '(1) was the employee dismissed? If so, (2) had the
requirements of the employer's business for employees to carry out work of a
particular kind ceased or diminished, or were they expected to cease or diminish? If so, (3) was the dismissal of the employee (the applicant before the
industrial tribunal) caused wholly or mainly by the state of affairs identified at
stage (2) above?'[10]

The following passage in the judgment of the EAT in *Burrell*[11] is both illumin- **4.06**
ating as to the general approach which must be taken and informative as to a
number of difficulties which had previously built up in the case law concerning
the application of what is now section 139(1):

(1) There may be a number of underlying causes leading to a true redundancy
situation: our stage (2). There may be a need for economies, a reorganisation in
the interests of efficiency, a reduction in production requirements, unilateral
changes in the employees' terms and conditions of employment. None of these
factors are themselves determinative of the stage (2) question. The only question to be asked is: was there a diminution/cessation in the employer's requirement for employees to carry out work of a particular kind, or an expectation of
such cessation/diminution in the future? (redundancy). At this stage it is irrelevant to consider the terms of the applicant employee's contract of employment.
That will only be relevant, if at all, at stage (3) (assuming that there is a
dismissal).

(2) At stage (3) the tribunal is concerned with causation: Was the dismissal
attributable wholly or mainly to the redundancy? Thus:

---

[6] cf the words of Lord Irvine in *Murray v Foyle Meats Ltd* [1999] ICR 827, 829: 'My Lords, the
language of paragraph (*b*) is in my view simplicity itself.'
[7] [1999] ICR 827.   [8] [1997] ICR 523.
[9] See *Burrell v Safeway Stores Ltd* [1997] ICR 523, 530, approving *Carry All Motors Ltd v
Pennington* [1980] ICR 806, EAT.
[10] *Burrell v Safeway Stores plc* [1997] ICR 523, 529.   [11] ibid, 538–540.

(a) Even if a redundancy situation arises, as in *Nelson v. British Broadcasting Corporation* [1977] I.C.R. 649, if that does not cause the dismissal, the employee has not been dismissed by reason of redundancy. In *Nelson* the employee was directed to transfer to another job as provided for in his contract. He refused to do so. That was why he was dismissed.

(b) If the requirement for employees to perform the work of a transport clerk and transport manager diminishes, so that one employee can do both jobs, the dismissed employee is dismissed by reason of redundancy: see *Carry All Motors Ltd. v. Pennington* [1980] I.C.R. 806. The same explanation applies, on the facts, to the eventual decision in *Robinson v. British Island Airways Ltd.* [1978] I.C.R. 304. In *Cowen v. Haden Ltd.* [1983] I.C.R. 1 the requirement for employees to do the work of a divisional contracts surveyor ceased. The post-holder was dismissed. That was a dismissal by reason of redundancy.

(c) Conversely, if the requirement for employees to do work of a particular kind remains the same, there can be no dismissal by reason of redundancy, notwithstanding any unilateral variation to their contracts of employment: see *Chapman v. Goonvean and Rostowrack China Clay Co. Ltd.* [1973] I.C.R. 310; *Lesney Products Co. Ltd. v. Nolan* [1977] I.C.R. 235; and *Johnson v. Nottinghamshire Combined Police Authority* [1974] I.C.R. 170.

(d) The contract versus function test debate is predicated on a misreading of both the statute and the cases of *Nelson* and *Cowen v. Haden Ltd.* Save for the limited circumstances arising from Nelson where an employee is redeployed under the terms of his contract of employment and refuses to move, and this causes his dismissal, the applicant/employee's terms and conditions of employment are irrelevant to the questions raised by the statute.

(e) This explains the concept of 'bumped redundancies'. Take this example, an employee is employed to work as a fork lift truck driver, delivering materials to six production machines on the shop floor. Each machine has its own operator. The employer decides that it needs to run only five machines and that one machine operator must go. That is a stage (2) redundancy situation. Selection for dismissal is done on the last in, first out principle within the department. The fork lift truck driver has the least service. Accordingly, one machine operator is transferred to driving the truck; the short service truck driver is dismissed. Is he dismissed by reason of redundancy? The answer is, 'Yes'. Although, under both the contract and function tests, he is employed as a fork lift driver, and there is no diminution in the requirement for fork lift drivers, nevertheless there is a diminution in the requirement for employees to carry out the operators' work and that has caused the employee's dismissal: see, for example, *W. Gimber Sons Ltd. v. Spurrett* (1967) 2 I.T.R. 308 and *Elliott Turbomachinery v. Bates* [1981] I.C.R. 218. In our judgment, the principle of 'bumped redundancies' is statutorily correct, and further demonstrates the flaw in the 'contract test' adumbrated in *Pink v. White (Earls Barton) Ltd.* [1985] I.R.L.R. 489.

(f) Our approach is also consistent with the decision of the Court of Appeal in *Murphy v. Epsom College* [1985] I.C.R. 80. There, the applicant was one of two plumbers employed by a school. His work consisted mainly of general plumbing work. The employers decided to employ a heating technician to maintain their improved heating system. They then decided to dismiss one of the two plumbers and selected the employee for dismissal. The Court of Appeal upheld the majority view of the industrial tribunal that the reason for dismissal was redundancy. The employer originally had two plumbers, now it only required one. The employee was dismissed by reason of redundancy.

In *Murray v Foyle Meats Ltd*,[12] Lord Irvine LC (with whose speech Lord Jauncey, **4.07** Lord Slynn, and Lord Hoffman agreed) said: 'I need to say no more than that I entirely agree with [Judge Peter Clark's] admirably clear reasoning and conclusions [in *Burrell*].' Lord Clyde, with whose speech Lord Jauncey and Lord Hoffman agreed, and whose judgment accordingly also forms part of the ratio of the decision in *Murray*, emphasised, however, the importance of simply applying the words of section 139(1) as they stand, without devising any further test to be applied when doing so.[13]

Lord Clyde also said that 'the provisions of the contracts of employment are **4.08** [not] necessarily irrelevant; in some circumstances they may be useful, for example in throwing light on the kinds of work carried out or the place of employment. But the contractual terms are not determinative of the application of the subsection.'[14] This was consistent with the decision of the EAT in *Bass Leisure v Thomas*,[15] which was approved by the Court of Appeal in *High Table Ltd v Horst*.[16] The combined effect of the latter cases is that, when deciding whether an employee was dismissed for redundancy by reason of the closure of the employee's normal workplace, the fact that the employee has a contractually binding mobility clause will not mean that the employee was dismissed for conduct rather than redundancy.

A slight muddying of the water: Shawkat

One case which casts a small shadow on the otherwise clear picture resulting **4.09** from the decisions in *Murray* and *Horst* is that of *Shawkat v Nottingham City Hospital NHS Trust (No 2)*.[17] There, the Court of Appeal declined to overturn an employment tribunal's decision that an employee was not redundant where his employer dismissed him for refusing to accept a post as a cardiac and thoracic surgeon when he had previously been employed as a purely thoracic surgeon. The court's ruling was based on the proposition that it was for the employment tribunal to decide whether, as a matter of fact, the employer's requirements for employees to carry out work of a particular kind had ceased or diminished, and that, since the tribunal had stated that it had done so and purported to apply *Murray*, its decision could not be overturned. But since the decision of the employment tribunal looks to have been inconsistent with *Murray* and therefore *Burrell*, *Shawkat* should be treated with caution.

---

[12] [1999] ICR 827, 830. [13] ibid, at 831–832. [14] ibid, 833.
[15] [1994] IRLR 104. [16] [1998] ICR 409. [17] [2002] ICR 7.

Situations which remain problematic

4.10 One difficult question which shows that, despite *Murray* and *Burrell*, all is not yet clear is whether an employer's requirement for one employee to reduce his hours of work involves a diminution in the employer's requirements for employees to do work of a particular kind. Certainly, there is a reduction in the requirements of the employer for one employee to do work of a particular kind. On one view, however, there is no reduction in the requirements of the employer for *employees* to do that work, since the same number of employees is required. However, if there had been two part-time employees spending an equal number of hours doing the work, and there was a need for the hours of only one of them, then there would clearly have been a situation falling within section 139(1) of the ERA 1996. Why, therefore, should the words 'employees to carry out' in section 139(1)(b) be determinative in other situations? It is suggested that it would be open to an employee sensibly to say that a redundancy payment should be made to him if he refused to accept alternative employment on reduced hours in the envisaged circumstances. It is of note that the conclusions of the Divisional Court in *Hanson v Wood (Abingdon Process Engravers)*[18] and the EAT in *Barnsley Metropolitan Borough Council v Prest*[19] are consistent with this proposition. It is suggested here also that the proposition is not inconsistent with the approach of the Court of Appeal in *Johnson v Nottinghamshire Combined Police Authority*.[20] It is true that in that case Lord Denning MR said that 'If the employers require the same number of employees as before—for the same tasks as before—but require them at different hours, there is no redundancy situation.'[21] However, the case concerned a mere change in the hours at which the work was done, not the number of hours of work given to, or required of, the employees. Lord Justice Cairns, while expressing agreement with Lord Denning's judgment, merely said this about the crucial issue: 'Where, as in the cases we are considering, the actual tasks to be performed are unchanged and the total hours are unchanged and the only difference is between the parts of the day when work is done and the number of days over which the work is spread, I am of the opinion that the work remains the same.'[22] Further, Stephenson LJ, while expressing agreement with the judgments of both Lord Denning and Cairns LJ, said this: 'In effect, has the particular kind of work which the applicants were required to do come to an

---

[18] [1967] 3 ITR 46.   [19] [1996] ICR 85.   [20] [1974] ICR 170, CA.
[21] ibid, 177.
[22] ibid, 178. He started his judgment with these words (at 177): 'I agree. Paragraph (b) of section 1(2) of the Redundancy Payments Act 1965 is not an easy paragraph to construe.'

end or grown less: or is the same kind of clerical work being done without diminution by their successors?'[23] Accordingly, *Johnson* is not good authority for the proposition that a reduction in an employee's hours does not by itself give rise to a right to a redundancy payment.

A further difficulty may arise where an employer decides to require employees **4.11** to 'hot-desk', ie share a reduced number of desks and a reduced amount of space at the original workplace, on the basis that the employees can all work at home for some of the time. In that case, it could sensibly be said that the employer has a diminished requirement for employees to carry out work of a particular kind in the place where the employees were originally employed. On that basis, all of the affected employees could be said to be dismissed for redundancy, with all of them being redeployed to work both at that place *and* elsewhere.

Some clarifications

An employee's qualifications are irrelevant to the determination of whether the **4.12** employer has a diminished requirement for employees to do work of the kind done by that employee.[24] So is his pay, so that a dismissal for refusing to accept a reduction in pay is not a dismissal for redundancy.[25] Equally, a dismissal for a refusal to accept a change in shift pattern is not for redundancy.[26]

It is irrelevant that an employee knows at the time of taking a job that he will be **4.13** dismissed from that job for redundancy.[27] An employee may be required to accept changes to his working practices, but 'if new methods alter the nature of the work to be done it may follow that no requirement remains for employees to do work of the particular kind which has been superseded and that they are truly redundant'.[28] The desire of the employer to continue the activity of the dismissed employee is irrelevant when deciding whether the employee was dismissed for redundancy if the employer was forced by a shortage of funds to cease that activity.[29] Thus the cause of what is often referred to as the 'redundancy

---

[23] ibid, 178.
[24] cf *Pillinger v Manchester Area Health Authority* [1979] IRLR 430, EAT.
[25] *Chapman v Goonvean and Rostowrack China Clay Co Ltd* [1973] ICR 310, CA.
[26] *Johnson v Nottinghamshire Combined Police Authority* [1974] ICR 170, CA; *Lesney Products & Co Ltd v Nolan* [1977] ICR 235, CA. Cf, however, *Macfisheries Ltd v Findlay* [1985] ICR 160, 163, where the EAT said that an employment tribunal can properly have regard to 'the impact of night work on the ordering of [the employees'] personal or domestic lives' when deciding whether or not night-shift work is different from day-shift work. This is surely inconsistent with the leading cases cited at the beginning of this footnote.
[27] *Lee v Nottinghamshire County Council* [1980] ICR 635, CA.
[28] *North Riding Garages Ltd v Butterwick* [1967] 2 QB 56, 63, DC.
[29] *Association of University Teachers v University of Newcastle-upon-Tyne* [1987] ICR 317, EAT.

situation'[30] is irrelevant: 'it is the "fact of redundancy" not the "reason for redundancy" that is a material matter'.[31] Nevertheless, there may be a 'redundancy situation' which has led to an employee not being replaced, but if he would have been kept on if he had worked faster, then his dismissal will not be for redundancy, it will be for capability.[32] In contrast, however, if (1) an employee ceases to do his usual work and is engaged by his employer in other work and that other work comes to an end; and (2) the employee is dismissed because that other work comes to an end, then the employee's dismissal will be for redundancy.[33] The employer's belief as to the reason for the dismissal is not conclusive.[34] Rather, the test is an objective one.[35]

Statutory aids to the construction of, and provisions supplementing, section 139(1)

4.14 There are several statutory aids to the construction of section 139(1) of the ERA 1996.

'Business'

4.15 The word 'business' is defined by section 235(1) of the ERA 1996 to include 'a trade or profession and . . . any activity carried on by a body of persons (whether corporate or unincorporated)'.[36] By virtue of section 139(2) of the ERA 1996, for the purposes of section 139(1), 'the business of the employer together with the business or businesses of his associated employers shall be treated as one (unless either of the conditions specified in paragraphs (a) and

---

[30] The term 'redundancy situation' does not appear in the ERA 1996, and as Lord Denning rightly cautioned in *Lesney Products & Co Ltd v Nolan* [1977] ICR 235, 238, having referred to *Johnson v Nottinghamshire Combined Police Authority* [1974] ICR 170, where he himself used the phrase: 'While I adhere to what I there said, I think the phrase "a redundancy situation" may be misleading. It is shorthand: and it is better always to check it by the statutory words. The dismissal must be attributable to "the fact that the requirements of that business for employees to carry out work of a particular kind . . . have ceased or diminished," etc.'

[31] *Association of University Teachers v University of Newcastle-upon-Tyne* [1987] ICR 317, 325. See too *James W Cook & Co (Wivenhoe) Ltd v Tipper* [1990] ICR 716, 729, per Neill LJ with whom Farquharson LJ and Sir Roger Ormerod agreed. Similarly, the fact that the dismissed employee 'caused' the 'redundancy situation' is irrelevant: *Sanders v Ernest A Neale Ltd* [1974] ICR 565, 573, NIRC.

[32] *Hindle v Percival Boats Ltd* [1969] 1 WLR 174, CA.

[33] *Tipper v Roofdec Ltd* [1989] IRLR 419, EAT.

[34] *Mumford v Boulton and Paul (Steel Construction) Ltd* (1970) 6 ITR 76, CA.

[35] *Baxter v Limb Group of Companies* [1994] IRLR 572, CA.

[36] See *Barbar Indian Restaurant v Rawat* [1985] IRLR 57, EAT, for the application of this definition to the situation in which partners own several businesses and dismiss an employee at one business to make way for an employee of one of the other businesses which they own, but which they close. There, the EAT ruled that the dismissed employee was not dismissed for redundancy, as the partners (the employers) did not have a reduced need for employees in the business in which the employee had been employed.

(b) of that subsection would be satisfied without so treating them)'. Further, as a result of section 139(3), for the purposes of section 139(1), 'the activities carried on by a local education authority with respect to the schools maintained by it, and the activities carried on by the governing bodies of those schools, shall be treated as one business (unless either of the conditions specified in paragraphs (a) and (b) of that subsection would be satisfied without so treating them)'. Since almost all maintained schools have delegated budgets within the meaning of Chapter IV of the School Standards and Framework Act 1998, section 139(1)(a) and (b) are likely to be satisfied without the assistance of section 139(3) in relation to persons who are employed to work solely at a particular school. This is the result of two factors: (1) the governing body of a voluntary aided, foundation, or foundation special school is the employer for all relevant purposes of the staff of the school;[37] and (2) the governing body of a school with a delegated budget rather than the local education authority has the power to decide whether persons employed at the school (other than school meals staff) should be dismissed.[38]

The definition of 'dismissal' for the purposes of the law of redundancy

The definition of dismissal for the purposes of section 139 is set out in section **4.16** 136(1) of the ERA 1996, and it is almost the same as the definition (in section 97(1) of the ERA 1996, which applies for the purposes of Part X of the ERA 1996) of dismissal for the purposes of the law of unfair dismissal: ie a dismissal occurs where (a) the employer terminates the contract of employment, whether with or without notice; (b) the employee is employed under a 'limited-term contract' and that contract terminates by virtue of the limiting event without being renewed under the same contract; or (c) the employee terminates the contract (with or without notice) in circumstances in which he is entitled to terminate it without notice by reason of the employer's conduct (unless—and here the definition differs from that which is in section 97(1)—the employee terminates the contract 'without notice in circumstances in which he is entitled to do so by reason of a lock-out by the employer').

The circumstances in which an employee can give a counter-notice of termin- **4.17** ation of the contract of employment, and yet be treated as having been dismissed by his employer for the purposes of the law relating to redundancy payments, differ more markedly from those provided for by the ERA 1996 for the purposes of the law of unfair dismissal. Under Part X, as a result of section 95(2) of the ERA 1996, an employee merely has to give notice after his employer has

---

[37] Education Act 2002, s 36(2).
[38] See reg 17 of the School Staffing (England) Regulations 2003, SI 2003/1963. As to school meals staff, see reg 18 of SI 2003/1963.

given him notice, although, as one would expect, the employee's notice must be given during the period of the employer's notice and must take effect before the end of the notice period given by the employer. In contrast, under Part XI, as a result of section 136, the employee must give a counter-notice within 'the obligatory period of notice', as defined by section 136(4).[39] That 'obligatory period' is either the minimum required (either by statute—currently section 86 of the ERA 1996—or, if greater, by the contract of employment), or, if the notice given by the employer was longer than the minimum, the period working backwards from the date when the notice takes effect to the beginning of that minimum period.

4.18 Further, where the employee gives a counter-notice which satisfies the requirements of section 136, the employer may, before the date when the employee's notice expires, give the employee a notice in reply under section 142(1). In order to fall within section 142(1) a notice (which could be called a 'counter-counter-notice') must (1) require the employee (a) to withdraw his notice and (b) to continue working until the date when the employer's notice of dismissal takes effect; and (2) state that, unless the employee does so, the employer will contest any liability to pay him a redundancy payment in respect of the termination of his contract of employment.[40] An employment tribunal may then be asked by the employee to decide whether the employer should pay any proportion, or all, of the redundancy payment to which the employee would be entitled if he left the employment in accordance with the employer's original notice.[41] The question to be asked by the tribunal in that regard is whether it appears to it to be 'just and equitable that the employee should receive' such payment.[42]

4.19 Section 136(5) provides:

> Where in accordance with any enactment or rule of law—
>
> (a) an act on the part of an employer, or
> (b) an event affecting an employer (including, in the case of an individual, his death),
>
> operates to terminate a contract under which an employee is employed by him, the act or event shall be taken for the purposes of this Part to be a termination of the contract by the employer.

---

[39] ERA 1996, s 136(3). The notice need not be of any particular length: *Ready Case Ltd v Jackson* [1981] IRLR 312, EAT, decided in relation to Pt X of the ERA 1996, but applicable by analogy.

[40] ERA 1996, s 142(2).

[41] ERA 1996, s 142(3) and (4). It is of note that s 142(3) is written in terms which assume that the tribunal makes the decision before the employer's notice of dismissal takes effect. However, those words clearly do not impose any kind of time limit, since s 164 of the ERA 1996 (as to which, see para 4.55 onwards below) provides for time limits.

[42] ERA 1996, s 142(3).

Sections 174 and 175 of the ERA 1996 provide for the manner in which the   **4.20**
rest of Part XI applies where the employer dies. If the employee dies, then,
according to section 176(1), Part XI applies as if the employee's contract of
employment had been 'duly terminated by the employer by notice expiring
on the date of the employee's death'. The rest of section 176 makes appropriate
provision in relation to the rest of Part XI for the circumstance that the employee
dies before becoming entitled to, or receiving, a redundancy payment.

It was held in *Mowlem Northern Ltd v Watson*[43] that an employer and an   **4.21**
employee may agree to postpone the date of dismissal by reason of redundancy.
That case was referred to by the EAT without disapproval in *Lambert v Croydon
College*,[44] where one issue was whether an employer and an employee could
agree that the employee's employment was effectively terminated on a date
which was different from that on which, in the absence of such agreement, it
would have been effectively terminated for the purposes of what is now section
97 of the ERA 1996. The decision in *Lambert* is certainly consistent with that
in *Watson*. However, in *Fitzgerald v University of Kent at Canterbury*,[45] the
Court of Appeal overruled *Lambert v Croydon College*, and therefore probably
should be taken to have overruled *Watson*. Further, no reference was made in
Watson to what is now section 138(1) of the ERA 1996.[46] Thus, the question of
when an employee's dismissal takes effect for the purposes of Part XI of the
ERA 1996 should be determined only by reference to the terms section 136 of
that Act.

Renewal of contract or re-engagement under a new contract

If an employee's contract of employment is renewed (and, for the purposes   **4.22**
of the ERA 1996, a renewal 'includes extension'[47]), or (a) the employee is
're-engaged under a new contract of employment in pursuance of an offer
(whether in writing or not) made before the end of his employment under the
previous contract',[48] and (b) 'the renewal or re-engagement takes effect either

---

[43] [1990] ICR 751, EAT.   [44] [1999] ICR 409.   [45] [2004] ICR 737.
[46] Concerning which, see the next para below. There is a cogent criticism in *Harvey*, at paras
E[457] to E[467], of the decision in *Watson*.
[47] ERA 1996, s 235(1).
[48] The requirement for an offer to be made before the ending of the previous contract for a re-
engagement to be effective for this purpose was emphasised by the EAT in *S I (Systems &
Instrumentation) Ltd v Grist* [1983] ICR 788, 797–798. The difference between the renewal of a
contract of employment and re-engagement under a new contract is relevant only in this context
and that of s 141 of the ERA 1996. There is an extensive discussion in *Harvey* at para E[1518]
onwards of the difference between a new contract and a renewed contract. It is suggested
here that, given the terms of s 138(2), which assume that the terms of a renewed contract as well as
those of a new contract may differ from those of the previous contract, there is probably no
practical difference between a renewed contract and a new contract, but that the difference lies—as

immediately on, or after an interval of not more than four weeks after, the end of that employment', then (subject to an exception, referred to in paragraph 4.24 below) the employee is not regarded for the purposes of section 139(1) as dismissed by reason of the ending of the employment under the previous contract.[49] For this purpose, the renewed or new contract of employment may be made with an associated employer within the meaning of section 231 of the ERA 1996.[50] Such an associated employer may (and may only) be (1) a company which either controls, or is controlled by, the original employer (which for this purpose must also be a company); or (2) a company which is controlled by the same person as the person who (whether directly or indirectly) controls the original employer. The offer of re-engagement must be sufficiently detailed to allow the employee to see the differences between the old and the new contracts of employment.[51] It must also be an offer of viable, or genuine, new employment.[52] Further, it must be communicated to the employee effectively.[53]

4.23 It was held by the EAT in *Ranger v Brown*[54] that employees who remain in their employment (ie working in effect for the business in which they are employed) after an alleged dismissal for redundancy by reason of the death of the employer are not necessarily to be taken to have been re-engaged or employed under a renewed contract. Difficult though it may be to reconcile that ruling with the wording of section 138 of the ERA 1996, it is a pragmatic ruling which, unlike the approach taken in *Mowlem Northern Ltd v Watson*,[55] it is difficult sensibly to criticise.

Statutory trial period where new terms differ

4.24 The exception to the general rule mentioned in paragraph 4.22 above occurs in the following circumstances, which are provided for by section 138 of the ERA

---

suggested in para E[1523] of *Harvey*—in whether or not the employer agrees to treat the employee in all respects as if he had not been dismissed. Any other approach would, for the reasons set out in *Harvey*, be inconsistent with the wording of s 138.

[49] See ERA 1996, s 138(1) (and see s 146(2) for the position where the employment ends on a Friday, Saturday, or Sunday). This 'disappearing dismissal' expressly applies only for the purposes of Pt XI. Thus, it does not apply for the purposes of the law of unfair dismissal: *Hempell v W H Smith & Sons Ltd* [1986] ICR 365, approved by the Court of Appeal in *Jones v Governing Body of Burdett Coutts School* [1999] ICR 38, 43.

[50] See ERA 1996, s 146(1).

[51] *Havenhand v Thomas Black Ltd* [1968] 1 WLR 1241, 1244, DC, in effect approved by the House of Lords in *McCreadie v Thomson & MacIntyre (Patternmakers) Ltd* [1971] 1 WLR 1193, 1196. See too *Curling v Securicor Ltd* [1992] IRLR 549, para 23, where the EAT commented that 'A multiplicity of insufficiently specific offers may well not be an adequate substitute for an offer of a single suitable alternative employment.'

[52] *Kane v Raine & Co Ltd* [1974] ICR 300, NIRC.

[53] *McCreadie v Thomson & MacIntyre (Patternmakers) Ltd* [1971] 1 WLR 1193, 1196, HL.

[54] [1978] ICR 603.   [55] See para 4.21 above.

1996. These are where (1) the provisions of the contract as renewed or the new contract concerning either the capacity and place in which the employee is employed, or the other terms and conditions of his employment, differ (wholly or in part) from the corresponding provisions of the previous contract; and (2) during the period (known as the 'trial period'[56]) of four weeks[57] (or such longer period—if and only if it is for the purpose of retraining[58]—as the employer and employee agree for the purpose pursuant to section 138(6) of the ERA 1996[59]) from the start of the employee's work under the renewed or new contract, either (a) the employee terminates or gives notice to terminate the new contract (and it terminates as a result) for any reason, or (b) the employer, 'for a reason connected with or arising out of any difference between the renewed or new contract and the previous contract' terminates or gives notice to terminate the new contract (and it terminates as a result). Accordingly, in the circumstances described in this paragraph, the employee is to be regarded as dismissed for the purposes of section 139 of the ERA 1996.

If there is a successful trial period, and the contract of employment is again **4.25** renewed or a new contract of employment is again entered into, then there is no right to a further trial period.[60]

The requirements of section 138(6) are that the agreement for a longer period **4.26** of retraining (1) is in writing; (2) is made between the employer and the employee or the employee's representative before the employee starts work under the contract as renewed, or the new contract; (3) specifies the date on which the period of retraining ends; and (4) specifies the 'important'[61] terms and conditions of employment which will apply in the employee's case after the ending of the retraining period.

Common law trial period

One oddity resulting from the application of the law relating to the termination **4.27** of a contract to the situation as a result of section 136(1)(c) of the ERA 1996 is that an employee who is dismissed 'constructively' by the imposition of new terms of employment, in circumstances to which section 138(1) applies, has

---

[56] ERA 1996, s 138(3).
[57] This means calendar weeks, irrespective of any holiday shutdown during those four weeks: *Benton v Sanderson Kayser Ltd* [1989] ICR 136, CA.
[58] This is the clear effect of the wording of s 138(3)(b)(ii), but that the purpose must indeed be for retraining was emphasised by the EAT in *Meek v J Allen Rubber Co Ltd* [1980] IRLR 21, EAT.
[59] See para 4.26 below concerning s 138(6).   [60] ERA 1996, s 138(5).
[61] *McKindley v William Hill (Scotland) Ltd* [1985] IRLR 492, EAT, para 6.

what has been called a 'common law trial period' in addition to (and which runs before) the statutory trial period: *Turvey v C W Cheney & Sons Ltd.*[62]

D. Entitlement to a Redundancy Payment

The general entitlement

4.28 The right to a redundancy payment is conferred by section 135 of the ERA 1996. It arises where the employee is dismissed for redundancy (ie in the circumstances discussed above, but subject to the qualifications discussed below) or where the employee is eligible by virtue of being laid off or on short-time working, in the circumstances described below.[63]

Continuous employment

4.29 An employee is entitled to a redundancy payment only if he has been continuously employed for at least two years.[64] Although the conditions for there to be two years' continuous employment are outside the scope of this book, one unusual situation is worth mentioning here, given the subject of the book. That is that an employee may have continuity of employment as a result of the application of section 218(2) of the ERA 1996 where there is a transfer of a trade, business or undertaking which does not give rise to a transfer under TUPE of the employee's contract of employment. Section 218(2) is a re-enactment of paragraph 17(2) of Schedule 13 to the Employment Protection (Consolidation) Act 1978. It was largely superseded by the enactment of TUPE 1981, but fills a gap in those circumstances.[65]

4.30 An employee who has been continuously employed for at least two years is nevertheless not entitled to a redundancy payment in two circumstances. One is that he received a redundancy payment (or is to be treated as if he had received such a payment in accordance with section 214(5) of the ERA 1996) in respect of (1) a dismissal; (2) lay-off; or (3) short-time, where the employment

---

[62] [1979] ICR 341, EAT, applying *Air Canada v Lee* [1978] ICR 1202, EAT.

[63] The following list of conditions or exceptions is not exhaustive. For example, it is unlikely to be necessary for the reader to take into account the position of a domestic servant, or the impact of the death of the employer. As to those cases, reference should be made to (1) s 161; and (2) ss 174 and 175 of the ERA 1996, respectively.

[64] ERA 1996, s 155. An employee cannot rely for the purposes of the ERA 1996 on an employer's promise to treat him as having continuous employment greater than that to which the relevant statutory provisions entitle him: *Secretary of State v Globe Elastic Thread Co Ltd* [1980] AC 506; [1979] ICR 706.

[65] See for example *Clark and Tokeley Ltd v Oakes* [1999] ICR 276, CA.

in question ended within the preceding two years and the employment was renewed (whether by the same or another employer) or the employee was re-engaged under a new contract of employment (whether by the same or another employer).[66] The other circumstance is that the employee received a payment in accordance with a scheme under section 1 of the Superannuation Act 1972 or arrangements falling within section 177(3) of the ERA 1996 (which apply to civil service and related employment) and commenced new or renewed employment.[67]

Upper age limit

Until 1 October 2006, an employee does not have a right to a redundancy payment if before the date giving rise to the alleged entitlement he has attained either sixty-five or (if less) the normal retiring age in the business for the purposes of which he was employed for an employee holding the position which the redundant employee held.[68] The normal retiring age is determined objectively.[69] It cannot properly be determined by an employment tribunal to be lower than the contractual retiring age.[70]   **4.31**

After 1 October 2006, section 156 of the ERA 1996 will be repealed by paragraph 30 of Schedule 8 to the Employment Equality (Age) Regulations 2006.[71] Similarly, section 162(4), (5), and (8) will be repealed by paragraph 32 of that Schedule.   **4.32**

Summary dismissal and strikes [72]

If an employee is dismissed in the circumstances that (1) the employer is entitled to dismiss the employee summarily (ie because the employee has fundamentally breached or repudiated his contract of employment[73]); and (2) the employer gives either (a) no notice, (b) short notice, or (c) proper notice including or accompanied by a statement in writing that the employer was entitled by reason of the employee's conduct to terminate the contract without   **4.33**

---

[66] ERA 1996, ss 145 and 214(2) and (4). For the position where an employee is reinstated in certain relatively limited circumstances (given the repeal of ERA 1996, s 219(3) and (4) by the Employment Rights (Dispute Resolution) Act 1998), see the Employment Protection (Continuity of Employment) Regulations 1996, SI 1996/3147 (as amended).

[67] ERA 1996, s 214(3).

[68] ERA 1996, s 156(1). The age must be the same for men and women: ibid.

[69] See *Cross v British Airways plc* [2005] IRLR 423, EAT.

[70] *Royal and Sun Alliance Insurance Group plc v Payne* [2005] IRLR 848, EAT.

[71] SI 2006/1031.

[72] For the definition of a 'strike' in this context, see ERA 1996, s 235(5).

[73] This is the test at common law (as stated in *Western Excavating (ECC) Ltd v Sharp* [1978] ICR 221). The question is not whether the employer dismissed the employee fairly (ie within the meaning of s 98(4) of the ERA 1996): *Bonner v H Gilbert Ltd* [1989] IRLR 475.

notice, then, subject to an exception, the employee is not entitled to a redundancy payment.[74] The exception is that the employee is not deprived of his entitlement to a redundancy payment by reason of his dismissal in those circumstances if (1) the entitlement of the employer to terminate the contract without notice arises because the employee is taking part in a strike; (2) the employer dismisses the employee 'by reason of his taking part in the strike'; and (3) before the strike started, the employer had given notice of termination of the contract on account of redundancy, or the employee had given notice of an intention to claim a redundancy payment by reason of being laid off or short-time working.[75] Where that exception does not apply, an employee who is dismissed in the circumstances stated in the first sentence of this paragraph may nevertheless ask an employment tribunal to determine that the employer should pay either part or the whole of the redundancy payment to which the employee would have been entitled if he had not been so dismissed.[76] Such a determination may be made only if it appears to the tribunal to be just and equitable in the circumstances of the case that the employee should receive such a payment.[77]

4.34   If, after an employer has given an employee notice to terminate the employee's contract of employment and before the notice takes effect the employee takes part (whether or not during the 'obligatory period') in a strike, then the employer may serve a notice on the employee requesting him to extend his contract of employment by the number of working days lost by striking.[78] The 'extension' notice must indicate the reasons for the request and state that the employer will contest any liability to pay the employee a redundancy payment in respect of the dismissal effected by the notice of termination unless either (1) the employee complies with the request; or (2) the employer is 'satisfied that, in consequence of sickness or injury or otherwise, the employee is unable to comply with it or that (even though he is able to comply with it) it is reasonable

---

[74] ERA 1996, s 140(1).

[75] ERA 1996, s 140(2). Where the employer has given notice, the employee's participation in the strike must occur during the 'obligatory period of notice': s 140(5). The analysis in *Harvey* at paras E[1286]ff (concerning the effect of the line of cases including *Sanders v Ernest A Neale Ltd* [1974] ICR 565, NIRC, and *Simmons v Hoover Ltd* [1977] ICR 61, EAT) is highly persuasive. Thus the best view is that s 140 of the ERA 1996 applies where an employer dismisses an employee for misconduct, but only if the employee would, if he had not been dismissed for misconduct, have been dismissed for redundancy.

[76] See ERA 1996, s 140(3) and (4). Where the employer has given notice, the employee's summary dismissal must have occurred during the 'obligatory period of notice': s 140(5).

[77] ERA 1996, s 140(3). An employment tribunal has a wide discretion when determining whether it is so just and equitable: *Lignacite Products Ltd v Krollman* [1979] IRLR 22, EAT.

[78] See, generally, ERA 1996, ss 143 and 144. The definition of 'working days lost by striking' is in s 144(2).

in the circumstances for him not to do so'.[79] If the employee does not comply with the request,[80] then he is not entitled to a redundancy payment by reason of the dismissal effected by the notice of termination, unless (1) the employer agrees to pay the employee such a payment; or (2) an employment tribunal decides that either the employee was unable to comply with the request or, although he was able to so do, it was reasonable in the circumstances for him not to comply with the request.[81] The tribunal may decide that the employee should be paid less than the full amount of the payment to which he would have been entitled if he had complied with the request.[82] The tribunal might decide that the employee should receive less than the full amount because the employee only attended his usual or proper workplace for part of the period covered by the extension notice. In any event, the notice of termination is deemed to take effect as if it had been extended either to the end of the period of the extension or, if the employee only works for part of that period, to the last day on which the employee 'attends at his proper or usual place of work and is ready and willing to work'.[83]

Exemption orders

An employee is not entitled to a redundancy payment if an exemption order **4.35** made by the Secretary of State under section 157 of the ERA 1996 is in place. Such an order may be made only where there is an agreement between (1) one or more employers or organisations of employers; and (2) one or more trade unions representing employees, under which employees to whom the agreement applies have a right 'in certain circumstances to payments on the termination of their contracts of employment'.[84] The Secretary of State may make an order under section 157 only where the agreement to which the order relates 'indicates (in whatever terms) the willingness of the parties to it to submit to an [employment] tribunal any question arising under the agreement' as to the right of an employee to a payment on the termination of his employment, or the amount of the payment.[85]

---

[79] ERA 1996, s 143(2). The extension must be by a period comprising as many 'available' days (defined by ERA 1996, s 144(3)) as the number of days lost by striking during the period beginning with the date of service of the notice of termination and the ending of the period of notice as originally given by the employer: ERA 1996, ss 143(2) and 144(2) and (3).

[80] An employee complies with the request by attending at his proper or usual place of work and being ready and willing to work, whether or not he has signified his agreement to the request in any other way: ERA 1996, s 144(1).

[81] ERA 1996, s 143(3)–(5).   [82] ERA 1996, s 143(5) and (6).

[83] ERA 1996, s 143(7) and (8).   [84] ERA 1996, s 157(2).

[85] ERA 19996, s 157(4).

Pension regulations which exclude the right to a redundancy payment

4.36 Section 158 of the ERA 1996 permits the making of regulations which exclude the right to a redundancy payment, or reduce the amount of the payment, where an employee has a right or claim to a periodical payment or lump sum by way of pension, gratuity, or 'superannuation allowance' which is to be paid by reference to the employee's employment by a particular employer and is to be paid, or began to be paid, at the time when the employee leaves the employment or within such period of leaving the employment as may be prescribed by regulations. The regulations may not affect an employee's entitlement to a redundancy payment if the periodical payment or lump sum in question represents 'compensation for loss of employment or for loss or diminution of emoluments or of pension payments' and 'is payable under a statutory provision'.[86]

Public officers

4.37 A person who is employed in a public office within the meaning of section 39 of the Superannuation Act 1965 (which includes employment in the civil service), or which is for the purposes of pensions and other superannuation benefits treated (whether by virtue of that Act or otherwise) as employment in the civil service, does not have a right to a redundancy payment in respect of that employment.[87] However, the Secretary of State may by regulations made under section 171 of the ERA 1996 provide that such employment is to be treated as employment under a contract of employment. Regulations made (or treated as having been made) under section 171 include the Redundancy Payments Office Holders Regulations 1965.[88]

Overseas government employment

4.38 Employees of the government of any territory or country outside the United Kingdom, or of 'any authority established for the purpose of providing or administering services which are common to, or relate to matters of common interest to, two or more overseas territories' are not entitled in respect of that employment to a redundancy payment.[89]

Lay-off or short-time

4.39 Entitlement to a redundancy payment by reason of lay-off or short-time arises under section 148 of the ERA 1996. For this purpose, an employee is laid off

---

[86] ERA 1996, s 158(3). The Redundancy Payments Pension Regulations 1965, SI 1965/1932 are treated as having been made udner s 158.
[87] ERA 1996, s 159.   [88] SI 1965/2007.   [89] See ERA 1996, s 160.

for a week if '(a) he is employed under a contract on terms and conditions such that his remuneration under the contract depends on his being provided by the employer with work of the kind which he is employed to do, but (b) he is not entitled to any remuneration under the contract in respect of the week because the employer does not provide any work for him'.[90] However, a week does not count if the lay-off or short-time 'is wholly or mainly attributable to a strike or lock-out (whether or not in the trade or industry in which the employee is employed and whether in Great Britain or elsewhere)'.[91] An employee is 'kept on short-time for a week' for these purposes if 'by reason of a diminution in the work provided for the employee by his employer (being work of a kind which under his contract the employee is employed to do) the employee's remuneration for the week is less than half a week's pay'.[92]

An employee is (subject to certain conditions, as to which see the following **4.40** paragraphs below) entitled to a redundancy payment by reason of being laid off or kept on short-time either for four or more consecutive relevant weeks or six or more relevant weeks of which no more than three are consecutive within a period of thirteen weeks,[93] where (1) the employee subsequently gives notice in writing to his employer 'indicating (in whatever terms)' his intention to claim a redundancy payment; and (2) the employer does not within seven days give a counter-notice in writing stating that he will contest any liability to pay the employee a redundancy payment.[94] The employee's notice must be given either on the last day of the four-week or (as the case may be) thirteen-week period, or within four weeks of that last day.[95] If the employer gives a counter-notice within seven days as described above in this paragraph, and that counter-notice is not withdrawn by a subsequent notice in writing, then the employee is entitled to a redundancy payment by reason of his notice of intention to claim only if an employment tribunal so determines.[96]

Further, in order to be entitled to a redundancy payment by reason of being laid **4.41** off or short-time working, an employee must give notice of the termination of his contract of employment in accordance with his contract of employment, or, if there is no requirement under the contract, one week's notice of such

---

[90] ERA 1996, s 147(1).
[91] ERA 1996, s 154(b). For the definitions of 'lock-out' and 'strike', see ERA 1996, s 235(4) and (5), respectively.
[92] ibid, s 147(2).
[93] The employee may for this purpose be laid off for some weeks and kept on short-time on other weeks: ERA 1996, s 154(a).
[94] See ERA 1996, ss 148 and 149. If the employer gives such a counter-notice but subsequently withdraws it by a further notice in writing, then the employee is conclusively entitled to a redundancy payment: s 149(b).
[95] ERA 1996, s 148.   [96] ERA 1996, s 149.

termination.[97] Furthermore, this notice must be given (1) within four weeks of the giving by the employee of the notice of intention to claim a redundancy payment; (2) if the employer gives a counter-notice under section 149 and subsequently withdraws that notice by a further notice in writing, within three weeks of the service of the notice of withdrawal; or (3) if the employer gives such a counter-notice within the period of seven days of the giving of the employee's notice of intention to claim and the question whether the employee has the right to claim a redundancy payment is referred to an employment tribunal, within three weeks of the notification by the tribunal of its decision on that reference (irrespective of any subsequent appeal against that determination).[98]

4.42   An employment tribunal may decide that an employee is not entitled to a redundancy payment by reason of being laid off or kept on short-time where the employer has given a counter-notice of the relevant sort (ie within seven days of the service by the employee of a notice of intention to claim) only if the conditions stated above are not satisfied, or (subject to an exception) if on the date of the service of the employee's notice of intention to claim it was reasonably to be expected that the employee would within four weeks of remaining in the same employment 'enter on a period of employment of not less than thirteen weeks during which he would not be laid off or kept on short-time for any week'.[99] The exception in question is that the employee continues to be employed by the same employer for the period of four weeks following the giving by the employee of the notice of intention to claim, and is laid off or kept on short-time for each of those weeks. In the latter case, the employee remains entitled to a redundancy payment by reason of being laid off or kept on short-time (as long as the employee terminates the employment in the manner described in the preceding paragraph above).[100]

4.43   An employee who is dismissed by his employer is not entitled to a redundancy payment by reason of being laid off or kept on short-time, but may nevertheless be entitled to a redundancy payment by reason of that dismissal.[101] There being no implied contractual right to impose a period of short-time working,[102] such

---

[97] ERA 1996, s 150(1) and (2). This notice need not satisfy any particular formal requirements: *Faber Construction Ltd v Race* [1979] ICR 529, 533, EAT.
[98] ERA 1996, s 150(3) and (4).
[99] ERA 1996, s 152(1). The employment must be 'under the contract of employment in relation to which the employee was laid off': *Neepsend Steel & Tool Corporation Ltd v Vaughan* [1972] ICR 278, 281, NIRC.
[100] See ERA 1996, s 152(2).   [101] ERA 1996, s 151.
[102] *Miller v Hamworthy Engineering Ltd* [1986] ICR 846, 849, CA.

an imposition will constitute a repudiation of the contract of employment.[103] An employee will therefore be in a position to accept that repudiation and claim a redundancy payment on the basis that he has been dismissed within the meaning of section 136(1)(c) of the ERA 1996.[104]

E. Loss of the Right to a Redundancy Payment

An employee is not necessarily entitled to a redundancy payment under **4.44** the ERA 1996 where the definition of redundancy is satisfied. In addition to losing the right to a redundancy payment for the reasons set out above, an employee may lose his assumed entitlement to a redundancy payment in the following circumstances.

Unreasonable refusal

If an employer makes an offer to an employee before the end of his employment **4.45** (a) to renew the employee's contract of employment, or (b) to re-engage him under a new contract of employment, with the renewal or re-engagement 'to take effect either immediately on, or after an interval of not more than four weeks after, the end of his employment', then the employee may, as a result of section 141 of the ERA 1996, lose the right to a redundancy payment by reason of the ending of the original employment. If the provisions of the new contract or the contract as renewed[105] 'would not differ from the corresponding provisions of the previous contract', then the employee will lose the right to a redundancy payment by reason of the ending of the previous contract if he 'unreasonably' refuses the offer.[106] If the provisions of the contract as renewed or the new contract 'would differ from the corresponding provisions of the previous contract', then the employee will lose the right to a redundancy payment by reason of the ending of the previous employment only if (a) 'the offer constitutes an offer of suitable employment in relation to the employee', and

---

[103] cf *Cantor Fitzgerald International v Callaghan* [1999] ICR 639, 649, CA.

[104] See eg *A Dakri & Co Ltd v Tiffen* [1981] ICR 256, EAT.

[105] The terms 'new contract' and 'contract as renewed' are used in s 141(3)(a) of the ERA 1996. As noted above (in para 4.22, n 48), the difference between a new contract and a contract as renewed in the context of s 138 of the ERA 1996 is a little difficult to ascertain. It has been held that in order to fall within s 141(3)(a), an offer must be of identical employment (*Devonald v J D Insulating Co Ltd* [1972] ICR 209; *Cartin v Botley Garages Ltd* [1973] ICR 144, where reference was not made to *Devonald*, but the same result was arrived at), although (see *Allman v Rowland* [1977] ICR 201, where reference was made to neither *Devonald* nor *Cartin*) trivial differences can be ignored. Thus in this context there is no relevant difference between a new contract and a renewed contract.

[106] ERA 1996, s 141(2) and (3)(a).

(b) he refuses it unreasonably.[107] In the latter case (ie where the terms of the new or renewed contract of employment do differ from those of the previous contract), the employee will be entitled to a trial period of at least four weeks.[108] If the employee accepts the offer, but during the trial period he unreasonably terminates the contract or unreasonably gives notice to terminate it and the contract is in consequence terminated, then he loses the right to a redundancy payment.[109]

Suitability

4.46 The words of the statute (ie in section 141(3)(b)) are to be applied without the gloss put on them by Lord Parker CJ in *Taylor v Kent County Council*[110] that the test is whether the alternative employment is 'substantially equivalent'.[111] The question whether the alternative employment is suitable is a question of fact for the employment tribunal.[112] This does not mean that the only ground of appeal is perversity. As it was said (correctly, it is submitted) in *Standard Telephones and Cables Ltd v Yates*:[113]

> [An employment tribunal] will only go wrong in law if, having done what the statute requires it to do and considered whether the offer constitutes an offer of suitable employment, it is found that there was no evidence on which it could have come to the conclusion to which it did come; or that it took into consideration something which it should not have done; or left out of consideration something which it should have considered; or that its conclusion is so wildly out of line that it must have misdirected itself and so gone wrong in law
>
> — that being the form of error of law which is usually referred to as a 'perverse decision' in this jurisdiction.

4.47 Thus, the factors which may need to be taken into account include, in addition to the tasks which the employee would be required to carry out in the alternative employment:[114] the employee's status in the alternative employment as compared with the employment in respect of which notice of dismissal was given ('the original employment'),[115] and (although this appears to be more

---

[107] ERA 1996, s 141(2) and (3)(b).   [108] See paras 4.24–4.26 above.
[109] ERA 1996, s 141(4).   [110] [1969] 2 QB 560.
[111] *Standard Telephones and Cables Ltd v Yates* [1981] IRLR 21, para 9 (EAT).
[112] *Taylor v Kent County Council* [1969] 2 QB 560, 565.   [113] [1981] IRLR 21, para 9.
[114] If authority for the proposition that the job content is relevant to its suitability is required, it is to be found in *Standard Telephones and Cables Ltd v Yates* [1981] IRLR 21, EAT.
[115] *Taylor v Kent County Council* [1969] 2 QB 560. See, further, in relation to status *Kane v Raine & Co Ltd* [1974] ICR 300, NIRC, and *Eltringham v Sunderland Co-operative Society Ltd* (1971) 6 ITR 121, DC, but note that in *Cambridge and District Co-operative Society Ltd v Ruse* [1993] IRLR 156, at para 18, the EAT held that it was acceptable on the facts of that case to decide that, although the alternative employment was generally suitable, the employee did not act unreasonably in refusing it because of his perception that its acceptance would involve a loss of status.

relevant to the question of the reasonableness of refusing the offer of alternative employment) changing from day-shift to night-shift work.[116]

Reasonableness

The question of suitability is (as is clear from the wording of section 141) **4.48** separate from the question of whether it was reasonable to refuse the alternative employment, and the necessity for asking these two questions (rather than rolling them up into a single question) has been emphasised by the EAT.[117] However, as the Court of Appeal pointed out in *Spencer v Gloucestershire County Council*,[118] some factors may be relevant to both questions. The facts of that case are illustrative of this.[119] The employer wanted to reduce the number of cleaners employed at a school and the number of hours worked by those cleaners who were retained. Although Neill LJ, with whom Sir John Donaldson MR and Balcombe LJ agreed, accepted that 'it is for the employer to decide what is the appropriate standard of work that he wants carried out',[120] he also said this:[121]

> it cannot be right to say as a general proposition that it is not a good reason for an employee to refuse to do work because he considers that the work he is being asked to do does not come up to a standard which he himself wishes to observe. It all depends on the facts of the case. There may well be cases where an employee wishes to apply a wholly unreasonable standard to the work, and say, 'I am only prepared to work to that standard'. But it seems to me that this is eminently a matter for the Industrial Tribunal to evaluate in the particular circumstances.

In deciding whether it was unreasonable to refuse the alternative employment, **4.49** the following factors are relevant: (1) the pay in the alternative employment as compared with that in the original employment;[122] (2) the employee's domestic circumstances,[123] which must include the daily travelling time from the

---

[116] *Kykot v Smith Hartley Ltd* [1975] IRLR 372, para 20, per Phillips J.

[117] See most recently and most clearly *Knott v Southampton and South-West Hampshire Health Authority* [1991] ICR 480, 485, EAT. The case concerned provisions in a Whitley Council agreement, which included the words used in the predecessor to what is now s 141.

[118] [1985] IRLR 393, at para 13.

[119] See too *Cambridge and District Co-operative Society Ltd v Ruse* [1993] IRLR 156, EAT.

[120] ibid, para 11.   [121] At para 14.

[122] It is surely correct that a difference in pay cannot make an alternative job unsuitable, but would instead be relevant to the question whether the employee's refusal of it was unreasonable. However, in *Hindes v Supersine Ltd* [1979] ICR 517, the EAT held on the facts of that case (which were relatively unusual) that a reduction in pay was relevant to the question whether the alternative employment was suitable. Nevertheless, in *Kennedy v Werneth Ring Mills* [1977] ICR 206, the EAT regarded the difference in pay as being relevant to the reasonableness of the employee's refusal of the alternative employment, rather than to its suitability.

[123] *Bass Leisure Ltd v Thomas* [1994] IRLR 104, EAT, at para 18. Although there was a contractual obligation on the employer in that case to consider the employee's domestic circumstances, such circumstances were implicitly recognized by the EAT in that paragraph to be relevant. That recognition was surely correct.

employee's home to the alternative employment as compared with the original employment;[124] (3) the employee's future prospects in the alternative employment;[125] (4) the fact that the alternative employment is temporary;[126] (5) the timing of the offer of alternative employment;[127] and (6) the fact that the employee has found employment with a new employer by the time when the original employer makes the offer of alternative employment.[128]

4.50 In deciding whether an employee unreasonably refused an offer of suitable alternative employment, the employment tribunal must put itself in the shoes of the employee and ask that question by reference to the facts as they appeared or ought reasonably to have appeared to him at the time when the decision had to be made.[129]

4.51 The question of the reasonableness of refusing alternative employment is clearly a matter which can be determined only in relation to each employee individually.[130] However, it is also necessary to decide whether employees who were offered alternative employment collectively refused it unreasonably by reference to the circumstances of each employee, and not those of the group.[131]

Specific provisions applicable to the health and local government sectors

4.52 Mention must be made here of the application to employment with a new employer (1) for employees in local government employment of the Redundancy Payments (Continuity of Employment in Local Government, etc) (Modification) Order 1999;[132] and (2) for employees in the national health service of the Redundancy Payments (National Health Service) (Modification) Order 1993.[133]

---

[124] *Bass Leisure Ltd v Thomas* [1994] IRLR 104, EAT, at para 18.

[125] *Thomas Wragg & Sons v Wood* [1976] ICR 313, EAT; *Paton Calvert & Co v Westerside* [1979] IRLR 108, para 17, EAT.

[126] *Dutton v Hawker Siddeley Aviation Ltd* [1978] ICR 1057, EAT.

[127] *Thomas Wragg & Sons v Wood* [1976] ICR 313, EAT.

[128] *Paton Calvert & Co v Westerside* [1979] IRLR 108, para 17, EAT.

[129] *Everest's Executors v Cox* [1980] ICR 415, 418, EAT.

[130] However, it was necessary for O'Connor J specifically to state that in *John Fowler (Don Foundry) Ltd v Parkin* [1975] IRLR 89, para 5.

[131] *John Fowler (Don Foundry) Ltd v Parkin*, paras 3–5.

[132] SI 1999/2277, as amended on a number of occasions.

[133] SI 1993/3167, as amended by SI 2000/694, SI 2002/2469, SI 2004/696, SI 2005/445, SI 2005/1622, and SI 2005/2078.

F. Claiming a Redundancy Payment[134]

The jurisdiction of an employment tribunal

The questions whether (1) an employee has a right to a redundancy payment; **4.53** and (2), if so, the amount of the payment, are ultimately determinable by an employment tribunal, pursuant to section 163(1) of the ERA 1996.[135] If an employee has been dismissed, then it must be presumed, unless the contrary is proved, that the reason for the dismissal was redundancy.[136] This presumption operates for the purposes of the law of redundancy only (ie and not for the purposes of the law of unfair dismissal).[137] Where an order under section 157 is in force in respect of an agreement,[138] the question whether an employee is entitled to a payment under the agreement is determinable by an employment tribunal under section 163(1).[139]

It was argued at one time in *Harvey*[140] that a claim for a redundancy payment **4.54** under section 163 of the ERA 1996 does not fall within section 32 of the Employment Act 2002 ('EA 2002'), because section 163 does not refer to 'claiming' a redundancy payment, the operative word in section 163 being 'referred'. However, since section 163 is expressly included in Schedule 4 to the EA 2002, it is suggested here that that argument was mistaken, and that an employee must first comply with the statutory grievance procedure in Part 2 of Schedule 2 to the EA 2002 before making a claim to an employment tribunal for a redundancy payment.

---

[134] Claims made to the Secretary of State for a redundancy payment under Ch VI of Pt XI of the ERA 1996 (ie ss 166–170) are outside the scope of this book.

[135] See s 163(3) in relation to the question whether an employee 'will become entitled to a redundancy payment if he is not dismissed by his employer and he terminates his contract of employment as mentioned in section 150(1)', ie the employee resigns by reason of being laid off or kept on short-time. The question then falls within s 163(1).

[136] ERA 1996, s 163(2). If several employees are dismissed and at least one is dismissed for redundancy, but it is impossible to say which one was so dismissed, then all of them must be presumed to have been dismissed for redundancy: *Willcox v Hastings* [1987] IRLR 298, CA. It has to be said that the facts of that case were relatively unusual.

[137] This is evident from the language of s 163(2) of the ERA 1996, but was confirmed by the NIRC in *Midland Foot Comfort Centre Ltd v Moppett* [1973] ICR 219. There, the industrial tribunal was unable, because of the vagueness of the employer's evidence, to decide the true reason for the employee's dismissal. As a result of the presumption which is now in s 163(2), the employee was entitled to a redundancy payment, but, since the employer had not shown the reason for the dismissal, the dismissal was deemed to have been unfair.

[138] See para 4.35 above concerning s 157.   [139] ERA 1996, s 163(4).

[140] Para E[2118.01], as published in 2005.

The time limit for claiming

4.55 Unusually (ie unlike the usual three-month time limit for making a claim to an employment tribunal), the primary time limit for making a claim to an employment tribunal for a redundancy payment is six months from a date ('the relevant date') which varies according to the circumstances which it is claimed gave rise to the right to a redundancy payment. This is the result of sections 145, 153, and 164(1)(c) of the ERA 1996. However, an employee may also acquire the right to a redundancy payment if within the period of six months starting with the relevant date such a payment is agreed and (rather oddly) paid.[141]

4.56 Further, an employee satisfies the primary time limit for claiming a redundancy payment where within six months of the relevant date he makes a claim for the payment 'by notice in writing given to the employer'.[142] An employee who is dismissed and makes a claim of unfair dismissal under section 111 of the ERA 1996 within six months of the dismissal also satisfies the primary time limit for claiming a redundancy payment.[143]

4.57 Where an employee complies with the primary time limit for claiming a redundancy payment, he may refer to an employment tribunal the question of the amount of the payment at any time subsequently.[144]

---

[141] ERA 1996, s 164(1)(a). It is of interest that in *Bentley Engineering Co v Crown & Miller* [1976] ICR 225, Phillips J, at 234, said in relation to the predecessor to s 164(1), namely s 21 of the Redundancy Payments Act 1965, which was in materially the same terms as s 164(1) (except that there was in it, at least at that time, no reference to the making of a claim of unfair dismissal): 'I confess I share the general puzzlement as to precisely how this section works. In particular, the meaning and purpose of paragraph (a), "the payment has been agreed and paid," seem far from clear.' Further, also at 234, Phillips J said this: 'Everybody who has had anything to do with this case—that is to say, counsel, myself, the tribunal and all involved—are agreed at least on one thing, and that is that this section is obscure.' His plea in the passage which followed that sentence, for 'consideration to be given to the replacement of section 21 by a section which will make quite plain to employees and employers precisely what are their rights and obligations in this respect', was clearly not heeded.

[142] ERA 1996, s 164(1)(b). Such notice need not be in any particular form: *Price v Smithfield & Zwanenberg Group Ltd* [1978] ICR 93, EAT. Thus a claim may be made in a 'without prejudice' letter: ibid, at 97. However, the writing which is claimed to constitute a notice within the meaning of s 164(1)(b) must be reasonably capable of being regarded as claiming a redundancy payment. In *Hetherington v Dependable Products Ltd* (1971) 6 ITR 1, CA, a trade union representative's letter asking for a meeting to discuss the position of the employee 'who was made redundant whilst off on the sick' was held not to constitute such a notice.

[143] ERA 1996, s 164(1)(d). The fact that the unfair dismissal claim is out of time is irrelevant for this purpose: *Duffin v Secretary of State for Employment* [1983] ICR 766, EAT. It should be borne in mind that an employee who is expressly dismissed is not obliged to follow the grievance procedures in Pt 2 of Sch 2 to the EA 2002 before making a claim of unfair dismissal: Employment Act 2002 (Dispute Resolution) Regulations 2004, SI 2004/752, regs 2(1) and 6(5).

[144] *Bentley Engineering Co Ltd v Crown and Miller* [1976] ICR 225, 235–236, Phillips J. This approach was followed by the EAT in *Price v Smithfield and Zwanenberg Group Ltd* [1978] ICR 93, 96.

An employee who fails to comply with the primary time limit of six months for **4.58** claiming a redundancy payment has a further six months within which he may be permitted to make such a claim. This is the result of section 164(2) of the ERA 1996, which provides that if an employee (a) makes a claim for a redundancy payment by notice in writing given to the employer, or (b) 'refers'[145] to an employment tribunal 'a question as to his right to, or the amount of, the payment', or (c) 'presents a complaint relating to his dismissal under section 111', then the tribunal must decide that the employee should receive a redundancy payment 'if it appears to the tribunal to be just and equitable' for him to do so. In so deciding, the tribunal must 'have regard' to (a) the reason 'shown' (not merely stated) by the employee for not making his claim within the primary time limit of six months, and (b) 'all the other relevant circumstances'.[146]

According to the EAT in *Watts v Rubery Owen Conveyancer Ltd*,[147] a claim made **4.59** before the termination of the employment in respect of which a redundancy payment is claimed is premature, and an employment tribunal will have no jurisdiction to hear the claim. There are, however, good reasons for saying that that decision should be treated with some caution.[148]

Right to a written statement

An employer is obliged by section 165(1) of the ERA 1996 to give an employee **4.60** a written statement indicating how a redundancy payment has been calculated, unless an employment tribunal has specified the amount of the payment to be made. A failure to comply with that obligation without a reasonable excuse is a criminal offence, the maximum penalty for which is a fine at level 1 on the standard scale.[149] The employee may then, after such failure, serve a written notice on the employer requiring him to give the employee a written statement complying with the requirements of section 165(1) within a period specified in the notice, which must be of not less than one week.[150] If the employer fails without reasonable excuse to comply with that notice, then the employer commits a further offence and is liable on summary conviction to pay a fine of a maximum of level 3 on the standard scale.[151]

---

[145] This word should be read as meaning 'presents', so that the claim must be received by the employment tribunal within the relevant period: *Secretary of State for Employment v Banks* [1983] ICR 48.

[146] ERA 1996, s 164(3).   [147] [1977] ICR 429.

[148] See paras E[2085]–E[2097.04] of *Harvey*, the analysis in which is cogent.

[149] ERA 1996, s 165(2). Level 1 is currently £200.   [150] ERA 1996, s 165(3).

[151] ERA 1996, s 165(4). Level 3 is currently £1,000.

5

EMPLOYEES' INDIVIDUAL STATUTORY RIGHTS WHERE THERE IS NO TRANSFER

A. Introduction

5.01 The main statutory employment right of employees where there is a business reorganisation but no TUPE transfer is the right not to be unfairly dismissed. The employer could dismiss fairly only for redundancy or 'some other substantial reason' within the meaning of section 98(1)(b) of the ERA 1996. A considerable body of case law has been developed in relation to dismissals where it is claimed by the employer that the dismissal was fair for either or both of those reasons, and the effect of that case law is described in this chapter. There is in addition some protection of employees under the law of discrimination which needs to be mentioned, not least because there are some specific provisions relating to the redundancy of women who are on maternity leave.

B. Fairness of a Dismissal for Redundancy

Introduction and overview

5.02 The fairness of a dismissal for redundancy now falls to be considered against the backdrop of a considerable body of case law, the emphasis of which has changed over time. The overall test, when applying section 98(4) of the ERA 1996, is the now standard test of whether the dismissal was within the range of reasonable responses of a reasonable employer.[1]

5.03 However, it is for the employer to show the reason for the dismissal,[2] and thus, if the employer claims that the reason for the dismissal was redundancy, then the employer will have to satisfy the employment tribunal that the definition of redundancy is satisfied.[3]

A summary of the principles applicable when determining whether a dismissal for redundancy was unfair

5.04 Certain reasons for selecting an employee for redundancy are automatically unfair. They are all of those reasons which make a dismissal automatically unfair. They are mentioned below.[4] This section is concerned with the 'ordinary' law

---

[1] *Duffy v Yeomans & Partners Ltd* [1995] ICR 1, 5, CA.   [2] ERA 1996, s 98(1).
[3] See para 4.03 onwards above for the definition of 'redundancy'.
[4] See para 5.52. It should be noted that an employee who is dismissed for any of the reasons mentioned in that para does not need a year's continuous employment in order to be able to claim unfair dismissal: ERA 1996, s 108(3). Nor does the upper age limit provided for by s 109 of that Act apply: see s 109(2). Further, the impact of the law of discrimination on the situation, including the provisions applicable to women who are absent through pregnancy or childbirth, which are mentioned at the end of this chapter (paras 5.61 to 5.63), should not be overlooked.

of unfair dismissal, namely the principles to be derived from the current case law concerning the application of section 98(4) of the ERA 1996. Before turning to that case law, mention must be made of the need to comply with the relevant statutory procedure in Schedule 2 to the EA 2002. Thus if there is an express dismissal (ie a dismissal within the meaning of section 95(1)(a) or (b) of the ERA 1996), then, subject to the exceptions referred to in the following sentence below, the employer will be obliged to comply with the relevant disciplinary and dismissal procedure ('DDP') in Part 1 of Schedule 2.[5] The main relevant exceptions are set out in regulation 4 of the Employment Act 2002 (Dispute Resolution) Regulations 2004. These are that (1) all of the employees of the description or category to which the dismissed employee belongs have been dismissed and offered new terms to take effect either before or on the termination of the original contracts of employment; or (2) 'the dismissal is one of a number of dismissals in respect of which the duty in section 188 of the 1992 Act (duty of employer to consult representatives when proposing to dismiss as redundant a certain number of employees) applies'. A failure by the employer to follow the relevant DDP will make the dismissal automatically unfair,[6] although the compensation payable for the dismissal will not necessarily be substantial.[7] In order to comply with the DDP in relation to a dismissal for redundancy, it will be necessary to provide 'information as to both why the employer considers that there is, to put it colloquially, a redundancy situation and also why [the employee's selection is proposed]'.[8]

One principle which applies to the determination of the question whether a **5.05** dismissal for redundancy was unfair within the meaning of section 98(4) of the ERA 1996 is that a reasonable employer will both (1) warn an employee whose possible dismissal is under consideration that he may be dismissed for redundancy; and (2) consult him before making the decision to dismiss him. Where a trade union is recognised in respect of employees of the description of the employee whose possible dismissal for redundancy is under consideration, a reasonable employer will both warn and consult that trade union. Another principle applicable when determining whether a dismissal for redundancy was unfair is that a reasonable employer will make reasonable efforts to redeploy an employee before dismissing him for redundancy. A further relevant principle is that an employment tribunal cannot properly decide that an employee's

---

[5] See reg 3(1) of the Employment Act 2002 (Dispute Resolution) Regulations 2004, SI 2004/752, read with reg 2(1) of those regulations. The applicability of the relevant DDP to a dismissal for redundancy was confirmed by the EAT in *Alexander v Brigden Enterprises Ltd* [2006] IRLR 422.

[6] ERA 1996, s 98A(1).   [7] See para 5.55 below.

[8] *Alexander v Brigden Enterprises Ltd* [2006] IRLR 422, para 41; see further paras 41–9.

dismissal for redundancy was unfair because the employer's decision to dismiss one or more employees for redundancy was itself unreasonable. Another relevant principle is that if it was necessary to select one or more employees for redundancy because there was more than one employee doing the work of a particular kind that the dismissed employee did before his dismissal, then the employer must apply proper selection criteria. All of these principles are considered in more detail below.

5.06 Before turning to that detail, attention can usefully be drawn to the fact that, in *Langston v Cranfield University*,[9] the EAT stated that where a claimant complains of unfair dismissal by reason of redundancy, 'it is implicit in that claim, absent agreement to the contrary between the parties, that the unfairness incorporates unfair selection, lack of consultation and failure to seek alternative employment on the part of the employer'. This echoes what was said by Lord Bridge in *Polkey v A E Dayton Services Ltd*:[10]

> in the case of redundancy, the employer will normally not act reasonably unless he warns and consults any employees affected or their representative, adopts a fair basis on which to select for redundancy and takes such steps as may be reasonable to avoid or minimise redundancy by redeployment within his own organisation.

The extent to which a decision to dismiss employees for redundancy can be challenged

5.07 In *James W Cook & Co (Wivenhoe) Ltd v Tipper*,[11] Neill LJ, with whom Farquharson LJ and Sir Roger Ormerod agreed, said this:

> It seems to me . . . that a distinction has to be drawn between the case of an individual employee where some compensation may be awarded to take account of a further period of consultation which would have been appropriate to deal with his particular situation and a case such as the present where a whole business is closed down. In my judgment it is not open to the court to investigate the commercial and economic reasons which prompted the closure. It may be that in order to ensure fairness for the workforce the court should have this power, but in my view it does not have this power at present.

5.08 However, as he also said:[12] 'The industrial tribunal is of course entitled to consider whether the closure of a business is in fact genuine.' Thus if an employer who asserts redundancy as the reason for the dismissal of an employee fails to show that the employee was in fact dismissed for redundancy, then the dismissal will be unfair. This will be because the employer has failed to show the reason for the dismissal.[13]

---

[9] [1998] IRLR 172, para 30.   [10] [1988] ICR 142, 162–163.
[11] [1990] ICR 716, 729.   [12] ibid, 729.   [13] ERA 1996, s 98(1).

Warning and consultation

The general position

Where there is no relevant recognised trade union, a reasonable employer will **5.09** almost always both warn and consult an employee whose dismissal for redundancy is under consideration before deciding whether to dismiss him. The fact that there is a duty both to warn and to consult was emphasised by the EAT in *Rowell v Hubbard Group Services Ltd*.[14] However, having been referred to that case, the EAT, in *Elkouil v Coney Island Ltd*,[15] said that 'the submission that there is a separate duty to warn is not made out', but that the 'consultation process should commence with a warning that the employee is at risk'. This seems to be a distinction without a difference. Nevertheless, an employer is not under a duty to warn an employee whose attendance record is relatively poor that he will be more likely to be selected for redundancy than his colleagues because of that record.[16]

The only time when consultation in respect of a proposed dismissal for redundancy will not be necessary is when a reasonable employer could have failed **5.10** to consult in the circumstances.[17] Where the employee(s) whose dismissal for redundancy is proposed is/are represented by an independent trade union recognised by the employer, a reasonable employer will usually give sufficient warning of impending redundancies 'so as to enable the union and employees who may be affected to take early steps to inform themselves of the relevant facts, consider possible alternative solutions, and, if necessary, find alternative employment in the undertaking or elsewhere'.[18] In addition, a reasonable employer will usually consult the union 'as to the best means by which the desired result can be achieved fairly and with as little hardship to the employees as possible'.[19] A reasonable employer 'will seek to agree with the union the criteria to be applied in selecting the employees to be made redundant'.[20] When

---

[14] [1995] IRLR 195, para 12.   [15] [2002] IRLR 174, para 13.
[16] *Gray v Shetland Norse Preserving Co Ltd* [1985] IRLR 53, para 9, EAT.
[17] *Duffy v Yeomans & Partners Ltd* [1995] ICR 1, 8, CA. In *Mugford v Midland Bank plc* [1997] ICR 399, 406, the EAT commented: 'Where no consultation about redundancy has taken place with either the trade union or the employee the dismissal will normally be unfair, unless the industrial tribunal finds that a reasonable employer would have concluded that consultation would be an utterly futile exercise in the particular circumstances of the case.'
[18] *Williams v Compair Maxam Ltd* [1982] ICR 156, 162. The EAT in *Rolls-Royce Motor Cars Ltd v Price* [1993] IRLR 203, para 31, warned against 'erecting what was said in *Williams v Compair Maxam* . . . into the terms of a statute'. The EAT in *Mugford v Midland Bank plc* [1997] ICR 399, 406 said: 'We would ourselves similarly adopt that approach [ie that of the EAT in *Price*] in this case.' The statements of principle drawn from *Williams v Compair Maxam* in the text below should be read accordingly.
[19] *Williams v Compair Maxam Ltd*, 162.   [20] ibid.

the selection has been made, the employer will 'consider with the union whether the selection has been made in accordance with those criteria',[21] and 'will consider any representations the union may make as to such selection'.[22]

5.11 Consultation with the trade union about the selection criteria will not of itself satisfy the duty to consult in relation to an impending redundancy or redundancies, since the employer will usually '[consider] with the employee individually his being identified for redundancy'.[23] 'It will be a question of fact and degree for the [employment] tribunal to consider whether consultation with the individual and/or his union was so inadequate as to render the dismissal unfair.'[24] 'The overall picture must be viewed by the tribunal up to the date of termination to ascertain whether the employer has or has not acted reasonably in dismissing the employee on the grounds of redundancy.'[25] If an employee is absent from work because she is on maternity leave, it will be a breach of the Sex Discrimination Act 1975 to fail to consult her where the reason (which need not be the only one) for the failure to consult her is her absence from work on maternity leave.[26]

5.12 Consultation 'should normally take place before a final decision to dismiss is reached'.[27] However, the 'high water mark of recent decisions',[28] namely that of the EAT in *Rowell v Hubbard Group Services Ltd*,[29] should probably be taken to require a little too much of an employer in terms of consultation (although in appropriate circumstances that which was there indicated as being requisite may be required). There, the EAT referred to the requirements applied by Hodgson J in *R v Gwent County Council, Ex parte Bryant*[30] to a public law case, namely that (a) consultation should take place when the proposals were still at a formative stage; (b) the body consulting should give (1) adequate information on which the consultee could respond, and (2) adequate time in which to respond, and (c) the body carrying out the consultation should conscientiously consider the response to the consultation. The EAT commented that these requirements would be 'of assistance to employers when they have to consult with staff in the context of dismissal for redundancy', but that there 'are no invariable rules as to

---

[21] *Williams v Compair Maxam Ltd*, 162.   [22] ibid.
[23] *Mugford v Midland Bank plc* [1997] ICR 399, 406.   [24] ibid.
[25] ibid, 407. Thus in theory it will be possible to give a conditional notice of dismissal, with the notice falling to be withdrawn before it takes effect if the employer is persuaded to withdraw it by what is said during the consultation process. However, in such a situation there will be a significant risk that an employment tribunal would conclude that the consultation was not genuine.
[26] *McGuigan v T G Baynes & Sons* (1998) 24 November, EAT; EAT/1114/97, transcript, p 10; the transcript is available at <www.bailii.org>. See para 5.61 below regarding the compensation payable for such discrimination.
[27] *Mugford v Midland Bank plc* [1997] ICR 399, 405.   [28] ibid, 403.
[29] [1995] IRLR 195.   [30] [1988] COD 19.

what is to be done in any given situation; everything will depend on its particular facts'.[31] Nevertheless, said the EAT in *Rowell*,[32] 'when the need for consultation exists, it must be fair and genuine, and should, we suggest, be conducted so far as possible as the passage from Glidewell LJ's judgment [in *R v British Coal Corporation and Secretary of State for Trade and Industry, ex parte Price*[33]] suggests'. There, having set out the relevant passage from Hodgson J's judgment in *Bryant*, Glidewell LJ said this:[34] 'Another way of putting the point more shortly is that fair consultation involves giving the body consulted a fair and proper opportunity to understand fully the matters about which it is being consulted, and to express its views on those subjects, with the consultor thereafter considering those views properly and genuinely.' While bearing it in mind that there will be circumstances in which it would be within the range of reasonable responses of a reasonable employer not to consult precisely in accordance with this statement, it is a helpful statement of that which proper consultation entails.

Some particular factors relating to consultation

However, while in some circumstances less thorough consultation may be required,[35] in other circumstances it will be particularly important to consult. For example, the more vague the selection criteria are, the more important it will be that the employer consults the employee and listens to his representations.[36] A failure to comply with a statutory duty to consult (such as under section 188 of the TULRA or regulation 13 of TUPE[37]) will be a relevant factor,[38] but it will not be conclusive.[39] The mere fact that at the end of an earlier set of dismissals for redundancy, having been consulted properly, the workforce as a whole said that they would have preferred simply being told

5.13

---

[31] *Rowell*, para 16.   [32] ibid.   [33] [1994] IRLR 72.   [34] ibid, para 25.

[35] See eg *Meikle v McPhail (Charleston Arms)* [1983] IRLR 351, EAT, concerning a dismissal for redundancy from the staff of a public house. At para 9, the EAT said that 'the so-called principles set out in *Williams v Compair Maxam Ltd* . . . must primarily refer to large organisations in which a significant number of redundancies are contemplated. In our view they should be applied with caution to circumstances such as the present where the size and administrative resources of the employer are minimal.' This does not mean that a small employer is under no obligation to consult an employee whose dismissal for redundancy is under consideration (assuming that it would not be 'utterly useless or futile to do so'): *De Grasse v Stockwell Tools Ltd* [1992] IRLR 269, paras 12 and 13, EAT.

[36] See *Graham v ABF Ltd* [1986] IRLR 90, EAT, where the criteria included 'the attitude of the persons evaluated to their work' (see para 3), and the principal ground on which the claimant was (because of the factors referred to in para 6 of the EAT's judgment) chosen to be dismissed for redundancy was his attitude to his work.

[37] See Chapters 6 and 7 below for the extent of these duties generally.

[38] *Williams v Compair Maxam Ltd* [1982] ICR 156, 164, EAT.

[39] *Hough v Leyland DAF Ltd* [1991] ICR 696, 708, EAT.

which of them were to be made redundant will not mean that the employer is not under a duty to consult when further redundancies are proposed.[40]

5.14 There is a duty to consult individual employees themselves about their proposed dismissal for redundancy not only because an employee may have representations to make about the application to him by the employer of work-related selection criteria, but also because only the employee will know about two particular factual matters. One is the employee's willingness to accept redeployment to a post on a lower grade and/or wage or salary.[41] The other is the employee's personal circumstances, the relevance of which was emphasised by the EAT in *Forman Construction Ltd v Kelly*.[42]

Appeals

5.15 While an employer is not under a duty, as far as the law of 'ordinary' unfair dismissal is concerned, to afford an employee an opportunity to appeal against his dismissal for redundancy,[43] if such an appeal occurs, then a procedural failing preceding the original decision to dismiss may be 'cured'.[44] However, given that the DDP in Schedule 2 to the EA 2002 now applies to dismissals for redundancy, it will be necessary to offer employees a right of appeal.[45]

The selection criteria

5.16 The selection criteria should be as objective as is reasonably possible.[46] Thus, 'the employer will seek to establish criteria for selection which so far as possible do not depend solely upon the opinion of the person making the selection but can be objectively checked against such things as attendance record, efficiency at the job, experience or length of service'.[47] In *Graham v ABF Ltd*,[48] the EAT went so far as to say this:

> we consider that there is a great deal of force in the criticisms which Mr Hughes has addressed to the adoption of 'attitude to work' as a criterion, certainly as a prominent criterion, for redundancy selection. It is dangerously ambiguous, particularly in a case like the present where the basis for redundancy selection had been agreed with the unions by word of mouth and there was nothing in writing

---

[40] *Ferguson v Prestwick Circuits Ltd* [1992] IRLR 266, para 19, EAT.
[41] See eg *Heron v Citylink-Nottingham* [1993] IRLR 372, para 24, EAT, and *De Grasse v Stockwell Tools Ltd* [1992] IRLR 269, para 14, EAT.
[42] [1977] IRLR 468, para 5.
[43] *Robinson v Ulster Carpet Mills Ltd* [1991] IRLR 348, para 22, NICA.
[44] *Taylor v OCS Group Ltd* [2006] EWCA Civ 702; [2006] IRLR 613.
[45] See paras 3 and 5 of Sch 2 to the EA 2002.
[46] *Williams v Compair Maxam Ltd* [1982] ICR 156, 162, EAT.
[47] ibid.   [48] [1986] IRLR 90, para 17.

at all. It is a highly relative term involving personal and subjective judgments, and it is dangerously vague. We trust we may be allowed to express a hope that so nebulous a criterion will not be found again in negotiated agreements for redundancy selection.

Nevertheless, the EAT found itself unable to say that the adoption of that **5.17** criterion made the dismissal unfair. Thus, the EAT concluded that it was not open to it to overturn the decision of the industrial tribunal that the dismissal was fair:

> Accepting all the criticisms we have made of this nebulous criterion, we neverthe-less do not consider that we can go to the lengths of saying that the conclusion reached by the Industrial Tribunal, that it was capable of founding a fair selection for redundancy, was one so startling that it would not have been open to any reasonable Tribunal properly directed in law.[49]

Ultimately, the selection criteria must be such that they fall within the band of **5.18** reasonable responses of a reasonable employer to the need to dismiss one or more employees by reason of redundancy.[50] Accordingly, given that (*Williams v Compair Maxam Ltd* apart) there are few clear statements of principle in the authorities concerning the choice of selection criteria, the citation of authority is unlikely to be of much assistance to an employment tribunal in that regard. One or two cases are of some assistance, however. One is that of *Forman Construction Ltd v Kelly*,[51] where the EAT emphasised the importance normally of taking into account the personal circumstances of candidates for redundancy. Another is that of *Jowett v Earl of Bradford (No 2)*,[52] where the EAT declined to criticise the industrial tribunal for regarding domestic arrangements as being important (and by implication relevant as a selection criterion).[53]

Application of the selection criteria

It is incorrect to say that '[an] employer is under no obligation, as a matter of law, **5.19** to look elsewhere among his employees, other than those employed in similar

---

[49] ibid.
[50] *N C Watling & Co Ltd v Richardson* [1978] ICR 1049, EAT, the approach in which was approved by the Court of Appeal (via its approval of *Iceland Frozen Foods Ltd v Jones* [1983] ICR 17) in *Foley v Post Office* [2000] ICR 1283.
[51] [1977] IRLR 468, para 5.   [52] [1978] ICR 431, 434.
[53] The approach in general terms of the EAT in *Jowett v Earl of Bradford (No 2)*, at 436, where the EAT rejected the submission that it was necessary to apply the test laid down in *Vickers Ltd v Smith* [1977] IRLR 11, must be seen as having been wrong, given the subsequent decision of the EAT in *N C Watling & Co Ltd v Richardson* [1978] ICR 1049, 1056–1057, where the EAT held that the range of reasonable responses of a reasonable employer test is applicable. Nevertheless, it must be right that an employee's domestic arrangements are a potentially fair selection criterion, given the importance of consulting an employee whose dismissal for redundancy is proposed, so that the employee can tell the employer about any domestic arrangements of which the employer is not aware.

positions' for a person to select for redundancy.[54] It is nevertheless, at least potentially lawful to confine the 'selection pool' to employees holding positions which are similar to those of the dismissed employee.[55]

5.20   It was said by Millett LJ in *British Aerospace plc v Green*[56] that it should normally be sufficient for an employer to satisfy an employment tribunal that the employer has set up 'a good system of selection and that it was fairly administered'. He also said that 'ordinarily there is no need for the employer to justify all the assessments on which the selection for redundancy was based'.[57] Waite LJ in that case based his decision that the industrial tribunal chairman had erred in ordering the disclosure of documents recording the results of the assessments relating to employees who had not been dismissed 'on grounds of policy and relevance',[58] and said that 'if a graded assessment system is to achieve its purpose it must not be subjected to an over-minute analysis'.[59] Stuart-Smith LJ agreed with Waite LJ as well as with Millett LJ,[60] but said this also:

> In cases of mass redundancy in my opinion it will be only in rare and exceptional cases that the assessment forms of other employees not made redundant will be relevant. This is because the tribunal is not considering whether those employees were unfairly not made redundant, but whether the applicant was unfairly dismissed. It is possible to envisage a case where for example all or the majority of employees in a certain category in one factory were made redundant, but all others, or the great majority, at the other sites were not. This might suggest that the criterion had not been fairly applied in their case. But this is something which will be known to the applicants or their union; and, if that is the case, it can be presented with proper particularity. Then, and only then, may it be relevant to look at the assessments of others in a similar category at other sites; but it cannot possibly be relevant to look at all the other assessments of employees in different categories. The truth of the matter here, as the appeal tribunal pointed out, is that this was a fishing expedition to see if any case could be discovered. That is what is not permitted.[61]

5.21   In contrast, the EAT ruled in *John Brown Engineering Ltd v Brown*[62] that the employer's failure to tell the employees the results of their individual assessments entitled the industrial tribunal to find that the employees' dismissals

---

[54] *Thomas & Betts Manufacturing Ltd v Harding* [1980] IRLR 255, para 9, CA. The EAT cast doubt on this approach in *Huddersfield Parcels Ltd v Sykes* [1981] IRLR 115, para 18. However, that doubt was based on the proposition that what is called 'bumping' in this context might be unlawful, and that is now clearly incorrect (see para 5.26 below).
[55] *Green v A & I Fraser (Wholesale Fish Merchants) Ltd* [1985] IRLR 55, para 13, EAT.
[56] [1995] ICR 1006, 1019.   [57] ibid.   [58] ibid, 1017.   [59] ibid, 1016.
[60] See ibid, 1020.   [61] ibid, 1020–1021.   [62] [1997] IRLR 90.

were unfair. Further, in *FDR Ltd v Holloway*,[63] the EAT (with Mummery J presiding) declined to overturn a decision of an industrial tribunal to order the disclosure of documents relating to all eight employees in a pool for selection for redundancy. There,[64] the EAT said this:

> The tribunal was not bound to accept the company's assertion that it had applied the criteria fairly. The role of the tribunal is to decide whether Mr Holloway was fairly selected. To do that the tribunal, of necessity, has to know Mr Holloway's markings and how they compare with the other seven employees in order to determine whether the system had been applied fairly and reasonably to him.

The logic of that passage cannot be faulted. The EAT was referred to, and considered the effect of, the decision of the Court of Appeal in *British Aerospace Plc v Green*. Accordingly, the best view appears to be that the question whether or not an employee should be enabled to see the results of the application of the selection criteria to other employees must be a matter which falls to be determined by an employment tribunal on the facts of the case in question. **5.22**

Redeployment

The statements of principle in *Langston v Cranfield University*[65] and *Polkey v A E Dayton Services Ltd*[66] mentioned in para 5.06 above show that it is now clear that an employer is under a duty to take reasonable steps to look for alternative employment for a potentially redundant employee within the employer's own organisation. **5.23**

Further, an employer may be required to look for alternative employment within the group of companies of which the employer forms a part.[67] Nevertheless, the obligation to look for alternative employment for an employee is not absolute.[68] Further, if an employee is willing to accept employment in a position with lower status or on a lower grade, then, it was said by the EAT in *Barratt Construction Ltd v Dalrymple*,[69] 'he ought, in fairness, to make this clear at an early stage so as to give his employer an opportunity to see if this is a feasible solution'. However, the EAT has also ruled that a decision by an industrial tribunal that a dismissal was unfair because the employer had not discussed with the dismissed employee the possibility of employment in a lower-paid job **5.24**

---

[63] [1995] IRLR 400.   [64] In para 11.   [65] [1998] IRLR 172, para 30.
[66] [1988] ICR 142, 162–163.   [67] *Vokes Ltd v Bear* [1974] ICR 1, 5, NIRC.
[68] See *British United Shoe Manufacturing Co Ltd v Clarke* [1978] ICR 70, 72, where the EAT said that 'industrial tribunals ought to avoid demanding some unreal or Elysian standard'. See too *MDH Ltd v Sussex* [1986] IRLR 123, para 20, where the EAT said that the industrial tribunal had been wrong to treat *Vokes* as 'virtually conclusive of unfairness'.
[69] [1984] IRLR 385, para 5.

was not unlawful.[70] The safer course would accordingly be to ask an employee about his willingness to accept a post on a lower grade.

5.25   In any event, if alternative employment is offered, enough information should be given to the employee for him to be able to 'make a realistic decision whether to take the job and stay, or whether to reject it and leave'.[71] Further, offering alternative employment on unreasonable terms is likely to make a dismissal for redundancy (as a consequence of the employee's declining the offer of alternative employment) unfair.[72]

5.26   An employer cannot properly refuse to consider whether to dismiss an employee other than the claimant, although on the facts a decision not to dismiss another employee may be fair.[73] The possibility of this kind of dismissal (sometimes referred to as 'bumping') was expressly contemplated as lawful by the EAT in *Burrell v Safeway Stores plc*[74] and the House of Lords in *Murray v Foyle Meats*.[75]

5.27   However, the obligation on an employer to make reasonable adjustments for disabled employees within the meaning of the Disability Discrimination Act 1995 ('DDA 1995') may affect the manner in which the employer seeks to redeploy redundant employees, and accordingly that obligation should be borne in mind here.[76] Equally, the position of the employee who is on maternity leave, and the obligation to offer her any alternative posts before they are offered to other employees,[77] should be borne in mind in this context.

Can an employer fairly require employees to apply for new posts in the reorganised business rather than selecting them for those posts?

5.28   In *Ball v Balfour Kilpatrick Ltd*,[78] an accounting department with five employees in it was closed and the employer had to choose which of the employees were to be offered posts in a new unit, to be 'formed under a separate company called Emform Ltd'.[79] The EAT accepted a submission made on behalf of the employer that there was in the circumstances no selection process involved. The following passage from the EAT's judgment is of particular interest:[80]

---

[70] *Huddersfield Parcels Ltd v Sykes* [1981] 115, paras 13 and 23; *Abbotts v Wesson-Glynwed Steels Ltd* [1982] IRLR 51, paras 16 and 17.

[71] *Modern Injection Moulds Ltd v Price* [1976] ICR 370, 374, EAT.

[72] See *Elliott v Richard Stump Ltd* [1987] ICR 579, 583, EAT.

[73] *Thomas & Betts Manufacturing Ltd v Harding* [1980] IRLR 255, para 16, CA.

[74] [1997] ICR 523.

[75] [1999] ICR 827. See para (2)(e) of the extract from the EAT's judgment in *Burrell*, as set out in para 4.06 above.

[76] See further para 5.60 below, where the case of *Kent County Council v Mingo* [2000] IRLR 90 is discussed.

[77] See paras 5.62–5.63 below.   [78] [1997] ICR 740.   [79] ibid, 742.

[80] ibid, 745.

In our judgment, the common sense view on the findings by the industrial tribunal is that the employers were not, in fact, selecting for redundancy at all. In our judgment, a position had been reached as a result of the reorganisation whereby, on application of section 81(2)(b) of the Act of 1978, all five employees in the accounts department were made redundant and there was, in reality, no selection process to be carried out. The true analysis, in our judgment, is that the employers were then embarking on what the industrial tribunal in effect held was the reasonable consideration of suitable alternative employment with Emform Ltd. of four out of those five who had already been made redundant by the employers and, in our judgment, it is clear on the authority of the decision of the Employment Appeal Tribunal in *Akzo Coatings Plc. v. Thompson* (unreported), 14 February 1996, of which we have seen a transcript, that the touchstone in such a situation is reasonableness, rather than the application of either agreed selection criteria for redundancy or the application of objective criteria.

It is suggested here that it would be wrong to regard this case as authority for **5.29** the proposition that it is always open to an employer to require employees to apply for posts of the same sort as those which they currently hold where a reorganisation is carried out. Rather, it should be regarded as authority for the proposition that where the posts in a restructured business or part of a business are genuinely different from those which they replace, it may be within the range of reasonable responses of a reasonable employer to require employees who are at risk of redundancy to apply for posts in the new structure. It would surely not be right to regard the case as authority for the proposition that where an employer has to dismiss for redundancy a number of employees from a larger number of employees, all of whom are doing the same or a similar job, it would be within the range of reasonable responses of a reasonable employer to dismiss all of the employees within the group and require those who wish to continue to be employed by that employer to apply for their 'old' job. Nevertheless, it is suggested here that even the dismissals in the latter circumstances would not necessarily be unfair: the determination of that question would depend on a proper consideration of all of the circumstances.

C. Compensation for Unfair Dismissal by Reason of Redundancy: General Principles

If an employee is dismissed for redundancy unfairly, then the compensation for **5.30** the unfair dismissal may be relatively low. This is for several reasons. One is that as long as the reason for the dismissal was indeed redundancy,[81] the basic award

---

[81] *Boorman v Allmakes Ltd* [1995] ICR 842, CA.

within the meaning of section 119 of the ERA 1996[82] is reduced to nil by any redundancy payment either paid or payable by the employer.[83] Another is that the only unfairness may have been a failure to consult, and it may be possible to show on the balance of probabilities that the employee would have been dismissed after appropriate consultation within a relatively short period of time. The employee should then receive compensation only for the loss of income from the employment for the period during which the consultation should have occurred.[84] However, in other cases, it may be impossible reasonably to say what would have happened if that which made the dismissal unfair had not occurred. In between these two extremes, it may be possible to say that there was a chance that the employee would have been retained in the employer's employment.

5.31   Where there is a chance that the employee would have been retained in the employment of the employer if the employer had acted fairly, the employment tribunal is obliged to assess the size, in percentage terms, of that chance. This is the clear effect of what was said by Browne-Wilkinson J in relation to that situation in *Sillifant v Powell Duffryn Timber Ltd*[85] as approved by Lord Bridge in *Polkey v A E Dayton Services Ltd*:[86]

> There is no need for an 'all or nothing' decision. If the industrial tribunal thinks there is a doubt whether or not the employee would have been dismissed, this element can be reflected by reducing the normal amount of compensation by a percentage representing the chance that the employee would still have lost his employment.

5.32   Where it is not possible reasonably to say what chance there was that the employee would not have been dismissed if a fair procedure had been followed, then the employment tribunal will have to 'decide whether the unfair departure from what should have happened was of a kind which makes it possible to say, with more or less confidence, that the failure made no difference, or whether the failure was such that one cannot sensibly reconstruct the world as it might have been'.[87] In this context, 'it is unhelpful . . . to characterise the defect in the employer's behaviour as either substantive or procedural'.[88]

---

[82] See paras 5.50 and 5.51 below concerning the calculation of the basic award.
[83] ERA 1996, s 122(4).   [84] See eg *Abbotts v Wesson-Glynwed Steels Ltd* [1982] IRLR 51.
[85] [1983 IRLR 91.
[86] [1988] ICR 142, 163. Lord Bridge's speech was not agreed with by the majority of the House of Lords, but this part of it was cited with implicit approval by Peter Gibson LJ, with whom Hutchison LJ agreed, in *O'Dea v ISC Chemicals Ltd* [1996] ICR 222, 233.
[87] *King v Eaton Ltd (No 2)* [1998] IRLR 686, Ct Sess, para 19, as approved by the Court of Appeal in *Lambe v 186K Ltd* [2005] ICR 307, 323, para 59.
[88] *Lambe*, ibid.

D. Dismissing for 'Some Other Substantial Reason'

Introduction

An employer wishing to change its employees' terms and conditions of employ-   **5.33**
ment relating to remuneration is likely initially to seek to obtain the employees'
agreement to the change. If the employer dismissed the employees for refusing
to accept the changes, or they resigned and successfully claimed that they had
been 'constructively' dismissed (ie dismissed within the meaning of section
95(1)(c) of the ERA 1996) as a result of the attempt to impose the changes on
them, then their dismissals would not be for redundancy.[89] The dismissals
could then be fair only if they could properly be said to have been for 'some
other substantial reason such as to justify the dismissal of an employee holding
the position which the employee held' within the meaning of section 98(1)(b)
of the ERA 1996. This is because the employer would otherwise be unable
to show the employment tribunal the reason for the dismissals.[90] If the
employer sought to impose the change without expressly dismissing the
employees, and an employee claimed successfully that he had been dismissed
as a result,[91] then the dismissal would be likely to be unfair, although it would
not necessarily be so.[92] An employer who merely offers new terms and informs
an employee that if the employee refuses to accept them then he will be
dismissed with proper notice and offered re-engagement on the new terms

---

[89] See *Chapman v Goonvean and Rostowrack China Clay Co Ltd* [1973] ICR 310, CA—as
approved ultimately by the House of Lords in *Murray v Foyle Meats Ltd* [1999] ICR 827, via its
approval of *Burrell v Safeway Stores Ltd* [1997] ICR 523 (see paras 4.04 and 4.06 above)—for the
proposition that dismissals in these circumstances are not for redundancy.

[90] cf *Pederson v Camden London Borough Council (Note)* [1981] ICR 674, CA, as analysed by
the EAT in *Farrant v The Woodroffe School* [1998] ICR 184, 196.

[91] See *Hogg v Dover College* [1990] ICR 39 concerning this possibility. The approach of the
EAT in *Hogg* was approved by the Court of Appeal in *Jones v Governing Body of Burdett Coutts
School* [1999] ICR 38, 42 (per Robert Walker LJ, with whom Morritt and Stuart-Smith LJJ
agreed). In *Hogg*, the EAT, at [1990] ICR 42, held that an employee who is being told by his
employer 'henceforth you are to be employed on wholly different terms which are in fact less than
50 per cent of your previous contract' is 'being told that his former contract of employment [is]
from that moment gone' and is accordingly being dismissed within the meaning of s 95(1)(a) of
the ERA 1996, but that if they (the EAT) were wrong about that, then there was a 'constructive
dismissal under [s 95(1)(c)]'.

[92] See *Savoia v Chiltern Health Farms Ltd* [1982] IRLR 166, CA, in relation to the proposition
that the dismissal could be fair, and *Stanley Cole (Wainfleet) Ltd v Sheridan* [2003] ICR 297,
para 82, EAT, for the proposition that the dismissal would be unlikely to be fair (the appeal to the
Court of Appeal in that case, reported at [2003] ICR 1449, not having concerned this issue). A
fair constructive dismissal following a reorganisation occurred in *Genower v Ealing, Hammersmith
and Hounslow Area Health Authority* [1980] IRLR 297, EAT.

should not to be taken without more to have repudiated the contract of employment.[93]

5.34 Assuming that the dismissal was not in breach of regulation 7(1) of TUPE,[94] then it could properly be held by an employment tribunal to be fair, but only if it was for 'some sound, good business reason'.[95] Eveleigh LJ commented in *Hollister v National Farmers' Union*[96] that it would not be right to lay down any kind of general rule about what would or would not be 'some other substantial reason' within the meaning of section 98(1)(b) ('SOSR'). Accordingly, the relevant cases in which it has been decided that a dismissal was for SOSR cannot be regarded as laying down principles. Nevertheless, they are illustrative of what may be regarded as SOSR in the context of a business reorganisation.

SOSR in the context of a reorganisation

5.35 In *D R Ellis v Brighton Co-operative Society Ltd*,[97] the EAT decided that a dismissal for refusing to accept new working practices, including longer working hours and increased duties which made the job 'slightly more, but not remarkably more, onerous',[98] was properly found by the industrial tribunal to have been for SOSR in the circumstances that (1) the trade union had agreed to the changes (although it did not act as Mr Ellis's agent[99]); and (2) the industrial tribunal appear to have concluded that the business would have been brought to a standstill if the changes were not accepted by all of the affected employees. The EAT commented that 'Where there has been a properly consulted-upon re-organisation which, if it is not done, is going to bring the whole business to a standstill, a failure to go along with the new arrangements may well—it is not bound to, but it may well—constitute "some other substantial reason".'[100]

5.36 Similarly, in *Bowater Containers v McCormack*,[101] the EAT allowed an appeal against a finding by an industrial tribunal that the fact that the imposition of additional duties on an employee, following a reorganisation, was a repudiation of his contract of employment meant that his dismissal was unfair. The EAT even went so far as to substitute a finding that the dismissal was fair. The case was not cited (although many others were) in *Farrant v The Woodroffe*

---

[93] *Kerry Foods Ltd v Lynch* [2005] IRLR 680, para 21, EAT. It is of interest that the EAT there expressed doubt about the correctness of the decision of the EAT in *Greenaway Harrison Ltd v Wiles* [1994] IRLR 380, but stated that it did not need to come to a firm conclusion as to its correctness: see *Lynch*, at para 20.

[94] See para 3.57 onwards above for the effect of reg 7(1).

[95] *Hollister v National Farmers' Union* [1979] ICR 542, 551, per Lord Denning MR, with whom Eveleigh LJ and Sir Stanley Rees agreed.

[96] ibid, 553.   [97] [1976] IRLR 491.   [98] See ibid, para 10.

[99] See ibid, para 6.   [100] ibid, para 9.   [101] [1980] IRLR 50.

School,[102] despite its relevance. However, the EAT in *Farrant* came to a similar conclusion. The case concerned an employee who was dismissed for gross misconduct when he refused to comply with an instruction to work to a new job description which he was not obliged to accept. Thus, the imposition of the new job description was a repudiation of the employee's contract of employment.[103] However, the EAT declined to overturn the industrial tribunal's decision that the dismissal was fair. The EAT also declined to distinguish between a deliberate contract breaker and an inadvertent contract breaker in this context.[104] It will be possible in both circumstances for the dismissal to be for SOSR.[105]

Although strictly speaking the imposition of a restrictive covenant does not constitute a business reorganisation, an employer may wish as part of, or as a result of, such a reorganisation to impose such a covenant on existing employees. As the NIRC put it in *R S Components Ltd v Irwin*:[106]   **5.37**

> it is not difficult to imagine a case where it would be essential for employers embarking, e.g., on a new technical process, to invite existing employees to agree to some reasonable restriction on their use of the knowledge they acquire of the new technique; and where it would be essential for the employer to terminate, by due notice, the services of an employee who was unwilling to accept such a restriction. A licensing agreement for a new process may impose on the licensee an obligation to protect the secret process in that way: see, for example, the terms of the licensing agreement in *Under Water Welders & Repairers Ltd. v. Street* [1968] R.P.C. 498. It would be unfortunate for the development of industry if an employer were unable to meet such a situation without infringing or risking infringement of rights conferred by the Industrial Relations Act 1971 [now the ERA 1996].

The same test is applicable when considering whether a dismissal for a refusal to accept a new restrictive covenant was for SOSR as the test which applies in relation to any other imposition of new contractual terms.[107]   **5.38**

An employer must adduce evidence to show (1) the reasons for a reorganisation; and (2) the advantages to the employer of the reorganisation, or alternatively that the employer considered the reasons for it to be important, before an employment tribunal can properly make a finding that a dismissal was for SOSR.[108] However, it is not necessary to show 'the quantum of improvement'   **5.39**

---

[102] [1998] ICR 184, EAT.   [103] See ibid, 189.   [104] ibid, 195.
[105] ibid, 195–196.   [106] [1973] ICR 535, 540.
[107] See *Willow Oak Developments Ltd (t/a Windsor Recruitment) v Silverwood* [2006] IRLR 28, Burton P, at paras 16 and 20, not following *Forshaw v Archcraft Ltd* [2006] ICR 70, EAT (Rimer J presiding). The Court of Appeal, in dismissing an appeal against the EAT's rulings in the *Willow Oak* case, expressly approved the approach of the EAT in that case; see [2006] EWCA Civ 660, [2006] IRLR 607, para 15.
[108] *Banerjee v City and East London Area Health Authority* [1979] IRLR 147, para 19, EAT.

which would be achieved if the proposed new terms and conditions were adopted.[109] Further, the 'hurdle of showing some other substantial reason for dismissal' is 'low'.[110] In *Gilham v Kent County Council (No 2)*,[111] Griffiths LJ said this:

> The hurdle over which an employer has to jump at this stage of an inquiry into an unfair dismissal complaint is designed to deter employers from dismissing employees for some trivial or unworthy reason. If he does so, the dismissal is deemed unfair without the need to look further into its merits. But if on the face of it the reason *could* justify the dismissal, then it passes as a substantial reason, and the inquiry moves on to section [98(4)], and the question of reasonableness.

5.40 The question whether the dismissal for the reason found to have been SOSR was fair, ie within the meaning of section 98(4) of the ERA 1996, must be asked only once it has been determined that there was SOSR for the dismissal.[112] Accordingly the most searching questions should be asked by an employment tribunal when deciding whether or not the dismissal was fair, and not when deciding whether or not there was SOSR for it.

Fairness of the dismissal when the reason is SOSR

5.41 Despite the firm disapproval by the Court of Appeal in *Lambe v 186K Ltd*[113] of distinguishing between 'substantive' and 'procedural' unfairness when considering the compensation which should be paid for an unfair dismissal by reason of redundancy, it is suggested here that such a distinction is helpful when considering whether a dismissal for SOSR was fair within the meaning of section 98(4) of the ERA 1996, namely within the range of reasonable responses of a reasonable employer.[114] This is because when considering the fairness of a dismissal for redundancy an employment tribunal cannot properly go behind the reasons of the employer for creating the 'redundancy situation' (assuming them to be genuine[115]), whereas it is clear from the cases referred to

---

[109] *Kerry Foods Ltd v Lynch* [2005] IRLR 680, para 14, EAT. No reference was made in that case to the previous case of *Orr v Vaughan* [1981 IRLR 63, where the EAT declined to interfere with an industrial tribunal's decision that there had not been enough analysis of the state of the business before carrying out a 'so-called reorganisation' (para 6), with the result that there was no SOSR. However, *Orr* is inconsistent with *Gilham v Kent County Council (No 2)* [1985] ICR 233, CA.

[110] *Kerry Foods Ltd v Lynch*, ibid, para 14.   [111] [1985] ICR 233, 239.

[112] This is the apparent effect of the judgment of Dillon LJ in *Gilham v Kent County Council (No 2)* ibid, 244.

[113] [2005] ICR 307, 323, para 59.

[114] In *Copsey v WWB Devon Clays Ltd* [2005] ICR 1789, 1812, para 71, Rix LJ indicated that the range of reasonable responses of a reasonable employer test applied in this context. This question was not referred to by the other members of the Court of Appeal in that case (Mummery and Neuberger LJJ), but the proposition that the test is whether the dismissal was within the range of reasonable responses of a reasonable employer is surely correct.

[115] See para 5.08 above.

below that an employment tribunal is obliged to consider the sufficiency of the employer's reasons for imposing the reorganisation when considering whether the dismissal was fair. It is of note that in *Copsey v WWB Devon Clays Ltd,*[116] which concerned a dismissal for (the employment tribunal decided[117]) SOSR, Mummery LJ stated: 'The article 9 point apart, the dismissal was procedurally and substantively fair.' However, it is necessary to bear in mind that such a distinction may in some circumstances be misleading, and that in any event the question whether an employer's reason for a dismissal is fair within the meaning of section 98(4) of the ERA 1996 is a question of fact.[118] Nevertheless, an employment tribunal, in determining this question of fact, must act lawfully, including by taking into account relevant factors, and not taking into account irrelevant factors.[119] In that regard, some useful guidance has been given in reported cases concerning both the reasonableness of relying on the relevant SOSR (or the 'substantive' fairness of the dismissal) and the reasonableness of the manner in which the employer imposed the change (or the 'procedural' fairness of the dismissal). The following principles can be derived from the reported cases.

Substantive fairness

If an employer proposes to carry out a reorganisation which would lead to a **5.42** reduction in the value to employees of their remuneration, or alternatively to other disadvantages to the employees as compared with their existing position, then the question for an employment tribunal hearing a claim of unfair dismissal brought by any employees who refuse to accept the change(s) will not be which of the employee's or the employer's interests should prevail. Rather, it will be whether the dismissal was within the range of reasonable responses of a reasonable employer.[120]

Although the general approach taken by the EAT in *Evans v Elemeta Holdings* **5.43** *Ltd*[121] was disapproved by a differently constituted EAT in *Chubb Fire Security Ltd v Harper,*[122] it must be correct that, as the EAT held in *Evans,* the imposition on an employee of new terms and conditions which include a requirement to work unlimited overtime hours as and when the employer pleases will be capable of placing the imposition of the new terms and conditions outside the range of reasonable responses of a reasonable employer. However, it is clear

---

[116] [2005] ICR 1789, 1803, para 41.   [117] See ibid, 1795, para 8.
[118] This was strongly emphasised by all of the members of the Court of Appeal in *Gilham v Kent County Council (No 2)* [1985] ICR 233.
[119] See para 2.17 above.
[120] *Richmond Precision Engineering Ltd v Pearce* [1985] IRLR 179, paras 30–31, EAT.
[121] [1982] ICR 323, EAT.   [122] [1983] IRLR 311, EAT.

from *Chubb Fire Security Ltd v Harper* and *Richmond Precision Engineering v Pearce* that the ruling in *Evans* that if it is reasonable for an employee to refuse to accept new terms and conditions, then it is unreasonable for the employer to impose them, was wrong. As the EAT said in *Richmond Precision Engineering Ltd v Pearce*:[123]

> The task of weighing the advantages to the employer against the disadvantages to the employee is merely one factor which the Tribunal have to take into account when determining the question in accordance with the equity and substantial merits of the case. Merely because there are disadvantages to the employee, it does not, by any manner of means follow, that the employer has acted unreasonably in treating his failure to accept the terms which they have offered as a reason to dismiss.

5.44 Similarly, the question when deciding whether a dismissal for refusing to accept new terms and conditions was substantively fair is not whether the change which the employer imposes was vital for the survival of the employer's business.[124] However, the fact that many employees have accepted a change in terms and conditions is relevant to the question of whether a dismissal for refusing to accept those new terms and conditions was substantively fair.[125] So is the fact that a relevant trade union recommended the change.[126] Further, economic factors are clearly relevant in determining whether the dismissal was substantively fair:

> The 'substantial reason' put forward by the employers was the need:
>
> > 'to achieve economies forced upon the employer by a national policy to reduce spending in the public sector and by offering new contracts on reduced terms to avoid a closure of all or major part of the school meals service'.
>
> It is quite impossible to argue that such a reason could not be a substantial reason for dismissing an employee. The hurdle over which the employer has to jump at this stage of an inquiry into an unfair dismissal complaint is designed to deter employers from dismissing employees for some trivial or unworthy reason. If he does so, the dismissal is deemed unfair without the need to look further into its merits. But if on the face of it the reason *could* justify the dismissal, then it passes as a substantial reason, and the inquiry moves on to section 57(3), and the question of reasonableness.[127]

---

[123] [1985] IRLR 179, para 32.

[124] *Catamaran Cruisers Ltd v Williams* [1994] IRLR 386, paras 19–23, EAT.

[125] *Catamaran Cruisers Ltd v Williams*, ibid, para 28(iv).   [126] ibid, para 28(v).

[127] See *Gilham v Kent County Council (No 2)* [1985] ICR 233, 239, per Griffiths LJ. It is true that neither Dillon LJ nor Waller LJ agreed with this statement of principle, but their judgments do not differ from it, and it was applied with approval by Burton P in para 17 of the EAT's judgment in *Scott & Co v Richardson* [2005] All ER (D) 87 (Jun); EATS/0074/2004. Further, the effect of the EAT's judgment in *Scott* (a) was stated without dissent by Judge Peter Clark in *Kerry Foods Ltd v Lynch* [2005] IRLR 680, para 14; and (b) was specifically approved by the Court of Appeal in *Willow Oak Developments Ltd (t/a Windsor Recruitment) v Silverwood* [2006] EWCA Civ 660, [2006] IRLR 607, para 15.

Where an employer seeks to impose a change in terms and conditions which **5.45** will have the effect of making it impossible for an employee in practice to comply with the requirements of his religion, such as attendance at church on Sundays, then it will be necessary for an employment tribunal, before which the employee claims that he has been unfairly dismissed, to take into account the employee's religious beliefs.[128]

Procedural fairness

A reasonable employer will almost always consult an employee about a proposal **5.46** to impose new terms and conditions on the employee. It is true that in *Hollister v National Farmers' Union*[129] the Court of Appeal held that consultation will not always be required,[130] but it is difficult to envisage circumstances in which it would not be required. It seems likely that only if the employer's need is genuinely urgent, or it would otherwise be futile to consult,[131] would it be within the range of reasonable responses of a reasonable employer to fail to consult the employee about the proposed change. This is consistent with what was said by Rix LJ in *Copsey v WWB Devon Clays Ltd*[132] concerning the imposition of a change in working hours which would prevent the employee from 'practising his sincere adherence to the requirements of his religion in the way of Sabbath observance'. This was that an employer 'may be acting unfairly if he makes no attempt to accommodate his employee's needs', and moreover that he could not conceive that a 'decent employer would not attempt to do so'.

If the employer complies with the relevant statutory procedure in Schedule 2 to **5.47** the EA 2002, then it is likely that the dismissal will be procedurally fair in any event. If there is an express dismissal (ie a dismissal within the meaning of section 95(1)(a) or (b) of the ERA 1996), then, subject to the exceptions referred to in the following sentence below, the employer will be obliged to comply with the relevant DDP in Part 1 of Schedule 2.[133] The relevant exceptions are set out in regulation 4 of the Employment Act 2002 (Dispute Resolution) Regulations 2004. These include that (1) all of the employees

---

[128] *Copsey v WWB Devon Clays Ltd* [2005] ICR 1789, CA. The Court of Appeal was divided on the question whether Art 9 of the European Convention on Human Rights was engaged. However, the result was the same whether or not Art 9 was engaged. There were, according to Mummery LJ in para 41, 'compelling economic reasons' for the imposition of the new terms.

[129] [1979] ICR 542.

[130] ibid, 552, per Lord Denning MR: 'It seems to me that consultation is only one of the factors.'

[131] cf *Duffy v Yeomans & Partners Ltd* [1995] ICR 1, 8, CA.

[132] [2005] ICR 1789, 1811, para 71.

[133] See reg 3(1) of the Employment Act 2002 (Dispute Resolution) Regulations 2004, SI 2004/752, read with reg 2(1) of those regulations.

of the description or category to which the dismissed employee belongs have been dismissed and offered new terms to take effect either before or on the termination of the original contracts of employment; or (2) 'the dismissal is one of a number of dismissals in respect of which the duty in section 188 of the 1992 Act (duty of employer to consult representatives when proposing to dismiss as redundant a certain number of employees) applies'. A failure by the employer to follow the relevant DDP will make the dismissal automatically unfair,[134] although the compensation payable for the dismissal will not necessarily be substantial.[135]

E. Compensation for an Unfair Dismissal Where the Employer Relied on SOSR

5.48 If a dismissal for SOSR was unfair because it was not within the range of reasonable responses for the employer to dismiss the employee for SOSR (ie unfair for substantive rather than procedural reasons), then, by analogy with the decision of the Court of Appeal in *Lambe v 186K Ltd*,[136] the employment tribunal will have to 'decide whether the unfair departure from what should have happened was of a kind which makes it possible to say, with more or less confidence, that the failure made no difference, or whether the failure was such that one cannot sensibly reconstruct the world as it might have been'. However, if the dismissal was unfair solely because of a failure to consult the employee and it is shown to the satisfaction of the employment tribunal that consultation would not have led to a different outcome, then the employee should receive only a basic award within the meaning of section 119 of the ERA 1996, and compensation for the loss of income during the period when consultation should have occurred.[137]

F. The Limits (Subject to Exceptions) on the Compensation Payable for an Unfair Dismissal

5.49 Generally, compensation for unfair dismissal consists of a basic award within the meaning of section 119 of the ERA 1996, and a compensatory award within the meaning of section 123 of that Act.

---

[134] ERA 1996, s 98A(1).   [135] See para 5.55 below.
[136] [2005] ICR 307, 323, paras 58 and 59.
[137] cf *Abbotts v Wesson-Glynwed Steels Ltd* [1982] IRLR 51.

The basic award

A basic award is calculated in the same way as a redundancy payment. The **5.50** payment is calculated by reference to the employee's length of service and his weekly remuneration, which is subject to the limit set by regulations made under section 227 of the ERA 1996.[138] The maximum number of years of employment which can be taken into account for this purpose is 20.[139] If the employee was over the age of 41 for any number of complete years of the employment, then the basic award in respect of those years is that number of years multiplied by 1.5.[140] If the employee was aged below 41 but above the age of 22 during the whole or any part of his employment, then the number of weeks' pay in respect of that period is the number of years of employment while the employee was of that age.[141] An employee who was below the age of 22 for all or any part of his employment will receive half a week's pay for each year of employment while he was below the age of 22.[142] By way of example, if an unfairly dismissed employee was employed continuously from the age of 19 for 23 years, then the employee will have been aged 42 at the date of his dismissal. He will then have been employed for one full year at the age of 41 or above, and the redundancy payment will be 20.5 times his weekly remuneration, unless it was above £290 gross, in which case it will be £5,945.

If an employee is above the age of 64 but below the age of 65, then, until 1 **5.51** October 2006, the basic award is reduced by one-twelfth for each whole month reckoned from the time when the employee attains the age of 64.[143] After then, it will not be so reduced.[144]

The compensatory award

The compensatory award is subject to a limit of (currently) £58,400,[145] **5.52** unless the dismissal was automatically unfair for certain reasons. These are that it was in breach of section 100 of the ERA 1996 (concerning dismissal in certain circumstances where the employee has sought to take action of some sort in relation to health and safety matters), or 103A of that Act (which

---

[138] Currently, the limit is £290 per week: see the Employment Rights (Increase of Limits) Order 2005, SI 2005/3352, which applies as from 1 February 2006. When calculating the employee's remuneration for this purpose, no account is taken of income tax or national insurance contributions.

[139] See ERA 1996, s 119(3).   [140] ERA 1996, s 119(2)(a).

[141] ERA 1996, s 119(2)(b).   [142] ERA 1996, s 119(2)(c).

[143] See ERA, s 119(4) and (5).

[144] See para 27 of Sch 8 to the Employment Equality (Age) Regulations 2006, SI 2006/1031.

[145] See ERA 1996, s 124(1), read with the Employment Rights (Increase of Limits) Order 2005, SI 2005/3352. This limit applies even if the employer fails to comply with the applicable dismissal procedure in Sch 2 to the Employment Act 2002.

concerns dismissal for a protected disclosure). All other automatically unfair dismissals are subject to the limit in section 124 of the ERA 1996. Those other automatically unfair dismissals (ignoring for this purpose a dismissal which is automatically unfair because of a failure by the employer to comply with the requirements of the relevant DDP in Part 1 of Schedule 2 to the EA 2002, the effect of which is mentioned where relevant above[146]) are (1) those which are contrary to the following sections of the ERA 1996: section 98B (concerning jury service), section 99 (read with regulation 20(1) and (3) of the Maternity and Parental Leave etc Regulations 1999,[147] which relate to leave for 'family reasons'), section 101 (which concerns dismissals for refusing to work on Sundays), section 101A (which relates to dismissals for taking action in relation to the Working Time Regulations 1998[148] and related regulations), section 102 (which protects employees who are trustees of occupational pension funds), section 103 (which protects employees who are, seek to become, or propose to act as, employee representatives), section 104 (which protects employees who assert a relevant statutory right), section 104A (which relates to the national minimum wage), and section 104B of the ERA 1996 (which relates to tax credits); (2) those which are contrary to the following provisions of TULRA: section 152 (concerning trade union activities and membership) and section 238A(2) (which provides for the partial protection of employees who take part in official industrial action); and (3) those which are contrary to a number of sets of regulations. The regulations are (1) the Transnational Information and Consultation of Employees Regulations 1999;[149] (2) the Part-Time Workers (Prevention of Less Favourable Treatment) Regulations 2000;[150] (3) the Fixed-Term Employees (Prevention of Less Favourable Treatment) Regulations 2002,[151] the European Public Limited-Liability Company Regulations 2004,[152] and the Information and Consultation of Employees Regulations 2004.[153]

5.53　Selection for redundancy is treated by section 99 of the ERA 1996 (read with regulation 20(2) of the Maternity and Parental Leave etc Regulations 1999) and section 105 of the ERA 1996 in a similar way to dismissal for all of these reasons with two exceptions, neither of which has any practical effect. One exception is that section 152 of TULRA is not affected by sections 99 and 105 of the ERA 1996. However, instead, protection against selection for redundancy on grounds related to trade union membership or activities is afforded by section 153 of TULRA. The other exception is that a woman who is taking maternity leave is given additional protection by regulation 10 of those

---

[146] Paras 3.59, 5.04, 5.15, and 5.47.　　[147] SI 1999/3312.
[148] SI 1998/1833.　　[149] SI 1999/3323, reg 28.　　[150] SI 2000/1551, reg 7.
[151] SI 2002/2034, reg 6.　　[152] SI 2004/2326, reg 42.　　[153] SI 2004/3426, reg 30.

regulations, the effect of which is considered in the final section of this chapter (which concerns the impact of the law of discrimination on business reorganisations generally). Ultimately, however, a dismissal which results from a failure to comply with the terms of regulation 10 is automatically unfair. This is because section 99 of the ERA 1996, read with regulation 20(1)(b) of the Maternity and Parental Leave etc Regulations 1999,[154] provides that an employee whose dismissal results from a failure to comply with the requirements of regulation 10 is unfairly dismissed.

Section 105 has the effect that an employee who is selected to be dismissed for **5.54** redundancy where 'it is shown that the circumstances constituting the redundancy applied equally to one or more other employees in the same undertaking who held positions similar to that held by the employee and who have not been dismissed by the employer', and the reason for the selection was the automatically unfair reason, is to be regarded as having been unfairly dismissed.

The impact of a failure to follow a statutory procedure within the meaning of the Employment Act 2002

An employee who is automatically unfairly dismissed by reason of a failure by **5.55** his employer to follow the relevant procedure in Schedule 2 to the EA 2002 is entitled to a minimum by way of a basic award of 4 weeks' pay (calculated by reference to the maximum provided for in section 227 of the ERA 1996), unless the employment tribunal determines that it would 'result in injustice to the employer' to impose that minimum.[155] Further, the employment tribunal must normally increase 'the award which it makes to the employee' (meaning, it seems clear, by 'award' all of the monetary compensation payable to the employee by reason of the unfair dismissal other than the basic award) by a minimum of 10 per cent and may increase it by a maximum of 50 per cent.[156] The tribunal is not under a duty to increase the award by 10 per cent 'if there are exceptional circumstances which would make [an] increase of that percentage unjust or inequitable', in which case the tribunal may make either no increase, or an increase of such a lesser percentage than 10 per cent as the employment tribunal 'considers just and equitable in all the circumstances'.[157]

An employee who is dismissed within the meaning of section 95(1)(a) or (b) of **5.56** the ERA 1996 is not obliged to follow the relevant grievance procedure in Part 2

---

[154] SI 1999/3312.   [155] ERA 1996, s 120(1A) and (1B).
[156] EA 2002, s 31(3). The maximum provided for by s 123 of the ERA 1996 is not affected, with the result that the compensatory award cannot be caused by s 31(3) to exceed that maximum.
[157] EA 2002, s 31(4).

of Schedule 2 to the EA 2002.[158] However, an employee who is 'constructively' dismissed, ie dismissed within the meaning of section 95(1)(c) of the ERA 1996, is obliged to follow such procedure.[159] Accordingly, an employee who fails to comply with the relevant procedure in Part 2 of Schedule 2 may not present a claim to an employment tribunal.[160] An employee who has complied with the requirement in paragraph 6 or 9 of Schedule 2 (whichever is applicable) may not then present to an employment tribunal a complaint in respect of the matter to which the grievance relates (assuming that it falls within a jurisdiction to which section 32 applies) before 28 days have elapsed since such compliance occurred.[161] An employee who has complied with that requirement more than one month after the end of the original time limit for making the complaint may also not then present to an employment tribunal a complaint under a jurisdiction to which section 32 applies.[162] However, in both of these situations, the original time limit is extended by regulation 15 of the Employment Act 2002 (Dispute Resolution) Regulations 2004.[163] The extension is to three months from the ending of the original time limit.

5.57　An employee who fails to comply with the applicable DDP (or, in the case of a 'constructive' dismissal within the meaning of section 95(1)(c) of the ERA 1996, the grievance procedure in Part 2 of Schedule 2 to the EA 2002[164]) but whose claim of unfair dismissal is successful may find that the award made to him by reason of the unfair dismissal is reduced by a minimum of 10 per cent and a maximum of 50 per cent.[165] A reduction should not be made 'if there are exceptional circumstances which would make a reduction . . . of that percentage unjust or inequitable', in which case the tribunal may make either no reduction or a reduction of such a lesser percentage than 10 per cent as the employment tribunal 'considers just and equitable in all the circumstances'.[166]

G. Extension of the Time Limit for Claiming Unfair Dismissal Where a Statutory Disciplinary or Dismissal Procedure Is Being Followed

5.58　Where an employee 'had reasonable grounds for believing, [at the time when the time limit for making a complaint of unfair or otherwise unlawful

---

[158] Employment Act 2002 (Dispute Resolution) Regulations 2004, SI 2004/752, reg 6(5), read with reg 2(1).

[159] See EA 2002, s 32 and Sch 4.　　[160] EA 2002, s 32(2).

[161] EA 2002, s 32(3).　　[162] EA 2002, s 32(4).

[163] SI 2004/752. See reg 15(1)(b) and (3).

[164] See reg 6(1) and (5) of SI 2004/752 and ss 31 and 40 of the EA 2002.

[165] See EA 2002, s 31(2).　　[166] EA 2002, s 31(4).

dismissal expired] that a dismissal or disciplinary procedure, whether statutory or otherwise (including an appropriate procedure for the purposes of regulation 5(2)[167]) was being followed in respect of matters that consisted of or included the substance of the tribunal complaint', the normal time limit for presenting the complaint is extended by three months.[168]

H. Discrimination

Introduction

It goes without saying that an employer will be liable for any unlawful dis-   **5.59**
crimination in relation to the dismissal of an employee, whether for redundancy or otherwise. The general principles of the law relating to, for example, sex discrimination or race discrimination are outside the scope of this book. However, there is some specific protection for women who are absent from work during maternity leave against dismissal by reason of redundancy during the period of maternity leave, and the relevant statutory provisions are described below.

Disability discrimination

First, however, the case of *Kent County Council v Mingo*[169] needs to be men-   **5.60**
tioned. There, the employee was unable to continue to work in his original job because of a disability. He was redeployed initially in a temporary supernumary post, but then, when the post ended, he was dismissed for incapability. The employer had a redeployment policy, which was 'designed to match internal job vacancies within the council with existing redeployees.'[170] The policy provided for two categories of employee. Category A employees were those at risk, or under notice of, redundancy. Category B staff included 'staff to be deployed on capability/ill health'.[171] Category A staff were better placed than category B staff in relation to redeployment. The EAT upheld the employment tribunal's decision that the employer had unlawfully discriminated against the employee. The key ruling can be seen from the following passage:

> It seems to us that the tribunal were entitled to consider that the redeployment procedures of the council did not adequately reflect the statutory duty on

---

[167] This is defined by SI 2004/752, reg 5(3). It must give the employee 'an effective right of appeal against dismissal or disciplinary action taken against him' and '[operate] by virtue of a collective agreement made between two or more employers or an employers' association and one or more independent trade unions'.

[168] Employment Act 2002 (Dispute Resolution) Regulations 2004, SI 2004/752, reg 15(1)(a).

[169] [2000] IRLR 90.   [170] ibid, para 5.   [171] ibid.

employers under the Act. The council's policy was to give preferential treatment to redundant or potentially redundant employees. That meant that those with disabilities were relatively handicapped in the system of redeployment.[172]

Sex discrimination

5.61 In *Webb v Emo Air Cargo*,[173] the European Court of Justice ruled that the dismissal of a woman who was pregnant because she would be absent from work during the pregnancy constituted direct discrimination on the ground of sex. Accordingly, an employee may be able to claim that a breach of her right, under section 99 of the ERA 1996, not to be unfairly dismissed is also direct discrimination against her on the ground of her sex. If so, then she would be able to claim unlimited compensation for that dismissal, as opposed to compensation limited currently[174] to £58,400.

Redeployment during maternity leave

5.62 An employee who is absent from work on maternity leave, whether 'ordinary' or 'additional' maternity leave within the meaning of the Maternity and Parental Leave etc Regulations 1999,[175] is given protection from dismissal by regulation 10 of those regulations. If it is 'not practicable by reason of redundancy for her employer to continue to employ her under her existing contract of employment', then, where there is

> a suitable available vacancy, the employee is entitled to be offered (before the end of her employment under her existing contract) alternative employment with her employer or his successor, or an associated employer, under a new contract of employment which complies with paragraph (3) (and takes effect immediately on the ending of her employment under the previous contract).[176]

5.63 The new contract must be such that the work done under it is 'of a kind which is both suitable in relation to the employee and appropriate for her to do in the circumstances'.[177] Further the provisions of the new contract as to the capacity and place in which the employee is to be employed, and the other terms and conditions of her employment under the new contract, must not be 'substantially less favourable to her than if she had continued to be employed under the previous contract'.[178]

---

[172] *Kent County Council v Mingo* [2000] IRLR 90, para 23.   [173] [1994] QB 718.
[174] See para 5.52 above.   [175] SI 1999/3312.   [176] Regulation 10(1) and (2).
[177] Regulation 10(3)(a).   [178] Regulation 10(3)(b).

6

COLLECTIVE CONSULTATION AND NOTIFICATION IN RELATION TO PROPOSED DISMISSALS

A. Introduction

6.01 In this chapter, the principal statutory obligations of an employer towards representatives of his or its employees, where redundancies above a certain minimum are proposed, are considered. There is a parallel obligation imposed on the employer to notify the Secretary of State about the proposed dismissals, and that obligation is considered also in this chapter, after the obligation to consult with appropriate representatives and the sanction for a failure to do so have been described.

The definition of 'redundant' in this context

6.02 An employer (other than the Crown[1]) who is 'proposing to dismiss as redundant 20 or more employees at one establishment within a period of 90 days or less' is obliged by section 188(1) of Trade Union and Labour Relations (Consolidation) Act 1992 ('TULRA') to 'consult about the dismissals all the persons who are appropriate representatives of any of the employees who may be affected by the proposed dismissals or may be affected by measures taken in connection with those dismissals'. The word 'redundant' here has a meaning which is wider than that which it is given by section 139 of the ERA 1996 for the purposes of the law of redundancy. The words 'dismiss as redundant' are defined for the purposes of Chapter II of Part IV of the TULRA (ie sections 188–198) by section 195(1) of TULRA to mean 'dismissal for a reason not related to the individual concerned or for a number of reasons all of which are not so related'. This was not the original wording of section 195 and its predecessor (section 126(6) of the Employment Protection Act 1975); section 195 originally defined redundant in the same way as it is defined now by section 139 of the ERA 1996. A dismissal is for redundancy under section 139(1) if the *principal* reason satisfies the requirements of that subsection. Under section 195(1) of TULRA, *none* of the reasons may relate to the individual. As suggested in *Harvey*,[2] there may be room for a de minimis exception to this requirement. In any event, whenever an employer is proposing to dismiss employees in a reorganisation, even if the dismissals will not lead to redundancies within the meaning of section 139 of the ERA 1996, the employer must consult in accordance with section 188 of TULRA.

---

[1] See TULRA, s 273(2).   [2] Paragraph E[2497].

Persons whose employment is not affected by Chapter II of Part IV of TULRA

Short-term employees as defined by section 282 of TULRA are excluded **6.03** from the scope of Chapter II of Part IV of TULRA, ie sections 188–198.[3] A short-term employee for this purpose is employed under a contract for a fixed term of three months or less, or under a contract made in contemplation of the performance of a specific task which is not expected to last for more than three months, and (in both cases) the employee has not been continuously employed (within the meaning of Chapter 1 of Part XIV of the ERA 1996) for a period of more than three months. Share fishermen within the meaning of section 284 of TULRA are also excluded from the scope of Chapter II of Part IV of TULRA,[4] as are persons in 'police service' as defined by section 280,[5] namely 'service as a member of any constabulary maintained by virtue of an enactment, or in any other capacity by virtue of which a person has the powers or privileges of a constable'.[6]

Presumption of redundancy

For the purposes of any proceedings under Chapter II of Part IV of TULRA, if **6.04** an employee is dismissed or an employer proposes to dismiss an employee, it is to be presumed, unless the contrary is proved, that the employee is, or is proposed to be, dismissed as redundant.[7]

The definition of 'dismissal'

The word 'dismiss' is defined by section 298 of TULRA to mean that which it **6.05** means in Part X of the ERA 1996. Accordingly, it is defined by section 95 of the ERA 1996, and includes 'constructive' dismissal and dismissal by reason of the ending of a limited-term contract which is not renewed. It also includes the termination of a contract of employment with the offer of new terms and conditions.[8] The manner in which an employment tribunal should consider whether there has been a 'dismissal' for this purpose was stated helpfully in *Hardy v Tourism South East*,[9] where the EAT (having been referred to the relevant previous authorities[10]) said this:

> 17. In our judgment, therefore, an employer 'proposes to dismiss' an employee if on an objective consideration of what the employer says or writes, the employer is proposing to withdraw the existing contract of

---

[3] See TULRA, s 282(1).   [4] See s 284.   [5] Section 280(1).
[6] Section 280(2).   [7] TULRA, s 195(2).
[8] See *Hogg v Dover College* [1990] ICR 39, EAT, as approved by the Court of Appeal in *Jones v Governing Body of Burdett Coutts School* [1999] ICR 38, 42.
[9] [2005] IRLR 242.   [10] *Hogg* and *Alcan Extrusions v Yates* [1996] IRLR 327.

employment from the employee, or the departures which the employer is proposing from the existing contract are so substantial as to amount to the withdrawal of the whole contract.

18. It follows from what we have said that the mere fact that an employer proposes to redeploy an employee is not decisive. If the employer only proposes to keep the employee in his employment on what is in reality a different contract of employment, he will be proposing to terminate the existing one.

Obligations to consult under other statutory provisions where section 188 applies

6.06 An employer may be obliged to consult also under the Information and Consultation of Employees Regulations 2004[11] ('the ICE Regulations'), but may under regulation 20 of those regulations avoid the need to consult under those regulations in addition to under section 188. The means by which such avoidance is secured is by the employer notifying the 'information and consultation representatives in writing that he will be complying with his duty under [section 188], instead of under these Regulations, provided that the notification is given on each occasion on which the employer has become or is about to become subject to the duty'.[12] However, the duty to consult under the ICE Regulations applies no matter how many dismissals are proposed, although those regulations apply only to organisations above a certain size. The ICE Regulations are accordingly described in Chapter 10 below.

6.07 The duty of an employer to comply with the Transnational Consultation of Employees Regulations 1999[13] and to refer, in the 'report drawn up by the central management' which is put before a European Works Council in an 'information and consultation meeting', to 'collective redundancies',[14] is additional to that which arises under section 188 of TULRA. It cannot be avoided. The content of that duty is accordingly considered in Chapter 10 below.

Obligation to notify the Secretary of State

6.08 In addition to consulting under section 188 of TULRA, an employer must notify the Secretary of State under section 193 of that Act. It is of note that while a failure to comply with section 188 may lead to the making by an employment tribunal of what is called a 'protective award' within the meaning of section 189 of TULRA, a failure to comply with section 193 is a criminal offence.[15]

---

[11] SI 2004/3426.   [12] ibid, reg 20(5).   [13] SI 1999/3323.
[14] See ibid, Sch, paras 7 and 8.   [15] See TULRA, s 194.

The conditions for the application of these sanctions are considered in detail below.[16]

The impact of European Community law

All of the duties described in the preceding paragraphs of this chapter arise **6.09** from European Community ('Community') legislation. It is accordingly necessary when considering each duty to bear it in mind that the UK legislation may not fully implement the relevant Community legislation. That possibility arises somewhat acutely in relation to section 188 of TULRA, and, in the course of the discussion of the effect of the relevant Community legislation on situations to which section 188 applies, reference is made to general principles applicable to the application of Community law. By way of introduction, in outline, the situation is that a Community Directive is not directly effective against all employers: only certain provisions of relevant treaties and Community Regulations and Decisions are directly effective against all employers. Directives were originally intended to affect only the governments of the Member States of the Community, in that they directed those governments to make laws implementing the policies set out in the Directives.[17] Accordingly, Directives were never intended to be directly effective. However, it has been held by the ECJ that a Directive may be enforced against the State or what is termed an emanation of the State where one or more of the Directive's provisions is sufficiently, clear, precise, and unconditional to be interpreted as giving rise to rights on the part of individuals.

It is not always easy to determine what amounts to an emanation of the State. **6.10** It was held by the Court of Appeal in *National Union of Teachers v Governing Body of St Mary's Church of England (Aided) Junior School*[18] that the governing body of what is now a voluntary aided school within the meaning (now) of section 20 of the School Standards and Framework Act 1998 is an emanation of the state for the purpose of the enforcement of a Directive. The court did not apply the test laid down by the ECJ in *Foster v British Gas*[19] for what is an emanation of the state, in its entirety. The subsequent decision of the ECJ in *Kampelmann v Landschaftsverband Westfalen-Lippe*[20] confirms the correctness of that approach: emanations of the state are[21]

> organisations or bodies which are subject to the authority or control of the State or have special powers beyond those which result from the normal rules

---

[16] See para 6.46 onwards regarding protective awards and paras 6.81 and 6.82 below for the potential sanction for a failure to notify the Secretary of State.

[17] See Art 189 of the Treaty of Rome as originally made.   [18] [1997] ICR 334.

[19] [1991] ICR 84.   [20] Cases C–253/96 to C–258/96; [1998] IRLR 333.

[21] See ibid, 341, para 46.

applicable to relations between individuals, such as local or regional authorities or other bodies which, irrespective of their legal form, have been given responsibility, by the public authorities and under their supervision, for providing a public service.

6.11 However, it is possible, where the direct enforcement of a provision of a Directive is not possible, to claim compensation from the State (ie here the UK Government) for failing properly to transpose that provision, under the line of cases including *Francovich v Italian Republic*.[22]

General matters

6.12 Because of its practical importance, the effects of section 188, including the conditions for the making and enforcement of a protective award, are considered first below. The duty to notify the Secretary of State, and the impact of a failure to comply with it, are then described.

B. The Duty to Consult Under Section 188 of TULRA

The circumstances in which section 188 applies

6.13 The duty to consult under section 188 arises in strictly defined circumstances. The minimum requirement for section 188 to apply is that the employer is 'proposing to dismiss' as redundant (defined as stated in paragraph 6.02 above) 20 or more employees at one establishment within a period of 90 days or less. The consultation must begin 'in good time' and in any event 30 days before the first of the dismissals 'takes effect', unless the employer is proposing to dismiss as redundant 100 or more employees, in which case the consultation must begin at least 90 days before the first of the dismissals takes effect.[23]

6.14 In determining how many employees an employer is proposing to dismiss as redundant, as a result of section 188(3), no account is to be taken of employees in respect of whose proposed dismissals consultation has already begun (although naturally an attempt to avoid the application of section 188(1) by deliberately proposing to dismiss employees in stages should not succeed). This can lead to the odd result that if consultation occurs in respect of the proposed dismissal of, say, 30 employees, and then the employer concludes that it may have to dismiss a further 10 employees, there will be no need to consult in

---

[22] Cases C–6/90 and 9/90; [1995] ICR 722, ECJ. It is of interest that an unsuccessful attempt to rely on *Francovich* was made in *Alderson v Secretary of State for Trade and Industry* [2004] ICR 512, CA, where it was claimed that the claimants had suffered loss by reason of the original restriction of TUPE 1981 to the transfer of an undertaking which was in the nature of a commercial venture. In principle, the claim was sound, but it failed on the facts.

[23] TULRA, s 188(1A).

relation to the proposed dismissal of the further 10 employees. However, if the employer proposes to dismiss 10 employees and later, within 90 days, proposes to dismiss a further 10 employees, then the employer will be obliged by section 188(1) to carry out consultation in relation to the dismissals of all 20 employees.

It is the clear effect of the wording of section 188(1) that if several employers in the same group of companies simultaneously propose the dismissals of employees, section 188(1) can be applied only to the circumstances of each company. Thus the number of proposed dismissals to be made by several employers in the same group of companies should not be aggregated for the purposes of section 188(1).[24]   **6.15**

It may on occasion be in issue whether or not a person who has issued a proposal that employees should be dismissed by reason of redundancy can properly be said to have been acting on behalf of the employer in so doing. The discussion in paragraphs 28–30 of the decision of the EAT in *Leicestershire County Council v Unison*[25] is illuminating in this regard. As the EAT there noted, quoting the decision of HHJ Serota QC in *Dewhirst Group v GMB*:[26] 'there is no need for the person making the proposal to have the power to carry it out. In many cases (if not most) third party consent would turn a proposal into a determination.'   **6.16**

The impact of the Community legislation which section 188 purports to implement

Section 188 (as amended) purports to implement in the UK Article 2 of the Collective Redundancies Directive, 98/59/EC. That applies 'Where an employer is contemplating collective redundancies', and requires the employer to consult 'with the workers' representatives in good time with a view to reaching an agreement'. Article 2 does not mention any particular period before the first contemplated 'redundancy' by when the requisite consultation must start. Article 3(1) imposes an obligation to 'notify the competent public authority in writing of any projected collective redundancies'. This is the obligation which section 193 of TULRA was enacted to implement.[27] In contrast to the position in relation to Article 2, there is a specified time limit for the notification required by Article 3(1). This is provided for by Article 4(1), which provides that the 'Projected collective redundancies notified to the competent   **6.17**

---

[24] This was the explicit holding of the EAT in *E Green & Son (Castings) Ltd v Association of Scientific, Technical and Managerial Staffs* [1984] ICR 352.
[25] [2005] IRLR 920.
[26] [2003] All ER (d) 175 (Dec), at para 22, which is set out in para 29 of the EAT's judgment in *Leicestershire County Council v Unison*.
[27] See para 6.72 onwards below concerning s 193.

public authority shall take effect not earlier than 30 days after the notification referred to in Article 3(1) without prejudice to any provisions governing individual rights with regard to notice of dismissal.'

6.18 Two issues of interpretation can be seen to arise here. One is what is meant by the word 'contemplating' in Article 2(1), and the other is when does a dismissal 'take effect' for the purposes of Article 4(1)? Both of these issues have been recently considered by the ECJ, in *Junk v Kühnel*.[28] The case concerned the German law of employment, which distinguishes between the giving of notice and the taking effect of the notice. That was helpful from the point of view of the interpretation of the ECJ's decision in *Junk*. One of the key rulings (the others are referred to where relevant below) is that 'the obligations to consult and to notify arise prior to any decision by the employer to terminate contracts of employment'.[29] Thus, 'Articles 2 to 4 of the Directive must be construed as meaning that the event constituting redundancy consists in the declaration by an employer of his intention to terminate the contract of employment'.[30] The obligation imposed by Article 2(1) is therefore an obligation to consult before the giving of notice, and not merely to consult before the notice takes effect.[31]

6.19 The word 'contemplating' was not directly in issue in *Junk*, but its usage was relied upon by the ECJ in support of its rulings in that case. In paragraph 44 of its judgment, having concluded that the obligation imposed by Article 2 is an obligation to 'negotiate' (see further below), the ECJ said this:

> The effectiveness of such an obligation would be compromised if an employer was entitled to terminate contracts of employment during the course of the procedure or even at the beginning thereof. It would be significantly more difficult for workers' representatives to achieve the withdrawal of a decision that has been taken than to secure the abandonment of a decision that is being contemplated.

6.20 Accordingly, the case law concerning the significance of the difference between the word 'proposing' in section 188 and 'contemplating' in Article 2(1) has been overtaken, and is now probably otiose. That case law included *Re Hartlebury Printers Ltd*[32] and *MSF v Refuge Assurance plc*.[33] The proposition that that case law is now otiose is supported by the first decision of an appellate

---

[28] C–188/03; [2005] IRLR 310.   [29] ibid, para 37.
[30] Paragraph 39. Thus the ruling of the EAT in *Middlesbrough Borough Council v TGWU* [2002] IRLR 332, para 38, that the word 'dismiss' means the expiry and not the giving of notice, should now be regarded as overruled.
[31] See *Junk*, para 41.   [32] [1992] ICR 559, Ch D.
[33] [2002] ICR 1365, EAT. At para 45, the EAT approved of the following words of the employment tribunal: 'We find that proposing to dismiss means more than a mere contemplation of, or consideration of, dismissal during the formulation and adoption of a business plan but is something less than a final decision.'

UK court to apply *Junk*, namely that of the EAT in *Leicestershire County Council v Unison*.[34] There, the EAT said this (albeit that it was obiter[35]), having referred to *MSF v Refuge Assurance plc*:

> We consider that effect must be given to the construction of the Directive which aims to avoid dismissal for redundancy and which requires there to be consultation at a stage before decisions on dismissal for redundancy are made. There is no straining of the language of s.188 in order to give effect to this purpose by construing 'proposing to dismiss' as 'proposing to give notice of dismissal'.

This does not mean that notices of the termination of relevant employees' **6.21** contracts of employment may not be served before the end of the period of (say) 90 days. Rather, such notices may safely be served once the process of consultation (and negotiation) required by section 188 has been completed and notification of the Secretary of State in accordance with section 193 has occurred.[36]

It was said (also in fact obiter) by the EAT in *MSF v Refuge Assurance plc*[37] that **6.22** the word 'establishment' in section 188 is inconsistent with Article 1(1)(a) of Directive 98/59/EC. That provides that Member States may implement the threshold requirements for the application of the obligation to consult in relation to redundancies in either of two ways. The option which the UK Government has taken is in the following terms:

> For the purposes of this Directive:
>
> (a) 'collective redundancies' means dismissals effected by an employer for one or more reasons not related to the individual workers concerned where, according to the choice of the Member States, the number of redundancies is: . . . over a period of 90 days, at least 20, whatever the number of workers normally employed in the *establishments* in question. [Emphasis added.]

However, held the EAT, section 188(1) of TULRA could not be interpreted **6.23** in accordance with the Directive without distorting its meaning, with the result that the EAT applied section 188(1) as it stood. In any event, it is by no means clear that the EAT's obiter statement that section 188(1) fails properly to implement Article 1(1) is correct. This is because of the use of the word 'establishment' in Articles 3(1) and 4(4) of the Directive. In any event, the obiter statement can have no direct practical effect, since the Directive does not apply to 'workers employed by public administrative bodies or by

---

[34] [2005] IRLR 920. [35] See paras 31–32.
[36] See for the avoidance of doubt *Junk v Kühnel* C–188/03; [2005] IRLR 310, paras 43–54.
[37] [2002] ICR 1365, para 52. As noted in para 6.20 above, the main ruling in the case has been overtaken by the decision of the ECJ in *Junk v Kühnel* C–188/03; [2005] IRLR 310.

establishments governed by public law',[38] and since (as was recognized by the EAT in *MSF v Refuge Assurance plc*[39]) an employee of a private sector body could not enforce the Directive against his employer. Only if a valid *Francovich* claim could be made against the UK Government would the use of the word 'establishment' in section 188 instead of 'establishments' have a practical effect.[40]

6.24 The word 'establishment' was interpreted by the ECJ in *Rockfon A/S v Special-arbejderforbundet i Danmark*[41] 'as designating, depending on the circumstances, the unit to which the workers made redundant are assigned to carry out their duties'. Further, said the ECJ: 'It is not essential, in order for there to be an "establishment", for the unit in question to be endowed with a management which can independently effect collective redundancies.'[42] The word 'assigned' was taken directly from the judgment of the ECJ in *Botzen v Rotterdamsche Droogdok Maatschappij BV*,[43] so the case law concerning assignment to an undertaking for the purposes of the ARD is relevant in this context also.[44]

6.25 The EAT in *MSF v Refuge Assurance plc*[45] said that the word 'establishment' in section 188(1) must be interpreted in accordance with *Rockfon*, but said also that it was 'unconvinced that [certain] domestic authorities [on the meaning of the word "establishment", including in particular *Lord Advocate v Babcock & Wilcox (Operations) Ltd*[46] and *Barratt Developments (Bradford) Ltd v Union of Construction, Allied Trades and Technicians*[47]] lead to a meaning that differs from the *Rockfon* meaning'.

6.26 The actual ruling in *MSF v Refuge Assurance plc* is dubious. The employment tribunal's original ruling was that although each member of the employer's home insurance field sales staff was assigned to a local branch, the 'establishment' was the 'entire field staff'. This was said by the EAT to have made 'very good industrial relations sense' but nevertheless was overruled because the tribunal had concluded that the sales staff were assigned to the local branches. This could be said to have been an overliteral approach to the application of the word 'assigned' as used in *Rockfon*, especially since (1) the ECJ prefaced its definition of the word 'establishment' by the words 'depending on the circumstances'; and (2) the approach of the ECJ was adopted with a view to maximising rather than minimising the extent of the application of the Directive.

---

[38] Article 1(2)(b).   [39] ibid, para 42.
[40] See para 6.11 above concerning the possibility of the making of a claim under the *Francovich* line of cases.
[41] Case C–449/93; [1996] ICR 673, 689, para 32.   [42] ibid.
[43] [1985] ECR 591; [1986] 2 CMLR 50.
[44] See para 3.04 onwards above for the effects of the current case law.
[45] [2002] ICR 1365, para 54.   [46] [1972] 1 WLR 488.   [47] [1978] ICR 319.

What are 'appropriate representatives'?

The 'appropriate representatives of any affected employees' are defined by
sections 188(1B) and 196 of TULRA. An 'affected employee' is an employee
'who may be affected by the proposed dismissals or who may be affected by
measures taken in connection with such dismissals'.[48] If the affected employees
are 'of a description in respect of which an independent trade union is recognised by their employer', then the appropriate representatives are 'officials or
other persons authorised by the trade union to carry on collective bargaining
with the employer'.[49] If the affected employees are not of such a description,
then the appropriate representatives are:

6.27

whichever of the following representatives the employer chooses—

(i) employee representatives appointed or elected by the affected employees
otherwise than for the purposes of this section who (having regard to the
purposes for and the method by which they were appointed or elected)
have authority from those employees to receive information and to be
consulted about the proposed dismissals on their behalf;

(ii) employee representatives elected by the affected employees, for the
purposes of this section, in an election satisfying the requirements of
section 188A(1).[50]

The requirements of section 188A(1) are these:

6.28

(a) the employer shall make such arrangements as are reasonably practical to
ensure that the election is fair;

(b) the employer shall determine the number of representatives to be elected
so that there are sufficient representatives to represent the interests of all
the affected employees having regard to the number and classes of those
employees;

(c) the employer shall determine whether the affected employees should be
represented either by representatives of all the affected employees or by
representatives of particular classes of those employees;

(d) before the election the employer shall determine the term of office as
employee representatives so that it is of sufficient length to enable information to be given and consultations under section 188 to be completed;

(e) the candidates for election as employee representatives are affected
employees on the date of the election;

(f) no affected employee is unreasonably excluded from standing for
election;

---

[48] Section 196(3).
[49] Sections 188(1B)(a) and 196(2). It is beyond the scope of this book to state the manner in
which such a trade union representative is appointed and authorised to act on behalf of the union.
It is sufficient for present purposes to emphasise that the union must be independent within the
meaning of s 5 of TULRA and that the terms 'recognised' and 'collective bargaining' are defined
for the purposes of TULRA by s 178 of that Act.
[50] Section 188(1B)(b).

(g) all affected employees on the date of the election are entitled to vote for employee representatives;

(h) the employees entitled to vote may vote for as many candidates as there are representatives to be elected to represent them or, if there are to be representatives for particular classes of employees, may vote for as many candidates as there are representatives to be elected to represent their particular class of employee;

(i) the election is conducted so as to secure that—

(i) so far as is reasonably practicable, those voting do so in secret, and

(ii) the votes given at the election are accurately counted.[51]

6.29 If, after an election which satisfies these requirements has been held, one of the elected representatives ceases to act as an employee representative and any of the affected employees are no longer represented, then they (ie presumably the affected employees who are no longer represented[52]) 'shall elect another representative by an election satisfying the requirements of subsection (1)(a), (e), (f) and (i)'.[53] Section 196(1) of TULRA defines 'employee representatives' for the purposes of Chapter II of Part IV in terms which correspond with those of section 188A, but provides in addition that such representatives must be employed by the employer 'at the time when they are elected or appointed'.

Employment protection and time off work for appropriate representatives and candidates to be employee representatives

6.30 An employee representative has the right under section 47(1) of the ERA 1996 not to be subjected to a detriment by any act or deliberate failure to act on the part of his employer 'done on the ground that' (1) the employee is an employee representative within the meaning of section 188(1B), or is a candidate in an election in which any person elected will, on being elected, be such a representative; or (2) the employee performed or proposed to perform any functions or activities as such a representative or candidate. Section 47(1A) confers the same protection on an employee who participates in an election of employee representatives for the purposes of Chapter II of Part IV of TULRA. If such an employee is dismissed in either circumstance, then the dismissal is automatically unfair as a result of section 103 of the ERA 1996.

---

[51] Section 188A was inserted by the Collective Redundancies and Transfer of Undertakings (Protection of Employment) (Amendment) Regulations 1999, SI 1999/1925. It may be that the inclusion of a subparagraphs (i) and (ii) of paragraph (i) (ie s 188A(1)(i)(i) and (ii)) was inadvertent.

[52] Although it is not normally permissible to construe a statutory provision by reference to a later enactment, it is likely to be of assistance to an employment tribunal that the wording of reg 14(2) of TUPE uses words which are to the effect stated in the text to this note: see para 7.14 below.

[53] Section 188A(2).

A trade union representative is protected in the same way, but by the provisions **6.31** which protect all trade union representatives in relation to trade union activities, namely sections 146 and 152 of TULRA.

An employee representative or candidate in an election to be such a representa- **6.32** tive is allowed by sections 61 and 62 of the ERA 1996 to take a reasonable amount of time off (with pay) during the hours when he is required by his contract of employment to be at work in order to perform his functions as such an employee representative or candidate, or to undergo training to perform such functions. Trade union representatives are allowed paid time off for equivalent purposes, under sections 168 and 169 of TULRA.

What is the content of the duty to consult?

The consultation required by section 188 of TULRA must 'include consulta- **6.33** tion about ways of (a) avoiding the dismissals, (b) reducing the numbers of employees to be dismissed, and (c) mitigating the consequences of the dismissals', and must be undertaken 'with a view to reaching agreement with the appropriate representatives'.[54] The employer must give the appropriate representatives the information referred to in section 188(4) for the purposes of the consultation. That information is

(a) the reasons for [the] proposals,
(b) the numbers and descriptions of employees whom it is proposed to dismiss as redundant,
(c) the total number of employees of any such description employed by the employer at the establishment in question,
(d) the proposed method of selecting the employees who may be dismissed,[55]
(e) the proposed method of carrying out the dismissals, with due regard to any agreed procedure, including the period over which the dismissals are to take effect, and
(f) the proposed method of calculating the amount of any redundancy payments to be made (otherwise than in compliance with an obligation imposed by or by virtue of any enactment) to employees who may be dismissed.[56]

This information must be in writing and must be 'delivered' to the appropriate **6.34** representatives, or sent by post to an address notified by them to the employer

---

[54] TULRA, s 188(2).

[55] It will be insufficient to state merely that the method will be agreed with the appropriate representatives; rather, a proposed method must be stated: *E Green & Son (Castings) Ltd v Association of Scientific, Technical and Managerial Staffs* [1984] ICR 352, 360.

[56] Para (f) accordingly applies only to redundancy payments which are calculated in accordance with a relevant policy applied by the employer. The policy may or may not be contractual. See para 11.08 onwards below for the circumstances in which it may have become contractual.

or, where the representatives are representatives of a trade union, sent by post to the union at the address of its head or main office.[57] The employer is under an obligation to provide the information in writing pursuant to section 188(4) even if the appropriate representatives have the information already.[58]

6.35   The duty to consult in domestic law was stated most clearly by the Divisional Court in *R v British Coal Corporation, ex parte Price*,[59] where the court said:

> 24   It is axiomatic that the process of consultation is not one in which the consultor is obliged to adopt any or all of the views expressed by the person or body whom he is consulting. I would respectfully adopt the tests proposed by Hodgson J in *R v Gwent County Council ex parte Bryant*, reported, as far as I know, only at [1988] Crown Office Digest p.19, when he said:
>
> 'Fair consultation means:
>
> (a)   consultation when the proposals are still at a formative stage;
> (b)   adequate information on which to respond;
> (c)   adequate time in which to respond;
> (d)   conscientious consideration by an authority of the response to consultation.'
>
> 25   Another way of putting the point more shortly is that fair consultation involves giving the body consulted a fair and proper opportunity to understand fully the matters about which it is being consulted, and to express its views on those subjects, with the consultor thereafter considering those views properly and genuinely.

6.36   However, the ECJ went further in *Junk v Kühnel*,[60] where it said that Article 2 of the Directive appears to impose an obligation to negotiate. The statement of Glidewell LJ in *R v British Coal Corporation, ex parte Vardy*[61] that section 188 'does not require a consultation about the reasons for the redundancy, including whether or not a plant should close', is probably no longer correct. This is because *Vardy* was concerned with the original wording of section 188, which did not include an obligation to consult 'with a view to reaching agreement with the appropriate representatives' about 'ways of . . . avoiding the dismissals' (those words having been added by the Collective Redundancies and Transfer of Undertakings (Protection of Employment) (Amendment) Regulations 1995[62]).

6.37   On any view, an employer who decides that there will have to be a certain number of redundancies in any event before commencing consultation with

---

[57] Section 188(4) and (5).
[58] *Securicor Omega Express Ltd v GMB* [2004] IRLR 9, para 50.
[59] [1994] IRLR 72.   [60] C–188/03, [2005] IRLR 310, para 43.
[61] [1993] ICR 720, 752; [1993] IRLR 104, para 116.   [62] SI 1995/2587.

appropriate representatives where section 188(1) applies will be in breach of the subsection, even if consultation would have been futile.[63]

If an employer recognises a number of independent trade unions jointly in respect of a description of employees, then it will not be sufficient for the employer to consult only one of those unions.[64] Similarly, the employer is obliged to consult a relevant recognised trade union under section 188 in respect of the proposed dismissal of all of the employees of the relevant description, even if some of those employees are not members of that trade union.[65] **6.38**

If an employer has invited any of the affected employees to elect employee representatives and the invitation was issued 'long enough before the time when the consultation is required by subsection (1A)(a) or (b) to begin to allow them to elect representatives by that time, [then] the employer shall be treated as complying with the requirements of [section 188] in relation to those employees if he complies with those requirements as soon as is reasonably practicable after the election of the representatives'.[66] By implication, a failure to invite the affected employees to elect employee representatives will constitute a breach of the requirements of section 188.[67] **6.39**

An employer must allow the appropriate representatives access to the affected employees, and must afford to those representatives 'such accommodation and other facilities as may be appropriate'.[68] **6.40**

A duty to inform when there is no duty to consult

If an employer invites affected employees to elect representatives under section 188A but the affected employees do not do that within a reasonable time, the employer must give each affected employee the information set out in section 188(4).[69] However, the employer is not obliged by section 188 to consult the employees in those circumstances.[70] **6.41**

---

[63] *Susie Radin Ltd v GMB* [2004] ICR 893, para 49, per Longmore LJ, with whose judgment Laws LJ agreed; *Middlesbrough Borough Council v TGWU* [2002] IRLR 332, paras 45–47.

[64] *Governing Body of the Northern Ireland Hotel and Catering College v National Association of Teachers in Further and Higher Education* [1995] IRLR 83, paras 12, 13, and 30, NICA.

[65] ibid.   [66] Section 188(7A).

[67] *R v Secretary of State for Trade and Industry, ex parte UNISON* [1996] ICR 1003, 1020, DC, per Otton LJ. The EAT in *Howard v Millrise Ltd* [2005] IRLR 84, in para 16, came to the same conclusion in relation to the parallel provisions in TUPE, but without reference to the *UNISON* case.

[68] Section 188(5A).

[69] TULRA, s 188(7B). See para 6.33 above for the information which is set out in s 188(4).

[70] It is asserted in *Harvey* at para E[2529] that, in this situation, the employer may assert that there are special circumstances within the meaning of s 188(7) which rendered it not reasonably

The special circumstances exception

6.42 An employer is not obliged to consult and inform appropriate representatives under section 188(1A), (2), or (4) where there are 'special circumstances which render it not reasonably practicable for the employer to comply with' those obligations.[71] However, the employer must nevertheless 'take all such steps towards compliance with [the relevant] requirement as are reasonably practicable in those circumstances'.[72] Where an employer is controlled (whether directly or indirectly) by another person (which may be a body corporate[73]) and the decision leading to the proposals to make employees redundant is that of the person controlling the employer, a failure on the part of that other person to provide information to the employer does not constitute such special circumstances.[74] That information is not limited to that which is required by section 188(4) to be given to appropriate representatives.[75] The EAT in *GMB and Amicus v Beloit Walmsley Ltd (in administration)*[76] helpfully described the operation of section 188(7) in the following manner:

> A practical example will suffice to illustrate the operation of the exception. Suppose a parent company decides that a wholly-owned subsidiary operating one plant with 100 employees must cease trading. It makes that decision on day one, but does not inform its subsidiary until day 90. The subsidiary ceases trading on day 91 and dismisses all of its employees on that day. It cannot rely on the parent company's delay in notifying it of its decision as a special reason for non-compliance with its obligations under s.188. If, instead, the parent company's delay in informing its subsidiary was only 30 days, it would be only that shorter period of delay which would fall to be ignored. If the dismissals could not be avoided before a further 60 days had elapsed, the parent company's decision might still amount to a special reason for non-compliance by its subsidiary with its obligations under s.188, but not if the prompt provision of the information about its decision to its subsidiary would have permitted compliance.

---

practicable for the employer to comply with the relevant requirements of s 188. However, the obligation imposed by s 188(1) is to consult 'all the persons who are appropriate representatives of any of the employees'. If there are no such representatives, then there is no obligation to consult under s 188(1).

[71] TULRA, s 188(7).   [72] ibid.   [73] Interpretation Act 1978, Sch 1.

[74] TULRA, s 188(7). See *GMB and Amicus v Beloit Walmsley Ltd (in administration)* [2004] IRLR 18, EAT, for an illustration of the application of this aspect of s 188(7). It was there held that it is not necessary for this exception to the special circumstances 'defence' to arise that the person controlling the employer envisages a particular number of redundancies: *GMB and Amicus v Beloit Walmsley Ltd (in administration)*, paras 22 and 26. Thus all that is necessary is that the decision of the person controlling the employer causes, by giving 'rise to the occurrence of', the dismissals, 'and the person making the decision must contemplate that it will have that consequence': para 22. 'It is delay in communicating that decision which is the mischief at which the exception to the special circumstances defence in s.188(7) is aimed. The effect of the exception is to remove from consideration the time lost as a result of that delay': ibid.

[75] *GMB and Amicus v Beloit Walmsley Ltd (in administration)* [2004] IRLR 18, para 18, EAT.

[76] ibid, para 22.

Insolvency is not in itself a special circumstance for these purposes.[77] Subject to **6.43** this, whether there are special circumstances is a question of fact for the employment tribunal.[78] Thus most of the relevant reported cases are at best illustrative only of situations in which it was properly held, or alternatively wrongly held, that there were special circumstances within the meaning of section 188(7) of TULRA.[79] However, it is helpful that the EAT indicated in *Middlesbrough Borough Council v TGWU*[80] that the special circumstances defence could apply in relation to one aspect only of the duty to consult, ie as imposed by section 188(2)(a), (b), or (c), rather than only the timing of the consultation in general terms. It is also helpful that, in *Union of Construction, Allied Trades and Technicians v H Rooke & Son (Cambridge) Ltd*,[81] the EAT held that the mere fact that the employer is (in one sense) not at fault is insufficient to justify the conclusion that there are special circumstances. In that case, the employer was misinformed by the Department of Employment as to the need to consult, and that misinformation caused the failure to comply with the duty to consult. Accordingly, it is clear that ignorance of the law does not fall within the special circumstances defence.

In *MSF v Refuge Assurance plc*,[82] the EAT made a further helpful (albeit obiter) **6.44** statement. It said, in relation to a situation which was affected by 'the requirements of secrecy imposed by the Takeover Code' which applies where there is a merger of companies, that:

> it cannot be simply *assumed* that disclosure to, say, a senior union official on the like terms of confidence as would be applicable to the companies' directors would necessarily be so restrictive that it would be completely useless to him and that it would therefore represent a step that need not be taken by the employer, or that such an official would necessarily decline to accept information on such terms.

---

[77] *Clarks of Hove Ltd v Bakers' Union* [1978] ICR 1076, 1085–1086 and 1087, CA.

[78] ibid.

[79] The reported cases include *Hamish Armour v Association of Scientific, Technical, and Managerial Staffs* [1979] IRLR 24, where the EAT held that the non-arrival of a hoped-for central government grant could constitute special circumstances; *Amalgamated Society of Boilermakers v George Wimpey* [1977] IRLR 95, where the EAT held (in para 9) that 'the various difficulties which [the employer] encountered in forecasting the duration of [certain construction] contracts and consequent redundancies' could constitute such special circumstances; *USDAW v Leancut Bacon Ltd* [1981] IRLR 295, where, at para 22, the EAT held that the industrial tribunal had not erred in concluding that the withdrawal from negotiations of a purchaser of the employer, coupled with the immediate appointment by the employer's bank of a receiver, constituted special circumstances; and *GMB v Rankin* [1992] IRLR 514, where the EAT held that the making by a receiver of redundancies, in order to reduce the workforce so that the business was more attractive to a purchaser, was not a special circumstance.

[80] [2002] IRLR 332, paras 48–49.   [81] [1978] ICR 818.

[82] [2002] IRLR 324, para 55.

6.45 It is of interest that the 'special circumstances' defence in section 188(7) is not directly empowered by Directive 98/59/EC. However, the defence is consistent with the final words of Article 2(4), which gave rise to the second paragraph of section 188(7) and which imply that an employer may defend a claim of a breach of the obligation to consult by reference to factors of which there is no mention in the Directive.

C. Remedy for a Breach of Section 188: The Protective Award

Who may apply for a protective award?

6.46 The statutory sanction for a failure to comply with section 188 is a protective award, made under section 189. An application for a protective award may be made to an employment tribunal under section 189 only by certain persons. In the case of an application for a protective award in respect of a failure 'relating to the election of employee representatives', the application may be made by 'any of the affected employees[83] or by any of the employees who have been dismissed as redundant'.[84] In the case of 'any other failure relating to employee representatives', the application may be made by 'any of the employee representatives to whom the failure related'.[85] In the case of a failure 'relating to representatives of a trade union', the application may be made by the trade union.[86] In 'any other case', the application may be made by 'any of the affected employees or by any of the employees who have been dismissed as redundant'.[87]

Burden of proof in relation to employee representatives

6.47 Where the question whether or not an employee representative was an appropriate representative for the purposes of section 188 arises in relation to a complaint made under section 189(1) of TULRA, it is for the employer to prove that the employee representative had the authority to represent the affected employees.[88] Similarly, where a complaint is made under section 189(1)(a), namely of a failure in relation to the election of employee representatives, it is for the employer to prove that the requirements of section 188A have been satisfied.[89]

---

[83] For the definition of an affected employee, see para 6.27 above.
[84] TULRA, s 189(1)(a).   [85] Section 189(1)(b).   [86] Section 189(1)(c).
[87] Section 189(1)(d).   [88] Section 189(1A).   [89] Section 189(1B).

Employment tribunal's duty and power in the event of a successful claim for a protective award

If an employment tribunal finds that a complaint made under section 189(1) is **6.48** well founded, then it must make a declaration to that effect.[90] It may also make a protective award.[91]

The protective award

A protective award is an order to the employer to pay remuneration to **6.49** employees of one or more descriptions 'who have been dismissed as redundant, or whom it is proposed to dismiss as redundant, and . . . in respect of whose dismissal or proposed dismissal the employer has failed to comply with a requirement of section 188'.[92] The order is for the payment of remuneration 'for the protected period'.[93] That period 'begins with the date on which the first of the dismissals to which the claim relates takes effect, or the date of the award, whichever is the earlier'.[94]

The period is of 'such length as the tribunal determines to be just and equitable **6.50** in all the circumstances having regard to the seriousness of the employer's default in complying with any requirement of section 188'.[95] However, the period may not be longer than 90 days.[96]

Time limit for making a claim for a protective award

A claim for a protective award must be made before the date on which the last **6.51** of the dismissals to which the complaint relates takes effect, or during the period of three months beginning with that date.[97] That period may be extended by the employment tribunal, but only if it is 'satisfied that it was not reasonably practicable for the complaint to be presented during the period of three months'.[98] In such a case, the complaint must nevertheless be made 'within such further period as [the tribunal] considers reasonable'.[99] There is a

---

[90] Section 189(2).   [91] ibid.

[92] Section 189(3). Employees whose dismissal was proposed but whose dismissal is no longer proposed were said by the EAT in *Securicor Omega Express v GMB* [2004] IRLR 9, at para 55, to be outside the scope of s 189.

[93] ibid.

[94] Section 189(4)(a). There is a discussion in *Harvey* at paras E[2635]–E[2647] concerning the possibility that the commencement of the protected period is the date of the first proposed dismissal. Given (1) the words of s 189(4)(a); and (2) the factors to which reference is made in those paragraphs of *Harvey*, it is suggested that the protected period does not start on the date when the first of the proposed dismissals was first proposed to take effect. Rather, it starts either on the date when the first of the dismissals took effect or, if an award is made earlier than then, the date of the award.

[95] TULRA, s 189(4)(b).   [96] ibid.   [97] TULRA, s 189(5)(a) and (b).

[98] Section 189(5)(c).   [99] ibid.

body of case law concerning an extension of time under provisions containing these words. In summary, the effect of that case law is that the words 'reasonably practicable' do not mean 'reasonable'.[100] Nor do they mean 'merely what is reasonably capable physically of being done'.[101]

> Perhaps to read the word 'practicable' as equivalent of 'feasible' as Sir John Brightman did in *Singh's* case [1973] I.C.R. 437 and to ask colloquially and untrammelled by too much legal logic—'was it reasonably feasible to present the complaint to the [employment] tribunal within the relevant three months?'—is the best approach to the correct application of the relevant subsection.[102]

6.52 This question must be asked 'against the background of the surrounding circumstances and the aim to be achieved'.[103] Those surrounding circumstances

> will always include whether or not, as here, the claimant was hoping to avoid litigation by pursuing alternative remedies. In that context the end to be achieved is not so much the immediate issue of proceedings as issue of proceedings with some time to spare before the end of the limitation period. That being so, in assessing whether or not something could or should have been done within the limitation period, while looking at the period as a whole, attention will in the ordinary way focus upon the closing rather than the early stages.[104]

6.53 Thus the fact that the employee was ill during the final weeks of the three-month limitation period will be particularly important.[105] Further, although the answer to the question whether it was reasonably practicable to present a claim in time is 'pre-eminently an issue of fact for the [employment] tribunal'[106] and the question will be what was the 'substantial cause of the employee's failure to comply with the statutory time limit',[107] certain factors will be relevant, and a failure to take one or more of them into account will constitute an error of law. These will, where appropriate, include whether the employee was physically prevented from complying with the time limit, 'whether there has been any misrepresentation about any relevant matter by the employer to the employee', 'whether the employee was being advised at any material time and, if so, by whom', and 'whether there has been any substantial fault on the part of the employee or his adviser which has led to the failure to comply with the statutory time limit'.[108]

---

[100] *Palmer v Southend-on-Sea Borough Council* [1984] ICR 372, 384, CA.
[101] ibid.   [102] ibid, 385.
[103] *Schultz v Esso Petroleum Co Ltd* [1999] ICR 1202, 1209, per Potter LJ, with whom Brooke and Stuart-Smith LJJ agreed.
[104] ibid, 1209–1210.   [105] See *Schultz v Esso Petroleum Co Ltd.*
[106] *Palmer v Southend-on-Sea Borough Council*, ibid, 385.   [107] ibid.   [108] ibid.

Burden of proving that there were 'special circumstances'

If an employer asserts in defence of a claim made under section 189 for a   **6.54**
protective award that there were special circumstances which made it not
reasonably practicable for the employer to comply with any requirement of
section 188, or that the employer 'took all such steps towards compliance with
that requirement as were reasonably practicable in those circumstances', then 'it
is for the employer to show that there were and that he did'.[109]

The purpose and nature of a protective award

A protective award could be (and has been) regarded as compensatory in   **6.55**
nature, compensating employees for a failure by their employer to consult
properly under section 188. However, in *GMB v Susie Radin Ltd,*[110] the Court
of Appeal stated that the purpose of a protective award is to provide a sanction
for a breach by the employer of the obligations imposed by section 188.[111]
Thus, 'there is nothing in the statutory provisions to link the length of the
protected period to any loss in fact suffered by all or any of the employees'.[112]
'The required focus is not on compensating the employees but on the default of
the employer and its seriousness. It is that seriousness which governs what is
just and equitable in all the circumstances.'[113]

The decision of the Court of Appeal in *GMB v Susie Radin Ltd* was the first   **6.56**
of that court to consider the purpose of a protective award.[114] Longmore LJ
commented (in paragraph 49): 'It may at first sight seem surprising to say that
the fact that consultation would have been futile is something which an
employment tribunal should not take into account when assessing the length
of time for which a protective award should be made.' However, he was
'convinced' by the argument which he had heard

> (1) that there is nothing in the statutory wording which requires such futility to
> be taken into account and (2) that in a collective claim brought by a union it would
> be impossible to take such futility into account in a fair and practical way. If some
> employees are not affected at all and others are affected (perhaps some of them
> in different ways) there is no fair way in which it can be taken into account.[115]

Peter Gibson LJ said (in paragraph 40) that 'the more practical approach in a   **6.57**
case where there has been no consultation is to do what Mr Sirs suggested in the
Talke Fashions case[116] to be correct, viz to start with the maximum protected

---

[109] Section 189(6).   [110] [2004] EWCA Civ 180; [2004] ICR 893.
[111] ibid, para 25, per Peter Gibson LJ, with whom Laws and Longmore LJJ agreed.
[112] Paragraph 26.   [113] ibid.
[114] This was noted by Peter Gibson LJ in para 1 of his judgment.
[115] Paragraph 49.   [116] [1977] ICR 833.

period and reduce it if there are circumstances justifying a reduction'. Further, 'what the employer did by way of finding the employees other employment would [not] be a relevant consideration for the employment tribunal'.[117] Peter Gibson LJ suggested (in paragraph 45) that employment tribunals:

> in deciding in the exercise of their discretion whether to make a protective award and for what period, should have the following matters in mind. (1) The purpose of the award is to provide a sanction for breach by the employer of the obligations in section 188: it is not to compensate the employees for loss which they have suffered in consequence of the breach. (2) The tribunal have a wide discretion to do what is just and equitable in all the circumstances, but the focus should be on the seriousness of the employer's default. (3) The default may vary in seriousness from the technical to a complete failure to provide any of the required information and to consult. (4) The deliberateness of the failure may be relevant, as may the availability to the employer of legal advice about his obligations under section 188.[118] (5) How the tribunal assess the length of the protected period is a matter for the tribunal, but a proper approach in a case where there has been no consultation is to start with the maximum period and reduce it only if there are mitigating circumstances justifying a reduction to an extent which the tribunal consider appropriate.

6.58 In *Amicus v GBS Tooling Ltd (in administration)*,[119] the EAT held that an employment tribunal may properly take into account any consultation which occurred before the dismissals were proposed (19 February) and effected (20 February), and that it was open to the employment tribunal to decide that the protective period should be 70 days rather than 90 days because of that which had occurred before 19 February. The EAT commented:[120]

> Peter Gibson LJ directs the tribunal to address the seriousness of the breach. It appears to us clear that where, as here, there was no consultation and no information provided, after the date of the proposal, it must be relevant, in order to sanction or punish a company which is in breach, to look to see what the nature of that breach is, what the consequence of that breach is, and what the state of mind lying behind the breach is. Peter Gibson LJ explained, by way of example, in the passage to which we have referred at subparagraph 45(4), that the deliberateness of the failure may be relevant. A company which has deliberately set out to be secretive would appear to fall into a different category from a company which has completely failed to disclose information through negligence or misguidedness, or, as here, a company which has not completely failed to disclose

---

[117] *Talke Fashions* [1977] ICR 833, para 42, per Peter Gibson LJ.

[118] As it is said in *Harvey*, at para E[2654], 'surely the employer's ignorance of the law should not, of itself, be an excuse . . . Those who set up in business and take on employees should make it their business to find out what their obligations are. It is not as if the law on redundancy consultation is new or that there is a dearth of information available to employers.' However, as the editors of *Harvey* go on to say, it would be different if the employer was misinformed by eg ACAS or the matter was affected by a point of law which was controversial or unclear.

[119] [2005] IRLR 683, para 20.   [120] ibid.

information but has simply failed to disclose it at the right time and in the right context. An assessment of the seriousness of the breach must include those kind of questions.

In apparent contrast, in *Leicestershire County Council v Unison*,[121] the EAT **6.59** accepted 'the submission that any "consultation" prior to the making of the proposal to dismiss cannot be taken into account'. However, the failure by the relevant trade union to 'respond effectively' was held in that case to be material and to justify a reduction in the length of the protective period.[122]

Entitlement under a protective award

Introduction

An employee who is of a description to which a protective award relates is **6.60** entitled, subject to exceptions, to be paid remuneration by his employer for the protected period.[123] The rate of the remuneration is specifically provided to be 'a week's pay for each week of the period'.[124] Rather more helpfully, it is provided that 'remuneration in respect of a period less than one week shall be calculated by reducing proportionately the amount of a week's pay'.[125]

Effect of payment of (or entitlement to) contractual remuneration

An employer is not entitled to offset against a protective award any payments **6.61** made to the entitled employees under their contracts of employment. This is the result of the absence of any provision to the effect that such payments are to be so offset, coupled with the repeal (without any re-enactment) by section 34(3) of the Trade Union and Employment Relations Act 1993 of section 190(3) of TULRA. That repeal followed the determination of the ECJ in *Commission of the European Communities v United Kingdom*[126] that section 190(3) contravened the requirement in the EEC Treaty that the sanction for a breach of Community law be a sufficient deterrent.

Nevertheless, as a result of section 190(4) of TULRA, an employee is not **6.62** entitled to remuneration under a protective award in respect of a period during which he is employed by his employer 'unless he would be entitled to be paid by the employer in respect of that period—(a) by virtue of his contract of employment or (b) by virtue of sections 87–91 of the [ERA 1996]' (which confer the right to pay in the period of notice) if the protected period fell within the period of notice required to be given by section 86(1) of the ERA 1996. This rather convoluted provision is a re-enactment of section 102(4) of

---

[121] [2005] IRLR 920, para 41.   [122] See paras 42–43.   [123] TULRA, s 190(1).
[124] Section 190(2).   [125] ibid.
[126] Case C–383/92; [1994] ICR 664, 725–726, paras 42–43.

the Employment Protection Act 1975 ('EPA 1975'). At that time, section 102(3) of the EPA 1975, which was the predecessor to section 190(3) of TULRA, was enacted. Thus, the word 'would' in what is now section 190(4) of TULRA can be seen to have had a particular purpose, namely to make it clear that an employee whose employer had not paid him for a week falling within a protected period would be entitled to remuneration under the protective award only if the employee had a contractual entitlement to be paid, or an entitlement to be paid under what are now sections 87–91 of the ERA 1996. Thus, an employee who was absent from work on account of sickness and who had no contractual right to sick pay was not entitled under a protective award to remuneration unless (a) he had been continuously employed for at least a month, (b) he was under a period of notice which was required to be given by what is now section 86(1) of the ERA 1996, and (c) he had no contractual right to at least a week's more notice than is provided for now by section 86(1).[127] Presumably, section 190(4) must now be read as meaning that an employee is only entitled to payment under a protective award if he or she actually is entitled during the protected period to pay under his contract of employment or sections 87–91 of the ERA 1996. However, since the purpose of a protective award is to provide a sanction and not compensation,[128] and since the ECJ has held (as noted in the preceding paragraph above) that the UK failed to provide an effective sanction when it provided that a protective award was to be offset against an employee's contractual remuneration, the consistency of section 190(4) with Community law may be questioned.[129]

A week's pay

6.63 A week's pay is calculated for the purposes of a protective award in accordance with Chapter II of Part XIV of the ERA 1996.[130] It is therefore probably currently no more than £290.[131] The 'calculation date' for the purposes of that Chapter is the date on which the protective award was made or, in the case of an employee who was dismissed before the date on which the protective award was made, 'the date which by virtue of section 226(5) is the calculation date for the purpose of computing the amount of a redundancy payment in relation

---

[127] See now s 87. The effect of the third of the conditions stated in the text is curious. The curiosity of that effect was noted by the EAT in *The Scotts Co (UK) Ltd v Budd* [2004] ICR 299, paras 11–12, where the EAT referred to the 'seemingly curious result' of s 87(4).

[128] See *Susie Radin Ltd v GMB* [2004] ICR 893, concerning which, see paras 6.55–6.57 above.

[129] It is of note that there is no equivalent provision in TUPE to s 190(4). See further para 6.70 below.

[130] TULRA, s 190(5).

[131] See s 227 of the ERA 1996, as amended by SI 2005/3352. The reason for the use of the word 'probably' in the text is that it may be thought that the fact that s 227 applies only to specific provisions of the ERA 1996 precludes its application in this context.

to that dismissal (whether or not the employee concerned is entitled to any such payment)'.[132] Section 226(5) of the ERA 1996 has the effect that the calculation date is either (1) as defined by section 145(5) of that Act (which means that, where the notice period required by section 86 of that Act expires after the 'relevant date' as defined by section 145(1)–(4), the calculation date is the date of the expiry of that notice period); or (2) the date when notice would have been given if (a) the contract had been terminable on notice and such notice had been given by the employer as required by section 86, and (b) 'the notice expired on the effective date of termination, or the relevant date, (whether or not those conditions were in fact fulfilled)'. Thus, the calculation date is either postponed to the date when the notice required by section 86 would have expired, or, if such notice was not required to be given, it is the date when such notice would have been given (and not when it expired).

Effect of death of an employee

The death of an employee who is entitled to remuneration under a protective **6.64** award ends the protected period as far as he is concerned: 'the [protective] award has effect in his case as if the protected period ended on his death'.[133]

Fair dismissal or resignation during the protected period

An employee who is fairly dismissed for a reason other than redundancy (as **6.65** defined by section 195(1) of TULRA) during the protected period ceases to be entitled to remuneration under the protective award 'in respect of any period during which but for that dismissal ... he would have been employed'.[134] Thus, he continues to be entitled to remuneration under the protective award for the period during which he remained employed, but ceases to be entitled to remuneration under that award for so much of the protected period as falls after his dismissal takes effect but during which he would otherwise have been employed.

Similarly, if the employee 'unreasonably terminates the contract of employ- **6.66** ment', then, subject to exceptions, 'he is not entitled to remuneration under the protective award in respect of any period during which but for that ... termination he would have been employed'.[135]

Read literally, in both cases the employee will continue to be entitled to **6.67** remuneration under the protective award in respect of the period after the dismissal or termination takes effect and during which the employee would not have been employed by the employer in any event. Thus, if the employee is

---

[132] TULRA, s 190(5).   [133] TULRA, s 190(6).   [134] See s 191(1)(a) of TULRA.
[135] Section 191(1)(b).

given, say, 20 days' notice of dismissal for redundancy, he is dismissed fairly for a reason other than redundancy 10 days after the original notice was given, and the protected period is 90 days starting from the date when notice is given, then the employee will still, ie despite having been fairly dismissed for a reason other than redundancy, be entitled to the benefit of the protective award for the final 70 days of the protected period. This is an oddity, and is another indication that the UK legislation may not be consistent with the EC legislation which it was enacted to implement.[136]

Renewal of contract or re-engagement

6.68 An employee who is entitled to remuneration under a protective award and who has been dismissed or given notice of dismissal will lose the right to remuneration under the protective award in certain other circumstances. Where the employer makes an offer (whether or not in writing and whether before or after the ending of the employee's contract of employment) to renew the employee's contract of employment, or to re-engage the employee under a new contract of employment, in the circumstance that the renewal or re-engagement would take effect before or during the protected period and either '(a) the provisions of the contract as renewed, or of the new contract, as to the capacity and place in which he would be employed, and as to the other terms and conditions of his employment, would not differ from the corresponding provisions of the previous contract, or (b) the offer constitutes an offer of suitable employment in relation to the employee' and the employee refuses the offer, the employee may lose the right to remuneration under the protective award 'in respect of a period during which but for that refusal he would have been employed'.[137] This will be the case (ie the employee will lose the right to remuneration in respect of that period) if the employee 'unreasonably refuses the offer'.[138]

6.69 There is, however, a trial period in this situation, of the same sort as the trial period which applies where a potentially redundant employee is offered alternative employment.[139] Thus the trial period is of four weeks in length, or 'such longer period as may be agreed in accordance with [section 191(6)] for the purpose of retraining the employee for employment under that contract'.[140] The requirements of section 191(6) are that (a) the agreement is made between the employer and the employee or the employee's representative before the employee starts work under the renewed, or new, contract, (b) the agreement is in writing, (c) it specifies the date of the end of the trial period, and (d) it specifies the terms and conditions of employment which will apply in the employee's case after the end of that period. The employee's right to remuneration under

---

[136] cf the final sentence of para 6.62 above.   [137] Section 191(2) and (3).
[138] ibid.   [139] Section 191(4).   [140] See TULRA, s 191(5).

the protective award ends if he unreasonably terminates the contract, or unreasonably gives notice to terminate it and it terminates as a consequence.[141] However, if 'for a reason connected with or arising out of the change to the renewed, or new employment', the employer terminates or gives notice to terminate the contract of employment and the contract is terminated as a result of the giving of such notice, then the employee will remain entitled to remuneration under the protective award.[142]

It is of note that there is no provision in TUPE which is equivalent to those **6.70** whose effects are described in the preceding two paragraphs above. For similar reasons to those stated at the end of paragraph 6.62 above, the provisions the effects of which are described in the two preceding paragraphs above may be inconsistent with Community law. However, for the reasons stated at the end of paragraph 6.23 above, that inconsistency could give rise to a valid claim by an employee only if the employee was employed by a private sector employer, and the employee could make a claim only under *Francovich* against the UK Government.

Enforcement of a protective award

Where there is a trade union, only the union can apply for a protective award. **6.71** However, only an employee who is entitled to remuneration under a protective award may enforce the right to that remuneration. The employee enforces that right by making a complaint to an employment tribunal under section 192(1) of TULRA (and only by making such a complaint[143]). The time limit for doing so is three months from ('beginning with') the day '(or, if the complaint relates to more than one day, the last of the days) in respect of which the complaint is made of failure to pay remuneration', unless the tribunal is satisfied that it was not reasonably practicable for the complaint to be presented within the period of three months.[144] In the latter case, the complaint must be presented within 'such further period as [the tribunal] may consider reasonable'.[145]

D. Duty to Notify the Secretary of State

There is a duty to notify the Secretary of State which is parallel to the duty in **6.72** section 188 of TULRA, although the duty to notify the Secretary of State can be complied with only after the duty to consult has been complied with. This is

---

[141] Section 191(7)(a).   [142] Section 191(7)(b).   [143] TULRA, s 192(4).
[144] TULRA, s 192(2). See paras 6.51–6.53 above for a summary of the case law concerning an extension of time on the basis that it was not reasonably practicable to make the claim within three months.
[145] ibid.

not stated in the UK legislation, but it is the (reasonably) clear effect of Articles 2, 3, and 4 of Directive 98/59/EC. Article 2 imposes the duty to consult when the employer is 'contemplating' redundancies, and Article 3 requires notification of the 'competent public authority in writing of any *projected* collective redundancies' (emphasis added). Article 4(1) then provides that

> Projected collective redundancies notified to the competent public authority shall take effect not earlier than 30 days after the notification referred to in Article 3(1) without prejudice to any provisions governing individual rights with regard to notice of dismissal.

6.73 In addition, the analysis of the ECJ in *Junk v Kühnel*[146] is strongly supportive of the proposition that notification of the Secretary of State can occur only after the consultation process required by section 188 has been completed.

6.74 The duty to notify the Secretary of State is imposed by section 193 of TULRA. It is a duty to notify the Secretary of State in writing of any proposal 'to dismiss as redundant 100 or more employees at one establishment within a period of 90 days or less . . . at least 90 days before the first of those dismissals takes effect', and to notify the Secretary of State in writing of any proposal 'to dismiss as redundant 20 or more employees at one establishment within [a period of 90 days or less] . . . at least 30 days before the first of those dismissals takes effect'.[147] The definitions of 'redundant' and 'establishment' and the proper interpretation of 'takes effect' are the same as for section 188.[148]

6.75 No account is taken when determining how many employees an employer is proposing to dismiss 'of employees in respect of whose proposed dismissal notice has already been given to the Secretary of State'.[149] Accordingly, if an employer proposes to dismiss 30 employees within a period of 90 days and notifies the Secretary of State accordingly, but then proposes to dismiss a further 10 employees within that period, there will be no need to notify the Secretary of State of the second proposal. If, however, the employer subsequently proposes to dismiss a further 10 employees and the dismissals of those further 10 employees would take effect within 90 days of the dismissals of the first group of 10 dismissals, then there will be a duty to notify the Secretary of State of the proposal to dismiss 20 employees.

6.76 A notice under section 193 must be delivered to the Secretary of State, and

---

[146] C–188/03; [2005] IRLR 310, paras 45–52.

[147] TULRA, s 193(1) and (2). Short-term employees as defined by s 282(1) of TULRA are excluded for this purpose. See para 6.03 above for the effect of s 282(1).

[148] See para 6.02 above for the definition of 'redundant', paras 6.22–6.26 for the definition of 'establishment', and para 6.18 for the meaning of the words 'takes effect'.

[149] Section 193(3).

may be so delivered by post 'at such address as the Secretary of State may direct in relation to the establishment where the employees proposed to be dismissed are employed'.[150] Where there are representatives to be consulted under section 188, the notice must identify them and state the date when consultation with them began.[151] The notice must be 'in such form and contain such particulars' in addition 'as the Secretary of State may direct'.[152] The further information is set out on the HR1 form, which can be obtained from any Redundancy Payments Office or Jobcentre Plus office. It can also be downloaded from the DTI's website, at <www.dti.gov.uk/er/redundancy/hr1.pdf>. The information is similar to that which is required to be given to employees' representatives.

The Secretary of State is empowered by section 193(5) of TULRA to require the employer to give more information than is specified in the original notice given by the employer. The requirement must itself be in the form of a written notice, and the further information must be specified in the Secretary of State's written notice. **6.77**

The employer is obliged to give a copy of the HR1 to any representatives who must be consulted under section 188.[153] That copy must be delivered to them or sent by post to an address notified by them to the employer unless the representatives are of a trade union, in which case the copy must be sent by post to the union at the address of its head or main office.[154] **6.78**

There is a 'special circumstances' defence in this context in the same terms as the special circumstances defence to a claim of a breach of section 188.[155] Thus, it is a defence to a claim of a breach of section 193 for an employer to show that there were 'special circumstances rendering it not reasonably practicable for the employer to comply with any of the requirements of sub-sections (1) to (6)', although the employer must still 'take all such steps towards compliance with that requirement as are reasonably practicable in the circumstances'.[156] Further: **6.79**

> Where the decision leading to the proposed dismissals is that of a person controlling the employer (directly or indirectly), a failure on the part of that person to provide information to the employer shall not constitute special circumstances rendering it not reasonably practicable for the employer to comply with any of those requirements.[157]

---

[150] Section 193(4)(a).   [151] Section 193(4)(b).   [152] Section 193(4)(c).
[153] Section 193(6).   [154] ibid.
[155] Section 193(7). See paras 6.42–6.44 above for the parallel defence to a claim of a breach of s 188, and the case law concerning that parallel defence.
[156] Section 193(7).   [157] ibid.

6.80 Ignorance of the need to notify the Secretary of State is not a defence to a prosecution under section 194.[158]

E. Sanction for Breach of Duty to Notify the Secretary of State

6.81 A failure to comply with the duty to notify the Secretary of State under section 193 is a criminal offence, contrary to section 194. The offence is summary, and the maximum penalty for the offence is a fine not exceeding level 5 on the standard scale.[159] Proceedings for the offence may be instituted only by the Secretary of State or with the Secretary of State's consent or by an officer authorised for the purpose by 'special or general directions of the Secretary of State'.[160] Such an officer so authorised may prosecute or conduct proceedings for the offence before a magistrates' court despite not being a solicitor or a barrister.[161]

6.82 If the offence in section 194 is committed by a body corporate and it is proved to have been committed 'with the consent or connivance of, or to be attributable to the neglect on the part of, any director, manager, secretary or other similar officer of the body corporate, or any person purporting to act in any such capacity, he as well as the body corporate is guilty of the offence' and may be proceeded against and punished accordingly.[162] If the affairs of a body corporate are managed by its members, then the relevant member is treated for this purpose as if he were a director of the body corporate.[163]

F. Variation of the Periods for Consultation and Notification

6.83 The Secretary of State has power under section 197 by order made by statutory instrument to vary the length of the periods provided for by sections 188(2) and 193(1), concerning consultation and notification, and the periods referred to at the end of section 189(4), concerning the maximum protected period.[164] However, the periods provided for by sections 188(2) and 193(1) may not be reduced below 30 days.[165] Any such order is subject to the positive resolution procedure.[166]

---

[158] *Secretary of State for Employment v Helitron Ltd* [1980] ICR 523, 527, EAT.
[159] Section 194(1). Level 5 is currently £5,000: see Criminal Justice Act 1982, s 37(2), as substituted by the Criminal Justice Act 1991.
[160] Section 194(2).   [161] ibid.   [162] Section 194(3).   [163] Section 194(4).
[164] TULRA, s 197(1).   [165] ibid.   [166] See s 197(2).

7

COLLECTIVE OBLIGATIONS WHERE THERE IS A TUPE TRANSFER

A. Introduction

This chapter is primarily concerned with the obligations of TUPE transferors **7.01**
and transferees in relation to the provision of information to, and consultation
with, the representatives of affected employees or, where there are no such
representatives, the employees themselves. It is also concerned with the effect
of a TUPE transfer on any collective agreement made by or on behalf of the

transferor with a trade union which is recognised by the transferor in respect of any employee whose contract of employment is preserved by regulation 4(1).[1] The possible preservation of the recognition of a trade union which is recognized by the transferor 'in respect of employees of any description who, in consequence of the transfer become employees of the transferee' is also dealt with in this chapter. The latter two matters are considered below first. The obligations imposed on a TUPE transferor and a TUPE transferee in relation to the provision of information to, and consultation with, the representatives of 'affected' employees (defined as stated in the following paragraph below), or in certain circumstances the employees themselves, are then described. Finally, the financial consequences of a failure to comply with the obligations concerning the provision of information to, and consultation with, the representatives of affected employees or the employees themselves are stated.

The meaning of the term 'affected employees'

7.02   The term 'affected employees' is defined by regulation 13(1) for the purposes of regulations 13–15 'in relation to a relevant transfer', ie a transfer as defined by regulation 3, in the following terms:[2]

> any employees of the transferor or the transferee (whether or not assigned to the organised grouping of resources or employees that is the subject of a relevant transfer) who may be affected by the transfer or may be affected by measures taken in connection with it.

7.03   The fact that the word 'may' is used in regulation 13(1) and not 'will' is significant. The putative changes may in fact not be made, and employees may in fact not be affected by any changes which are made. If the employer (whether the transferor or the transferee, but not an associated employer[3] of either the transferor or the transferee) plans to take 'measures' in connection with the transfer in relation to some or all of his employees, then, it seems clear, the employees in question are 'affected employees' within the meaning of regulation 13(1).

7.04   There is no definition in TUPE of the word 'measures', for this or any other

---

[1] See para 3.37 onwards above for the effect of reg 4(1). The word 'recognised' is defined for the purposes of TUPE in accordance with s 178(3) of TULRA: see reg 2(1) of TUPE.

[2] See para 2.04 onwards above for the definition of a relevant transfer. It is noted here that the employees of an undertaking or business, or part of an undertaking or business, may ordinarily work 'outside the United Kingdom', although the undertaking, business, or part of an undertaking or business must 'immediately before the transfer' be situated in the UK: see reg 3(1) and (4). Regulation 13(1) of TUPE 1981 provided that regs 8, 10, and 11 of TUPE 1981 did not apply to 'employment where under his contract of employment the employee ordinarily works outside the United Kingdom'. The effect of reg 13(1) of TUPE 1981 was not repeated by the TUPE Regulations 2006.

[3] Within the meaning of s 231 of the ERA 1996.

purpose. Naturally it will include dismissal, including by reason of the imposition of new terms of employment which constitute a radical alteration to the employee's working conditions.[4] It will probably also include any change to the employee's terms and conditions of employment other than those which will necessarily occur as a result of the change of employer—subject, probably, to the de minimis principle, which is that 'the law is not concerned with very small things'.[5] It will probably also include a change to working practices which is more than trivial. It is of interest that it was 'common ground' in *Institution of Professional Civil Servants v Secretary of State for Defence*[6] that the word 'measures' is 'of the widest import, and includes any action, step or arrangement'.

A change to an employee's terms and conditions of employment of the sort **7.05** which will necessarily occur as a result of the change of employer will include that which occurred in *MITIE Managerial Services v French*,[7] where the EAT held that an employment tribunal had been wrong to conclude that transferred employees had the right to benefit from the transferor's profit-sharing scheme under which the transferor company had given its employees either a cash payment or shares in the transferor.[8]

The word 'employee' is defined by regulation 2(1) to mean for the purposes **7.06** of TUPE:

> any individual who works for another person whether under a contract of service or apprenticeship or otherwise but does not include anyone who provides services under a contract for services.

The fact that for the purposes of TUPE a person who works otherwise than **7.07** under a contract of 'service' (ie employment) may be an employee means that an office-holder such as a civil servant is within the scope of TUPE.

B. Effect of a TUPE Transfer on Collective Agreements

Regulation 5 of TUPE provides that where, at the time of a TUPE transfer, **7.08** 'there exists a collective agreement made by or on behalf of the transferor with a trade union recognised by the transferor in respect of any employee whose contract of employment is preserved by regulation 4(1) above',[9] then:

---

[4] See para 5.33, n 91 above for the authorities confirming that this amounts to a dismissal.
[5] That was how Dyson LJ described the maxim 'de minimis non curat lex' in *Omilaju v Waltham Forest London Borough Council* [2005] ICR 481, 488.
[6] [1987] IRLR 373, para 12, High Court, per Millett J.   [7] [2002] ICR 1395.
[8] See para 3.42 above for the obligation of the transferee in the circumstances.
[9] The terms 'collective agreement', 'collective bargaining', and 'trade union' are defined for the purposes of TUPE to have the same meanings as in TULRA: see reg 2(1) of TUPE.

(a) without prejudice to sections 179 and 180 of the 1992 Act[10] (collective agreements presumed to be unenforceable in specified circumstances) that agreement, in its application in relation to the employee, shall, after the transfer, have effect as if made by or on behalf of the transferee with that trade union, and accordingly anything done under or in connection with it, in its application in relation to the employee, by or in relation to the transferor before the transfer, shall, after the transfer, be deemed to have been done by or in relation to the transferee; and

(b) any order made in respect of that agreement, in its application in relation to the employee, shall, after the transfer, have effect as if the transferee were a party to the agreement.

C. Effect of a TUPE Transfer on Trade Union Recognition

7.09   Where there is a TUPE transfer and there is an independent trade union which is recognised to any extent by the transferor in respect of 'employees of any description who in consequence of the transfer become employees of the transferee', the transferee may be deemed to recognise the trade union also 'to the same extent in respect of employees of that description so employed'. This is the effect of regulation 6 of TUPE. Such deemed recognition by the transferee occurs only where, after the transfer, 'the transferred organised grouping of resources or employees maintains an identity distinct from the remainder of the transferee's undertaking'.[11] Nevertheless, even where such deemed recognition occurs, 'any agreement for recognition may be varied or rescinded' by the transferee.[12]

7.10   It is of interest that there is no specific reference made in TUPE to the transfer of the functions of employee representatives who have been elected by affected employees before a TUPE transfer. However, if there are such representatives in existence, then they will be eligible to be chosen by the transferee as appropriate consultees in relevant circumstances.[13]

D. Obligation Imposed on a Transferor to Provide Information

The persons to whom the information must be provided

7.11   A TUPE transferor is obliged by regulation 13(2) of TUPE to provide some specific information to the 'appropriate representatives of any affected

---

[10] ie TULRA.   [11] Regulation 6(1).   [12] Regulation 6(2).
[13] See eg reg 13(3)(b)(i) of TUPE, concerning which see para 7.12 below, and s 188(1B)(b)(i) of TULRA, concerning which see para 6.27 above.

employees'. This duty applies 'irrespective of whether the decision resulting in the relevant transfer is taken by the employer or a person controlling the employer'.[14] The definition of 'affected employees' for this purpose is stated in paragraph 7.02 above. The term 'appropriate representatives' is defined in the same way (albeit suitably modified and in several minor respects clarified) as it is defined for the purposes of section 188 of TULRA.

Who are the 'appropriate representatives'?

If the affected employees are 'of a description in respect of which an independent trade union is recognised by their employer', then the appropriate representatives are representatives of that trade union.[15] If the affected employees are not of such a description, then the appropriate representatives are: **7.12**

> whichever of the following employee representatives the employer chooses—
>
>   (i) employee representatives appointed or elected by the affected employees otherwise than for the purposes of this regulation who (having regard to the purposes for, and the method by which they were appointed or elected) have authority from those employees to receive information and to be consulted about the transfer on their behalf;
> (ii) employee representatives elected by any affected employees, for the purposes of this regulation, in an election satisfying the requirements of regulation 14(1).[16]

The requirements of regulation 14(1) are these: **7.13**

(a) the employer shall make such arrangements as are reasonably practicable to ensure that the election is fair;

(b) the employer shall determine the number of representatives to be elected so that there are sufficient representatives to represent the interests of all the affected employees having regard to the number and classes of those employees;

(c) the employer shall determine whether the affected employees should be represented either by representatives of all the affected employees or by representatives of particular classes of those employees;

(d) before the election the employer shall determine the term of office as employee representatives so that it is of sufficient length to enable information to be given and consultations under regulation 13 to be completed;

(e) the candidates for election as employee representatives are affected employees on the date of the election;

(f) no affected employee is unreasonably excluded from standing for election;

---

[14] TUPE, reg 13(12).

[15] TUPE, reg 13(3)(a). For this purpose, a representative of a trade union recognised by an employer is an official or other person authorised to carry on collective bargaining with that employer by that trade union: TUPE, reg 2(2).

[16] Regulation 13(3)(b).

(g) all affected employees on the date of the election are entitled to vote for employee representatives;

(h) the employees entitled to vote may vote for as many candidates as there are representatives to be elected to represent them or, if there are to be representatives for particular classes of employees, may vote for as many candidates as there are representatives to be elected to represent their particular class of employee;

(i) the election is conducted so as to secure that—

(i) so far as is reasonably practicable, those voting do so in secret, and

(ii) the votes given at the election are accurately counted.

7.14 If, after an election which satisfies these requirements has been held, one of the elected representatives ceases to act as an employee representative and as a result any of the affected employees are no longer represented, then 'those employees' (ie the affected employees who are no longer represented) 'shall elect another representative by an election satisfying the requirements of paragraph (1)(a), (e), (f), and (i)'.[17]

What is the position if there are no 'appropriate representatives'?

7.15 If an employer invites affected employees to elect representatives under regulation 14 but the affected employees do not do so within a reasonable time, the employer must give each affected employee the relevant information.[18]

The information which must be provided

7.16 The information which must be provided to the persons described in the preceding paragraphs above is stated in regulation 13(2) of TUPE, and it is this:

(a) the fact that the transfer is to take place, the date or proposed date of the transfer and the reasons for it;

(b) the legal, economic and social implications of the transfer for any affected employees;[19]

(c) the measures[20] which he envisages he will, in connection with the transfer, take in relation to any affected employees or, if he envisages that no measures will be so taken, that fact; and

(d) if the employer is the transferor, the measures, in connection with the transfer, which he envisages the transferee will take in relation to any affected employees who will become employees of the transferee after the transfer by virtue of regulation 4 or, if he envisages that no measures will be so taken, that fact.[21]

---

[17] Regulation 14(2).   [18] See reg 13(11).

[19] This terminology is used in Art 7(1) of Directive 2001/23/EC. It is not defined by TUPE in any way.

[20] See paras 7.04 and 7.05 above for what may be meant by the word 'measures'.

[21] Regulation 13(2).

The time at which the relevant information must be given

The relevant information must be given to the relevant person(s) 'long enough **7.17** before a relevant transfer to enable the employer of any affected employees to consult the appropriate representatives of any affected employees'.[22] There has been little consideration of what is meant by the words 'long enough' in this context. As it is said in *Harvey*,[23] there is at present 'a paucity of decided cases'. The meaning of the words was, however, in issue in *Institution of Professional Civil Servants v Secretary of State for Defence*,[24] where Millett J said:

> In relation to the information described in para.(d), therefore, the opening words of [the equivalent of what is now regulation 13(2) of TUPE] cannot sensibly be read as meaning 'As soon as measures are envisaged and in any event long enough before the transfer' but rather 'As soon as measures are envisaged and if possible long enough before the transfer'.

Millett J's justification for this statement was this: **7.18**

> if the company enters into discussions with the unions, it may well wish to develop or change the measures it has previously envisaged. In such a developing situation no criticism can be made of the company if, for reasons beyond its control, particular measures are not envisaged until shortly before the transfer, when there is insufficient time for effective consultations to take place.[25]

Duty imposed on the transferee to give information to transferor

The transferor will be unable to comply with the duty to give the relevant **7.19** person(s) the information referred to in regulation 13(2)(d) unless the transferee informs the transferor of any measures which the transferee envisages taking in relation to any employees who will become employees of the transferee by reason of the transfer.[26] The transferee is accordingly under a duty to give the transferor that information 'at such a time as will enable the transferor to perform the duty imposed on him by virtue of paragraph (2)(d)'.[27] The transferee is not entitled to give this information under the cloak of confidentiality, so that it cannot be given to the appropriate representatives.[28]

The manner in which the information must be given to the appropriate representatives

The information set out in regulation 13(2) must be given to each of the **7.20** appropriate representatives 'by being delivered to them, or sent by post to an

---

[22] ibid.   [23] Para F[206].   [24] [1987] IRLR 373, para 11.   [25] ibid.
[26] See paras 7.04 and 7.05 above for what may be meant by the word 'measures'.
[27] Regulation 13(4).
[28] *Institution of Professional Civil Servants v Secretary of State for Defence* [1987] IRLR 373, para 11, High Court, per Millett J.

address notified by them to the employer or (in the case of representatives of a trade union) sent by post to the trade union at the address of its head or main office'.[29]

E. Obligation to Consult Appropriate Representatives

7.21   In addition to the obligation to provide information described above, an employer (ie whether a transferor or a transferee) of an affected employee 'who envisages that he will take measures in relation to an affected employee, in connection with the relevant transfer, shall consult the appropriate representatives of that employee with a view to seeking their agreement to the intended measures'.[30] In the course of doing so, the employer must '(a) consider any representations made by the appropriate representatives; and (b) reply to those representations and, if he rejects any of those representations, state his reasons'.[31]

7.22   These duties are imposed not only on a TUPE transferee who intends to make changes to the employment of a transferred employee (including the employee's dismissal), but also on a transferor who proposes to make such changes. These duties apply 'irrespective of whether the decision resulting in the relevant transfer is taken by the employer or a person controlling the employer'.[32]

7.23   The word 'envisages' was considered by Millett J in *Institution of Professional Civil Servants v Secretary of State for Defence*,[33] where he said (obiter[34]) that it 'simply means "visualises" or "foresees" '. The following words in the passage of his judgment where he said that are of assistance:

> Despite the width of these words, it is clear that manpower projections are not 'measures' at all; though positive steps to achieve planned reductions in manpower levels otherwise than through natural wastage would be. The real argument revolved around the word 'will' and the degree of certainty which it entails. Mr Beloff, who appeared for the Secretary of State, submitted that it excludes contingencies, and confines 'measures' to those which are inevitable or at least non-negotiable. I reject that submission, which ignores the element of uncertainty involved in the choice of the word 'envisages' rather than 'intends'. But I accept that the use of the word 'will' rather than 'may' is apt to exclude mere hopes or possibilities. In my view it is not enough that there should be some possibility in contemplation; the company must have formulated some definite plan or proposal which it has in mind to implement, if necessary after

---

[29]   Regulation 13(5).
[30]   TUPE, reg 13(6). See paras 7.04 and 7.05 above for what may be meant by the word 'measures'. See paras 6.35 and 6.36 above for the meaning of the word 'consult'.
[31]   TUPE, reg 13(7).   [32]   TUPE, reg 13(12).   [33]   [1987] IRLR 373, para 12.
[34]   See the first sentence of para 14 of Millett J's judgment, which shows that all of the passages of his judgment to which reference is made below were obiter.

appropriate negotiation with the unions. I doubt that it is possible to be more precise than this.

It is said in *Harvey*[35] that 'taking measures' is unlikely to include transferring **7.24** employees under TUPE. That is, surely, correct. The effect of the application of TUPE is automatic,[36] so that it is the TUPE transfer itself which causes the employees' contracts of employment to transfer. Thus, the employer will not be envisaging taking any measures in relation to employees whose contracts of employment will transfer (automatically) under TUPE. Moving an employee into or out of the business or part of a business which will be transferred and which will cause TUPE to apply will, however, be a measure taken within the meaning of regulation 13(6) of TUPE.

Millett J in *Institution of Professional Civil Servants v Secretary of State for* **7.25** *Defence*[37] also addressed the extent of the obligation to consult which is imposed by regulation 13(6) and (7) of TUPE. That case concerned an enactment, section 1(6) to (9) of which re-enacted the operative provisions of regulation 10 of TUPE 1981, which regulation 13 of the TUPE Regulations 2006 replaced. Section 1(6) was, so far as material, in the same terms as regulation 13(2) of the TUPE Regulations 2006, and section 1(8) was in materially the same terms as regulation 13(6) except that (1) it did not contain a requirement to seek agreement with the consultees; and (2) it imposed an obligation only to consult the representatives of any independent trade union which was recognised by the Secretary of State (who was the transferor). Millett J's helpful analysis of the impact of that provision was this:[38]

> The second question which was canvassed before me was the extent of the obligation to consult which is placed upon the Secretary of State. That obligation is imposed by subsection (8), and it arises only where the Secretary of State envisages that he will be taking measures in connection with the transfer. Thus the Act evidently requires the Secretary of State to inform the unions of four different matters, but to consult them on only one of them. I was for some time oppressed by the apparent illogicality of this. Why should the Secretary of State be required to consult the unions where he envisages that he will take measures, but not when he envisages that he will take none? The unions may well wish to be consulted as much in the second case as in the first. And why is the Secretary of State required to inform the unions in time to enable effective consultations to take place of matters on which he is not required to consult them? Logically, the consultations referred to in the opening words of subsection (6) must include, but cannot be confined to, those referred to in subsection (8). On the other hand,

---

[35] At paras F[208].   [36] See para 2.15 above.   [37] [1987] IRLR 373.
[38] ibid, para 13.

Parliament can hardly have intended to compel the employer in the private sector to consult the unions on the desirability of the transfer itself or the sufficiency of the reasons for it. These are matters of business policy for the transferring employer to decide, and the unions cannot expect to participate in the decision. The reconciliation, in my view, is this. The consultations referred to in the opening words of subsection (6) are voluntary consultations, which the unions may seek on any topic once they have the requisite information, but which the transferring employer is not compelled to grant if he chooses not to do so. The only consultations which he is obliged by law to enter into are those referred to in subsection (8).

7.26 One aspect of Millett J's analysis of the position is, however, suspect. In relation to the words 'in connection with the transfer', as used in regulation 13(2)(c) and (d), he said this:

> The words 'in connection with the transfer' in para.(c) obviously mean 'on or before and with a view to the transfer'; and in para.(d) they must bear the corresponding meaning 'on or after and as a result of the transfer'. The connection is both temporal and causal. Measures, such as a planned reduction in the workforce, due to external circumstances which have nothing to do with the transfer, and which would have taken place irrespective of the transfer, are as much outside para.(c) and (d) as they are plainly outside para.(b). Mr Mann, who appeared for the unions, pointed out that the words 'in connection with the transfer' are not to be found in the Directive, but that fact does not raise an ambiguity or entitle me to ignore them. In any case, I am far from satisfied that they are not implicit in the Directive.

7.27 This passage is, surely, in part mistaken. This is because (a) it is possible for a transferor to take measures in connection with the transfer in relation to retained employees after the transfer (and that is often the case), and (b) a transferee may well envisage taking measures in relation to persons who are already the transferee's employees before a transfer, as well as after it. In any event, as noted above, this and all of the other passages from Millett J's judgment referred to above were obiter.

7.28 It is suggested in *Harvey*[39] that Millett J's 'comments upon causal connection are open to misinterpretation' also because, in saying that there would be no duty to consult about measures which were due to external circumstances which had nothing to do with the transfer, Millett J left out of account the possibility of a transferee intending to 'introduce changes for his existing workforce for reasons unconnected with the transfer', where 'those changes would not affect the employees transferred but for the transfer'. It is then submitted that, in those circumstances, 'a sufficient causal connection is made out'. Surely, this ignores the effect of the words 'in connection with the transfer'. The change envisaged

---

[39] At para F[210].

will, however, be a 'legal, economic [or] social' implication of the transfer, within the meaning of regulation 13(2)(b) of TUPE, so the transferor will, if he knows of the change, be obliged to inform the appropriate representatives of it.

Special circumstances defence

There is a 'special circumstances' defence here, as there is (in section 188(7) of **7.29** TULRA) in relation to the duty to consult imposed by section 188 of TULRA. As with section 188(7), there is no provision of the relevant Directive which specifically authorises the application of a 'special circumstances' defence. However, there is in this context, as in that context,[40] implicit authority for the application of such a defence.[41]

The 'special circumstances' defence in TUPE is in regulation 13(9) and is **7.30** in the same terms, appropriately adapted, as those of section 188(7) of TULRA. Accordingly, the case law which applies in that context is likely to be of assistance when interpreting the 'special circumstances' defence applicable in relation to TUPE.[42] Regulation 13(9) of TUPE provides:

> If in any case there are special circumstances which render it not reasonably practicable for an employer to perform a duty imposed on him by any of paragraphs (2) to (7), he shall take all such steps towards performing that duty as are reasonably practicable in the circumstances.

Accordingly, an employment tribunal may properly conclude that an employer **7.31** should not be liable for a failure to perform a duty imposed by regulation 13(2) to (7) because it was not reasonably practicable for the employer to do so, but only if the tribunal is satisfied that the employer has taken all such steps towards performing the duty as were reasonably practicable in the circumstances. The burden of proving both of these elements is placed by TUPE on the employer.[43]

A failure on the part of a person controlling (whether directly or indirectly) the **7.32** employer to provide information to the employer does not constitute special circumstances for the purposes of regulation 13(9).[44]

If it is claimed that a transferor has failed to comply with the duty imposed by **7.33** regulation 13(2)(d)[45] or to comply with the duty in regulation 13(9) 'so far as relating thereto', then the transferor will not be able to show that it was not

---

[40] See para 6.45 above.
[41] See the second paragraph of Art 7(4), which gave rise to reg 13(12) of the TUPE Regulations 2006. The word 'excuse' is used in Art 7(4) rather than the word 'defence', which is used in Art 2(4) of Directive 98/59/EC.
[42] See para 6.42 onwards above for the relevant case law concerning s 188(7) of TULRA.
[43] See reg 15(2).   [44] Regulation 15(6).
[45] Concerning which, see para 7.16 above.

reasonably practicable to perform the duty in question 'for the reason that the transferee had failed to give him the requisite information at the requisite time in accordance with regulation 13(4) unless he gives the transferee notice of his intention to show that fact'.[46] The giving of such notice makes the transferee a party to the proceedings.[47]

F. Employer's Obligations to Appropriate Representatives

7.34 The employer must allow the appropriate representatives access to any affected employees and must 'afford those representatives such accommodation and other facilities as may be appropriate'.[48] There is no definition in TUPE of the word 'facilities', but the guidance document issued in 2006 by the DTI in relation to the TUPE Regulations 2006 on page 28 suggests by way of example the use of a telephone and otherwise merely states (somewhat obviously) that 'What is "appropriate" will vary according to circumstances.'

7.35 'Appropriate representatives', ie employee representatives and trade union representatives, and candidates to be employee representatives, are protected from being subjected to a detriment or from being dismissed by reason of being, or seeking to be, such representatives, in precisely the same way that such representatives are protected in relation to section 188 of TULRA.[49]

G. Deemed Compliance with the Duty to Inform and Consult Where No Employee Representatives Are Elected

7.36 Regulation 13(10) of TUPE provides that where an employer has invited any of the affected employees to elect employee representatives and the invitation was issued 'long enough before the time when the employer is required to give information under paragraph (2) to allow them to elect representatives by that time', the employer is to be treated as having complied with the requirements of regulation 13 of TUPE in relation to those employees 'if he complies with those requirements as soon as is reasonably practicable after the election of the representatives'. In *Howard v Millrise Ltd*,[50] the EAT held that if an employer fails to invite the affected employees to elect representatives for the purposes of regulation 13, then there will be a breach of that regulation.[51] Thus there is an obligation imposed by TUPE on an employer 'to set the ball rolling by inviting

---

[46] Regulation 15(5).   [47] ibid.   [48] Regulation 13(8).
[49] See paras 6.30–6.32 above for the relevant provisions.   [50] [2005] IRLR 84.
[51] See in particular para 16.

affected employees (assuming there were no recognised trade union representatives or other elected or appointed representatives already in place) to elect representatives for the purposes of TUPE'.[52]

H. Sanctions for Failure to Give Information and/or Consult

Complaint to an employment tribunal

A failure by an employer to comply with any requirement of regulation 13 **7.37** or regulation 14 may be the subject of a complaint made to an employment tribunal under regulation 15. The complaint may be made in the case of a failure relating to the election of employee representatives by any of the employer's employees who are 'affected employees'.[53] In the case of any other failure relating to employee representatives, the complaint may be made by any of the employee representatives to whom the failure related.[54] In the case of a failure relating to representatives of a trade union, the complaint may be made by the trade union.[55] In any other case, the complaint may be made by any of the employer's employees who are 'affected employees'.[56]

The time limit for making a complaint of a failure to comply with a require- **7.38** ment of regulation 13 or regulation 14 is three months from the date when the relevant transfer was 'completed',[57] or within 'such further period as the tribunal considers reasonable in a case where it is satisfied that it was not reasonably practicable for the complaint to be presented before the end of the period of three months'.[58]

A complaint may be made under regulation 15 before the transfer to which it **7.39** relates takes place.[59] A complaint may also be made under regulation 15 if a proposed transfer does not in fact occur.[60] Similarly, such a complaint may be made if no employees are subsequently held to have been assigned to the business or undertaking, or part of a business or undertaking which is transferred.[61]

---

[52] ibid, para 14.
[53] Regulation 15(1)(a); see para 7.02 above for the definition of 'affected employees'.
[54] Regulation 15(1)(b). Thus, one union cannot complain that another union's representative was not consulted.
[55] Regulation 15(1)(c).   [56] Regulation 15(1)(d).   [57] Regulation 15(12)(a).
[58] Regulation 15(12), proviso. See paras 6.51–6.53 above for the principles which apply to the determination of whether it was 'not reasonably practicable' for the complaint to be made within three months.
[59] *South Durham Health Authority v UNISON* [1995] ICR 495, EAT.
[60] *Banking Insurance and Finance Union v Barclays Bank plc* [1987] ICR 495, EAT.
[61] The case of *London Borough of Lambeth v UCATT* EAT/115/96 is cited for this proposition in J McMullen, *Business Transfers and Employee Rights*, 3rd edn, 1998, looseleaf, at para 11[62]. That authority is not available on the EAT's website. The proposition is in any event sound.

Burden of proof in relation to claims concerning employee representatives

7.40   Where it is claimed that there has been a failure by an employer relating to the election of employee representatives, the employer is under the burden of proving where necessary that the requirements in regulation 14 have been satisfied.[62]

7.41   If the question arises in relation to a complaint of a failure to comply with the requirements of regulation 13 or 14 whether or not an employee representative was an appropriate representative for the purposes of regulation 13, it will be for the employer to show that the employee representative had the necessary authority to represent the affected employees.[63]

Duties and powers of the employment tribunal

Complaint against a transferee

7.42   If an employment tribunal finds a complaint made against a transferee under regulation 15(1) to be well founded, it must make a declaration to that effect.[64] It may also order the transferee to pay appropriate compensation to 'such descriptions of affected employees as may be specified in the award'.[65] The amount of the compensation is 'such sum not exceeding thirteen weeks' pay for the employee in question as the tribunal considers just and equitable having regard to the seriousness of the failure of the employer to comply with his duty'.[66] A week's pay for this purpose is determined in accordance with sections 220 to 228 of the ERA 1996, calculated as at the date of the transfer.[67]

Complaint against a transferor

7.43   If an employment tribunal finds a complaint made against a transferor under regulation 15(1) to be well founded, it must make a declaration to that effect.[68] It may also order the transferor to pay appropriate compensation to 'such descriptions of affected employees as may be specified in the award'.[69] However, the transferee will in that event be jointly and severally liable with the transferor to pay that compensation.[70] The amount of the compensation is 'such sum not exceeding thirteen weeks' pay for the employee in question as the tribunal

---

[62] Regulation 15(4).   [63] Regulation 15(3).   [64] Regulation 15(7).   [65] ibid.

[66] Regulation 16(3). See further para 7.45 below concerning the level of the compensation.

[67] See reg 16(4). It is therefore probably capped at (currently) £290, as provided for by s 227 of the ERA 1996. The only reason for doubting the applicability of that cap is that the words of s 227 are of limited application. However, if Parliament had intended s 227 not to apply, surely it would have applied 'sections 220–226 and 228' and not 'sections 220–228'.

[68] Regulation 15(8).   [69] Regulation 15(8)(a).

[70] Regulation 15(9). This was a new provision when the TUPE Regulations 2006 were enacted.

considers just and equitable having regard to the seriousness of the failure of the employer to comply with his duty'.[71] A week's pay for this purpose is probably capped at the level provided for by sections 220 to 228 of the ERA 1996, calculated as at the date of the transfer.[72]

If a complaint is made to an employment tribunal that a transferor did not inform the relevant representatives (or in the absence of such representatives the affected employees) of the measures, in connection with the transfer, which the transferor envisaged the transferee would take in relation to any affected employees who were to become employees of the transferee after the transfer by virtue of regulation 4 or, if he envisaged that no measures would be so taken, that fact (ie if the complaint is of a failure to comply with the duty imposed by regulation 13(2)(d)[73]), then the tribunal may order the transferee to pay appropriate compensation to 'such descriptions of affected employees as may be specified in the award'.[74] However, the tribunal may do so only if the transferor has given notice to the transferee under regulation 15(5),[75] and the transferor shows 'that it was not reasonably practicable for him to perform the duty in question for the reason that the transferee had failed to give him the requisite information at the requisite time in accordance with regulation 13(4)'.[76]

Is the sanction penal or compensatory?

Given the approach of the Court of Appeal in *GMB v Susie Radin Ltd*[77] to the manner in which an employment tribunal should determine the protective award payable under section 189 of TULRA for a breach of section 188 of TULRA, namely that it is penal and not compensatory, and given that the consultation obligations in TUPE and section 188 are drafted in very similar terms and must have similar aims, the proper approach in deciding what 'compensation' should be paid under regulation 15 must be penal. In *Sweetin v Coral Racing*,[78] the EAT expressly decided that the approach required by *GMB v Susie Radin Ltd* under section 189 of TULRA applies in determining the compensation payable under regulation 15 of TUPE for a failure to consult properly in relation to a TUPE transfer.

7.44

7.45

---

[71] Regulation 16(3). See para 7.45 below concerning the level of the compensation.
[72] See reg 16(4) and n 67 in the proceeding para above. This is currently £290.
[73] Concerning which, see para 7.16 above.
[74] Regulation 15(8)(b). The level of the compensation is determined in accordance with reg 16(3). See further the next paragraph below.
[75] See para 7.33 above for the effect of reg 15(5).
[76] Regulation 15(8)(b).
[77] [2004] EWCA Civ 180, [2004] ICR 893; see paras 6.55–6.57 above. See paras 6.58–6.59 for subsequent case law.
[78] [2006] IRLR 252.

Claims by employees to enforce the award of compensation

7.46 An order that a transferor or transferee should pay compensation for a failure to comply with a duty imposed by regulation 13 or 14 (referred to here as the original tribunal's order) is enforceable only by the making of a further complaint to an employment tribunal. The further complaint may be made only by one or more of the employees of a description to which the original tribunal's order relates.[79] If the further tribunal finds the complaint to be well-founded, then it must order the transferor or the transferee 'as applicable' to pay the employee 'the amount of the compensation which it finds is due to him'.[80] The transferor and the transferee are jointly and severally liable in respect of such compensation.[81]

7.47 The time limit for the making of a complaint by an employee to enforce an award in these circumstances is three months from the date of the original tribunal's order,[82] 'or within such further period as the tribunal considers reasonable in a case where it is satisfied that it was not reasonably practicable for the complaint to be presented before the end of the period of three months'.[83]

Appeal from a decision of an employment tribunal

7.48 An appeal to the EAT may be made against a decision of an employment tribunal made 'under or by virtue of' TUPE, but only on a question of law.[84]

---

[79] See reg 15(10).   [80] Regulation 15(11).

[81] See reg 15(9), which applies to compensation payable under both reg 15(8)(a) and reg 15(11), and which was a new provision when the TUPE Regulations 2006 were enacted.

[82] Regulation 15(12)(b).

[83] Regulation 15(12), proviso. See paras 6.51–6.53 above for the principles which apply to the determination of whether it was 'not reasonably practicable' for the complaint to be made within three months.

[84] See reg 16(2) of TUPE.

8

TUPE TRANSFEROR'S OBLIGATIONS TO THE TRANSFEREE

A. Introduction

The subject matter of this chapter is the obligation imposed for the first time by **8.01** regulation 11 of the TUPE Regulations 2006 on a TUPE transferor in relation to a TUPE transfer occurring on or after 19 April 2006 to notify to the transferee in writing or by otherwise making it available to the transferee 'in a readily accessible form' certain information concerning each employee who is 'assigned to the organised grouping of resources or employees that is the subject of a relevant transfer'.[1] The information is described below first. Regulation 12 of TUPE provides for a remedy for a breach of the obligation, and its effects are then stated. By design or otherwise, the obligation imposed by regulation 11 is strict in that there is no statutory excuse for a breach of the obligation (although the remedy for a breach of the obligation may not always be substantial).

---

[1] Regulation 11(1), read with reg 21(4).

B. Obligation to Provide Information to Transferee

Introduction

8.02 The information which a TUPE transferor is obliged by regulation 11 to provide to the transferee is the 'employee liability information' as defined by regulation 11(2). That is information of five kinds. The first is the 'identity and age of the employee'. The second is 'those particulars of employment that an employer is obliged to give to an employee pursuant to section 1 of the 1996 Act'. The third is information of any '(i) disciplinary procedure taken against an employee; [and/or] (ii) grievance procedure taken by an employee, within the previous two years, in circumstances where the Employment Act 2002 (Dispute Resolution) Regulations 2004[2] apply'. The fourth is 'information of any court or tribunal case, claim or action—(i) brought by an employee against the transferor, within the previous two years; [and/or] (ii) that the transferor has reasonable grounds to believe that an employee may bring against the transferee, arising out of the employee's employment with the transferor'. The fifth kind is 'information of any collective agreement which will have effect after the transfer, in its application in relation to the employee, pursuant to regulation 5(a)'.

8.03 Regulation 11 requires the transferor to come to an accurate view concerning the effect on the transfer of regulation 4(1) of TUPE. This is because, in order to know whether or not employee liability information needs to be given in relation to a person, it will be necessary to decide whether or not he is 'assigned to the organised grouping of resources or employees that is subject to [the] relevant transfer'. That may sometimes be a difficult question to answer.[3] An incorrect decision that a particular employee was not assigned to an undertaking or part of an undertaking which is transferred under TUPE, with the resulting incorrect conclusion that there is no need to provide employee liability information in relation to that employee, will attract liability for a breach of regulation 11(1).

8.04 Similarly, regulation 11(4) provides:

> The duty to provide employee liability information in paragraph (1) shall include a duty to provide employee liability information of any person who would have been employed by the transferor and assigned to the organised grouping of resources or employees that is the subject of a relevant transfer immediately before the transfer if he had not been dismissed in the circumstances described in regulation 7(1), including, where the transfer is effected by a series of two or more transactions, a person so employed and assigned or who would have been so employed and assigned immediately before any of those transactions.

---

[2] SI 2004/752.   [3] See para 3.03 onwards above.

The question whether a person was 'dismissed in the circumstances described **8.05** in regulation 7(1)' may also be difficult to answer.[4] An incorrect decision that a particular employee was not dismissed in the circumstances described in regulation 7(1), with the resulting incorrect conclusion that there is no need to provide employee liability information in relation to that employee, will also attract liability.

The impact of the Data Protection Act 1998

However, the employee liability information will constitute personal data **8.06** within the meaning of the Data Protection Act 1998 ('DPA 1998'). Thus, a mistaken decision that an employee is assigned to an undertaking or part of an undertaking which is transferred will lead to the provision of personal data without the authority of regulation 11 of TUPE, and therefore without the protection afforded by section 55(2)(a) of the DPA 1998 against a prosecution under section 55(3) of that Act. In order to avoid liability for the criminal offence provided for by section 55(3), it will be necessary to be able to satisfy the court that the person disclosing the data 'acted in the reasonable belief that he had in law the right to . . . disclose the data or information'.[5]

Time for giving the employee liability information

A little inelegantly, regulation 11(3) provides that **8.07**

> Employee liability information shall contain information as at a specified date not more than fourteen days before the date on which the information is notified to the transferee.

In other words, the employee liability information described in paragraph 8.02 **8.08** above must state the relevant matters as they stand as at a date which is no earlier than 14 days before the giving of the information. The notification of the information must be 'given not less than fourteen days before the relevant transfer or, if special circumstances make this not reasonably practicable, as soon as reasonably practicable thereafter'.[6] Thus the information may be of the situation as it stands 28 days before the transfer. However, it may also be of the situation as it stands rather earlier than 28 days before the transfer. It may also (where it is not reasonably practicable to give the information 14 or more days before the transfer) be of the situation as it stands less than 28 days before the transfer.

In any event, TUPE provides that subsequent changes to the information **8.09** must also be notified to the transferee. Regulation 11(5) requires the transferor to 'notify the transferee in writing of any change in the employee liability

---

[4] See para 3.57 onwards above.   [5] DPA 1998, s 55(2)(b).   [6] Regulation 11(6).

information'. It is of interest that a change in the employee liability information must be notified in writing, whereas that information may initially be given not only in writing but also by being made 'available . . . in a readily accessible form'.[7] It is also of interest that there is no stated time by which any change which occurs must be notified to the transferee.

Manner in which notification may occur

8.10 Any notification under regulation 11 (ie whether given under regulation 11(1) or regulation 11(5)) may be given in more than one instalment, and may be given 'indirectly, through a third party'.[8]

C. Remedy for Breach of the Obligation in Regulation 11

Manner of complaining of breach

8.11 The obligation imposed by regulation 11 of TUPE is enforceable by an employer making a complaint to an employment tribunal under regulation 12(1) of TUPE '[o]n or after a relevant transfer'. The time limit for the making of such an application is three months from the date of the transfer, unless the tribunal is 'satisfied that it was not reasonably practicable for the complaint to be presented before the end of that period of three months'.[9] It is noteworthy that this is one of the rare occasions when an employer rather than an employee can make a complaint to an employment tribunal.

Powers of the employment tribunal

8.12 Where it finds a complaint of a breach of regulation 11 to be well-founded, the tribunal must make a declaration to that effect, and may make an award of compensation to be paid by the transferor to the transferee.[10]

The amount of the compensation which the tribunal may award

8.13 The amount of the compensation awardable by an employment tribunal for a breach of regulation 11 must be 'such as the tribunal considers just and equitable in all the circumstances', 'having particular regard to— (a) any loss sustained by the transferee which is attributable to the matters complained of';

---

[7] See reg 11(1).   [8] Regulation 11(7).
[9] Regulation 12(2). See paras 6.51–6.53 above for the principles which apply to the determination of whether it was 'not reasonably practicable' for the complaint to be made within three onths.
[10] Regulation 12(3).

and (b) the terms of any relevant agreement between the transferor and the transferee, but may not be 'less than £500 per employee in respect of whom the transferor has failed to comply with a provision of regulation 11, unless the tribunal considers it just and equitable, in all the circumstances, to award a lesser sum'.[11] It is relevant that there is no reference here to the tribunal awarding nothing by way of compensation. However, regulation 11(6) provides that the tribunal must 'apply the same rule concerning the duty of a person to mitigate his loss as applies to any damages recoverable under the common law of England and Wales, Northern Ireland or Scotland, as applicable'. Presumably an employment tribunal which concludes that there has been a breach of regulation 11 will have to make a declaration to that effect and award a sum, however small, by way of compensation to the transferee for that breach, unless the transferee has failed to mitigate his or its loss.

The role of the Advisory, Conciliation and Arbitration Service

Regulation 12(7) of TUPE applies section 18 of the Employment Tribunals Act **8.14** 1996 to the right conferred by regulation 12 and to proceedings under regulation 12. Accordingly, a conciliation officer within the meaning of section 42 of that Act is obliged in the circumstances provided for by section 18(2) of that Act to attempt to promote a settlement of a claim that there has been a breach of regulation 11.

---

[11] See reg 12(4) and (5).

9

PENSION RIGHTS WHERE THERE IS A TUPE TRANSFER

A. Introduction

This chapter is mainly concerned with the obligations of a TUPE transferee in relation to the pensions (if any) of employees who transfer to the transferee's employment under the TUPE transfer in question. The position in that regard is now governed by sections 257 and 258 of the Pensions Act 2004 and the Transfer of Employment (Pension Protection) Regulations 2005.[1] Until those provisions were enacted, there was no obligation imposed on a TUPE transferee to provide any sort of pension for transferred employees. The only means by which it could credibly be argued that there was such an obligation was by relying on the predecessor to regulation 4(9) of TUPE.[2] Now, such reliance is specifically precluded, by regulation 10(3) of TUPE.[3] **9.01**

In addition, in common with the position under TUPE 1981, pension rights under a transferor's occupational pension scheme (within the meaning now of the Pension Schemes Act 1993) are specifically excluded by regulation 10(1) of the TUPE Regulations 2006 from the operation of regulation 4.[4] **9.02**

---

[1] SI 2005/649.   [2] See para 3.36 above for the effect of reg 4(9).
[3] See para 3.54 above.   [4] See para 3.53 above, including for the scope of this exception.

177

9.03   Brief mention is also made below of the litigation affecting part-time employees' pensions which was initiated following the 1994 decision of the ECJ in *Vroege v NCIV Instituut voor Volkshuisvesting BV*.[5]

B. Pension Protection Under the Pensions Act 2004

The protection in detail

9.04   Sections 257 and 258 of the Pensions Act 2004 give a measure of protection in relation to pension rights where there is a TUPE transfer. Section 257 provides for the circumstances in which such protection applies, and section 258 provides for the protection itself. Section 257 provides that it applies 'in relation to a person ("the employee")' where

- there is a relevant transfer within the meaning of TUPE;
- by virtue of the transfer the employee ceases to be employed by the transferor and becomes employed by the transferee; and
- at the time immediately before the employee becomes employed by the transferee, there is an occupational pension scheme[6] in relation to which the transferor is the employer (and for this purpose, and all other purposes of sections 257 and 258, references to the 'transferor' include 'any associate of the transferor'[7]), or there would have been such a scheme if the transferor had not taken action 'by reason of the transfer', and any one of three conditions is satisfied.[8]

9.05   The three conditions are set out in subsections (2), (3), and (4) of section 257. Taking these in turn, the first is that the employee is an active member of the occupational pension scheme, and, if any of the benefits that may be provided under the scheme are money purchase benefits (ie the scheme is not simply a final salary scheme), either the transferor is required to make contributions to the scheme in respect of the employee or the transferor is not so required but has made one or more such contributions.[9] The second condition is that the employee is not an active member of the scheme but is eligible to be such a

---

   [5] [1995] ICR 635.

   [6] As defined by s 1 of the Pension Schemes Act 1993, as substituted by s 239(3) of the Pensions Act 2004: see Pensions Act 2004, s 318(1).

   [7] See s 257(8) of the Pensions Act 2004. That subsection applies s 435 of the Insolvency Act 1986 to s 257 of the Pensions Act 2004, with the result that the word 'associate' falls to be interpreted in accordance with s 435.

   [8] Pensions Act 2004, s 257(1) and (5), as amended by the TUPE Regulations 2006.

   [9] Pensions Act 2004, s 257(2). In the case of an occupational pension scheme which is contracted-out by virtue of s 9 of the Pension Schemes Act 1993, references to 'contributions' in s 257(2) 'mean contributions other than minimum payments (within the meaning of [the Pension Schemes Act 1993]': Pensions Act 2004, s 257(7).

member, and, if any of the benefits that may be provided under the scheme are money purchase benefits, the transferor would have been required to make contributions to the scheme in respect of the employee if the employee had been an active member of it.[10] The third condition is that (a) the employee is not an active member of the scheme and is not eligible to be such a member, but would have been an active member of the scheme or eligible to be such a member 'if, after the date on which he became employed by the transferor, he had been employed by the transferor for a longer period', and (b) if any of the benefits that may be provided under the scheme are money purchase benefits, the transferor would have been required to make contributions to the scheme in respect of the employee if the employee had been an active member of it.[11]

The protection afforded by section 258 of the Pensions Act 2004 varies, as one **9.06** would expect, according to the circumstances. The protection takes the form of an entitlement, conferred on the employee as a condition of the employee's contract of employment.[12] The entitlement is to benefit from the result of compliance by the transferee with either of two sorts of obligations.

The simpler of these two obligations is to make 'relevant contributions' to a **9.07** stakeholder pension scheme of which the employee is a member, or at least to offer to do so (and not withdraw the offer).[13] Such contributions are as prescribed by regulations,[14] and the current regulations are the Transfer of Employment (Pension Protection) Regulations 2005.[15] Regulation 3(1) of those regulations provides that a relevant contribution for this purpose must be made 'in respect of each period for which the employee is paid remuneration, provided that the employee also contributes to the scheme in respect of that period'. The relevant contribution is either (a) at least the same as the employee's contribution or, (b) where the employee contributes 6 per cent or more of his remuneration to the pension scheme, at least 6 per cent of the

---

[10] ibid, s 257(3). In the case of an occupational pension scheme which is contracted-out by virtue of s 9 of the Pension Schemes Act 1993, references to 'contributions' in s 257(3) 'mean contributions other than minimum payments (within the meaning of [the Pension Schemes Act 1993]': Pensions Act 2004, s 257(7).

[11] ibid, s 257(4). In the case of an occupational pension scheme which is contracted-out by virtue of s 9 of the Pension Schemes Act 1993, references to 'contributions' in s 257(4) 'mean contributions other than minimum payments (within the meaning of [the Pension Schemes Act 1993]': Pensions Act 2004, s 257(7).

[12] See s 258(1). The employee and the transferee may, after the employee becomes an employee of the transferee, validly agree that the employee is not to be so entitled: s 258(6).

[13] See s 258(3)–(5). The term 'stakeholder pension scheme' is defined for this purpose by s 258(7) as 'a pension scheme which is registered under section 2 of the Welfare Reform and Pensions Act 1999'.

[14] See s 258(7).   [15] SI 2005/649.

employee's remuneration. Remuneration is calculated for this purpose in accordance with regulation 3(2), paragraph (a) of which provides that it means only the employee's basic pay, and that 'bonus, commission, overtime and similar payments shall be disregarded'. However, such basic pay is that to which the employee is entitled before the deduction of tax, national insurance, or pension contributions.[16] Where the scheme is contracted-out by virtue of section 9 of the Pension Schemes Act 1993, minimum payments within the meaning of that Act are disregarded when calculating the amount of the transferee's pension contributions for the purposes of regulation 3(1) of the Transfer of Employment (Pension Protection) Regulations 2005.[17]

9.08 The alternative obligation imposed on the employer by section 258 of the Pensions Act 2004 is to secure that, 'as from the relevant time,[18] the employee is, or is eligible to be, an active member of an occupational pension scheme in relation to which the transferee is the employer' and the scheme satisfies certain conditions.[19] If the scheme is a money purchase scheme, the transferee must make 'relevant contributions' to the scheme in respect of the employee, or, if the employee is not an active member of the scheme but is eligible to be such a member, the transferee would be required to make such contributions if the employee were an active member.[20] 'Relevant contributions' are defined for this purpose by the provisions stated in the preceding paragraph above,[21] and are therefore calculated in the manner stated in that paragraph. If the scheme is not a money purchase scheme, then it must either (a) satisfy 'the statutory standard referred to in section 12A of the Pension Schemes Act 1993',[22] or 'if regulations so provide' (b) comply with 'such other requirements as may be prescribed'.[23] Regulation 2(1) of the Transfer of Employment (Pension Protection) Regulations 2005 makes such provision. It provides that the alternative standard, ie alternative to 'the statutory standard referred to in section 12A of the Pension Schemes Act 1993', is satisfied if members are entitled to benefits the value of which is at least 6 per cent of the employee's pensionable pay[24] 'for each year

---

[16] Regulation 3(2)(b).   [17] Regulation 3(3).

[18] The 'relevant time' is defined by s 258(7). Where s 257(2) or (3) applies, the relevant time is 'the time when the employee becomes employed by the transferee'. Where s 257(4) applies, the relevant time is 'the time at which the employee would have been a member of the scheme referred to in subsection (1)(c)(i) of that section or (if earlier) would have been eligible to be such a member'. See para 9.05 above for the circumstances in which s 257(2), (3), and (4) apply.

[19] See s 258(2).   [20] Section 258(2)(b).

[21] See Pensions Act 2004, s 258(7) and reg 3(1) of the Transfer of Employment (Pension Protection) Regulations 2005, SI 2005/649.

[22] See s 258(2)(c)(i).   [23] Section 258(2)(c)(ii).

[24] 'Pensionable pay' is defined by reg 2(2) of SI 2005/649 for the purposes of reg 2(1) to mean 'that part of the remuneration payable to a member of a scheme by reference to which the amount of contributions and benefits are determined under the rules of the scheme'.

of employment together with the total amount of any contributions made by them', and, where members are required to make contributions to the scheme, the scheme requires them to make contributions at a rate which is no greater than 6 per cent of their pensionable pay.[25] The alternative standard is also satisfied if the transferee is obliged to make 'relevant contributions to the scheme on behalf of each employee of his who is an active member of it'.[26] A 'relevant contribution' for this purpose is defined and calculated in the same way as is stated in paragraph 9.07 above.[27]

A summary of the protection

By way of an overview, then, the effect of sections 257 and 258 of the Pensions **9.09** Act 2004 is that if an employee is a member of, or eligible to be a member of, an occupational pension scheme, then the transferee of that employee's contract of employment under TUPE is obliged to provide for, or offer to, the employee membership of an occupational pension scheme which satisfies certain requirements. For example, the transferee may be obliged to make contributions of the same amount as those which the employee makes, but there is a cap on the amount which the transferee may be obliged to contribute. That cap is 6 per cent of the employee's basic remuneration before the deduction of income tax, national insurance contributions, and pension contributions.

C. Equal Pay Claims Where There Is a TUPE Transfer

One of the issues which was highlighted by the ruling of the ECJ in *Vroege v* **9.10** *NCIV Instituut voor Volkshuisvesting BV*[28] was whether or not a TUPE transfer caused the time limit to start to run in relation to an equal pension claim in respect of employment with the transferor. In *Preston v Wolverhampton Healthcare NHS Trust (No 3)*,[29] the House of Lords decided that time starts to run in respect of such a claim on the date of the transfer. This was mainly because of the effect of regulation 7 of TUPE 1981 (now regulation 10(3) of the TUPE Regulations 2006).

---

[25] See reg 2(1)(a) of SI 2005/649.   [26] ibid, reg 2(1)(b).
[27] See reg 3(1) of SI 2005/649, which specifically states that it applies for the purposes of reg 2(1)(b) of those regulations.
[28] [1995] ICR 635.   [29] [2006] UKHL 13; [2006] ICR 606.

10

OTHER CONSULTATION OBLIGATIONS

A. Introduction

There are two further sets of regulations which impose obligations on an **10.01** employer to consult with representatives of the employer's workforce where a reorganisation is proposed. Both sets of regulations apply only to employers of a certain size. They are the Transnational Information and Consultation of Employees Regulations 1999[1] ('the TICE Regulations') and the Information and Consultation of Employees Regulations 2004[2] ('the ICE Regulations'). It is beyond the scope of this book to describe in detail all of the effects of those sets

---

[1] SI 1999/3323.   [2] SI 2004/3426.

of regulations. In this chapter the manner in which those sets of regulations may affect a business reorganisation is first described. The effects of the main relevant provisions concerning the application of the regulations are then stated. The main focus of what is said below is the initial pitfalls which may arise in the application of both sets of regulations.

10.02　The TICE Regulations are considered first below, partly because they were the first of the two sets of regulations to be enacted but also because the ICE Regulations in many respects follow the format of the TICE Regulations. There are, however, several major differences between the two sets of regulations, including that an employer can choose that the ICE Regulations are not to apply where either section 188 of TULRA or regulation 13 of TUPE applies.

B. The Transnational Information and Consultation of Employees Regulations 1999

Introduction and overview

10.03　The TICE Regulations impose obligations on undertakings (the word 'undertaking' is not defined by the regulations[3]) with at least 1,000 employees in Europe (to use the term loosely). The obligations are to inform and consult the workforce in relation to the current situation of, and intended or likely changes to, the employer's business.

10.04　Where a valid request for the purposes of the TICE Regulations has been made (but only where such a request has been made), the employer is under an obligation to initiate negotiations for the establishment of a vehicle by means of which the informing and consulting can be effected. That vehicle may be a European Works Council ('an EWC'), as provided for by regulation 17 of the TICE Regulations, or it may instead be 'an information and consultation procedure', which is established under the same regulation. The TICE Regulations envisage the employer voluntarily starting negotiations.[4] There is a duty on the part of both the employer and the employees' representatives to 'work in a spirit of co-operation with due regard to their reciprocal rights and obligations'.[5]

10.05　A failure to comply with a material obligation in relation to the establishment of the EWC or information and consultation procedure (as the case may be) may be the subject eventually of a penalty, payable to the Secretary of State under regulation 22 of the TICE Regulations, of a maximum of £75,000.

---

[3] But see para 2.05 above for a helpful statement made by the ECJ of what amounts to an ndertaking for the purposes of TUPE. That statement is surely applicable in this context.
[4] See para 10.30 below.　　[5] See reg 19.

When do the TICE Regulations apply?

Introduction

The TICE Regulations apply to an undertaking only where the undertaking has **10.06** at least 1,000 employees within the Member States (defined as 'a Contracting Party to the Agreement on the European Economic Area signed at Oporto on 2nd May 1991 as adjusted by the Protocol signed at Brussels on 17th March 1993'[6]) and 'at least 150 employees in each of at least two Member States'.[7] Such an undertaking is defined as a 'Community-scale undertaking'.[8] The TICE Regulations apply to a group of undertakings (defined by regulation 2(1) as 'a controlling undertaking and its controlled undertakings'[9]) only where the group has at least 1,000 employees within the Member States, at least two group undertakings in different Member States, and at least one group undertaking with at least 150 employees in one Member State and at least one other group undertaking with at least 150 employees in another Member State.[10] Such a group of undertakings is defined as a 'Community-scale group of undertakings'.[11]

The relevant obligations in the TICE Regulations (regulations 7 to 41) are **10.07** stated by regulation 4(1) to apply 'in relation to a Community-scale undertaking or Community-scale group of undertakings only where, in accordance with regulation 5, the central management is situated in the United Kingdom'. However, this is stated by regulation 4(1) to be subject to exceptions, and there are many. In the case of the exceptions, the obligation in question applies 'in relation to a Community-scale undertaking or Community-scale group of undertakings whether or not the central management is situated in the United Kingdom'. There is in regulation 4(2) a list of the regulations which so apply, some of which are stated to apply only to a limited extent.

The central management

The term 'central management' is defined by regulation 2(1) to mean **10.08**

(a) the central management of a Community-scale undertaking, or
(b) in the case of a Community-scale group of undertakings, the central management of the controlling undertaking,

or, where appropriate, the central management of an undertaking or group of undertakings that could be or is claimed to be a Community-scale undertaking or Community-scale group of undertakings.

---

[6] TICE Regulations, reg 2(1).   [7] ibid.   [8] ibid.
[9] See further reg 3, which is solely concerned with what is a controlled undertaking and a controlling undertaking.
[10] Regulation 2(1).   [11] ibid.

Initial obligations

10.09   Where they apply, the TICE Regulations in certain circumstances require the establishment by the central management of the conditions and means necessary for the setting up of an EWC or 'an information and consultation procedure'.[12] Those circumstances are that (a) 'the central management is situated in the United Kingdom', or (b) the central management is not situated in a Member State 'and the representative agent of the central management (to be designated if necessary) is situated in the United Kingdom', or (c) 'neither the central management nor the representative agent (whether or not as a result of being designated) is situated in a Member State and' either (i) there are more employees employed in a UK establishment of a Community-scale undertaking than in any other establishment which is situated in a Member State, or (ii) there are more employees employed by a group undertaking which is situated in the United Kingdom than are employed in any other group undertaking which is situated in a Member State, and (in all three of those cases) (d) the central management initiates, or is required by regulation 9(1) of the TICE Regulations to initiate, negotiations for an EWC or information and consultation procedure.[13] In the case of either (b) or (c), the central management is treated for the purposes of the TICE Regulations as being situated in the UK and as being in the case of (b) the representative agent and in the case of (c) the management of the UK establishment or (as the case may be) the UK group undertaking.[14]

Establishment

10.10   As with the word 'undertaking', the word 'establishment' is not defined by the TICE Regulations. However, the case law concerning the word 'establishment' as used in section 188 of TULRA is likely to be relevant in determining what is an establishment for the purposes of the TICE Regulations.[15]

Manner in which the TICE Regulations may affect a business reorganisation

10.11   A need to comply with the TICE Regulations may arise where there is a business reorganisation (or at least the possibility of one) because the Schedule to those Regulations may require an employer to give information to an EWC, and to consult it, about matters which relate to or are likely to give rise to a reorganisation of the employer's business or businesses. The Schedule applies in three sets of circumstances. Before they are described, it is necessary to state the definitions of several terms.

---

[12] See reg 5(1).
[13] ibid. See para 10.29 below for the manner in which an obligation may arise under reg 9(1).
[14] See reg 5(2).   [15] See paras 6.22–6.24 above for the relevant case law.

Definition of 'consultation' for the purposes of the TICE Regulations

The word 'consultation' is defined by regulation 2(1) to mean **10.12**

> the exchange of views and establishment of dialogue between members of a European Works Council in the context of a European Works Council, or information and consultation representatives in the context of an information and consultation procedure, and central management or any more appropriate level of management.

Definitions of 'information and consultation representative' and 'information and consultation procedure'

An 'information and consultation representative' is defined also by regulation **10.13** 2(1) as 'a person who represents employees in the context of an information and consultation procedure'. An 'information and consultation procedure' is also so defined, to mean

> one or more information and consultation procedures agreed under
>
> (a) regulation 17, or
> (b) where appropriate, the provisions of the law or practice of a Member State other than the United Kingdom which are designed to give effect to Article 6(3) of the Transnational Information and Consultation Directive [Council Directive 94/45/EC].

The circumstances in which the Schedule will apply

Where there is an EWC, or 'an information and consultation procedure **10.14** instead of' such a council, the parties may agree that the Schedule to the TICE Regulations applies.[16] The provisions of the Schedule will also apply if, 'within the period of six months beginning on the date on which a valid request referred to in regulation 9 was made, the central management refuses to commence negotiations'.[17] The provisions of the Schedule will in addition apply if 'after the expiry of a period of three years beginning on the date on which a valid request referred to in regulation 9 was made, the parties have failed to conclude an agreement under regulation 17 and the special negotiating body has not taken the decision under regulation 16(3)'.[18]

Obligations imposed by the Schedule to the TICE Regulations

Annual information and consultation meeting

The Schedule confers on an EWC constituted under the TICE Regulations, **10.15** a right

---

[16] See regs 17 and 18(1)(a) of the TICE Regulations.   [17] Regulation 18(1)(b).
[18] Regulation 18(1)(c). See para 10.32 below concerning the special negotiating body and the effect of reg 16(3).

to meet with the central management[19] once a year in an information and consultation meeting, to be informed and consulted, on the basis of a report drawn up by the central management, on the progress of the business of the Community-scale undertaking or Community-scale group of undertakings[20] and its prospects.[21]

10.16 Such a meeting must

relate in particular to the structure, economic and financial situation, the probable development of the business and of production and sales, the situation and probable trend of employment, investments, and substantial changes concerning organisation, introduction of new working methods or production processes, transfers of production, mergers, cut-backs or closures of undertakings, establishments or important parts thereof, and collective redundancies.[22]

Right to be informed and consulted additionally in exceptional circumstances

10.17 In addition to conferring on an EWC a right to be informed and consulted annually in the manner described in the preceding paragraphs above, the Schedule to the TICE Regulations confers on the select committee of such a council[23] (or, where there is no such committee, the council) a right to be informed and (at its request) consulted at an 'exceptional information and consultation meeting' where there are 'exceptional circumstances affecting the employees' interests to a considerable extent, particularly in the event of relocations, the closure of establishments or undertakings or collective redundancies'.[24] The meeting must be with either the central management 'or any other more appropriate level of management within the Community-scale undertaking or group of undertakings having its own powers of decision', and the purpose of the meeting must be to inform and consult the select committee or (as the case may be) the EWC 'on measures significantly affecting employees' interests'.[25]

10.18 Such a meeting must take place 'as soon as possible on the basis of a report drawn up by the central management or any other appropriate level of management of the Community-scale undertaking or Community-scale group of undertakings'.[26] It is specifically provided by the Schedule to the TICE Regulations that 'an opinion may be delivered at the end of the meeting or within a reasonable time' on the report.[27]

---

[19] The 'central management' is defined as stated in para 10.08 above.
[20] The definitions of 'Community-scale undertaking' and 'Community-scale group of undertakings' are stated in para 10.06 above.
[21] TICE Regulations, Sch, para 7(1).   [22] TICE Regulations, Sch, para 7(3).
[23] A 'select committee' of no more than three members must be elected from among the members of the European Works Council where the latter decides that its size warrants such election: TICE Regulations, Sch, para 2(6).
[24] TICE Regulations, Sch, para 8(1).   [25] ibid.   [26] Schedule, para 8(3).
[27] ibid.

If the meeting takes place with the members of the select committee of the **10.19**
EWC, then the members of the EWC 'who have been elected or appointed
by the establishments or undertakings which are directly concerned by the
measures in question shall also have the right to participate' in the meeting.[28]

Confidential information

The central management is not obliged to disclose any information or document **10.20**
to (a) a member of a special negotiating body or an EWC, (b) an information
and consultation representative, or (c) an expert who is assisting any of these
persons or bodies or the select committee of an EWC, 'when the nature of the
information or document is such that, according to objective criteria, the disclosure of the information or document would seriously harm the functioning
of, or would be prejudicial to, the undertaking or group of undertakings concerned'.[29] Any dispute as to whether the nature of the information or document
is of such a nature may be the subject of an application to the CAC (ie the
Central Arbitration Committee[30] as provided for by section 259 of TULRA) for
a ruling and, if the ruling is against the central management, for a declaration
and order accordingly.[31]

Obligations concerning the establishment of an EWC or information and consultation procedure

Introduction

An employer to whom the TICE Regulations apply comes under a duty to take **10.21**
steps towards the establishment of an EWC or an information and consultation
procedure within the meaning of the regulations only where a valid request
is made by a sufficient number of employees or their representatives, called
'employees' representatives'. Further, in order to ascertain whether the TICE
Regulations apply to an employer, it is necessary to know how many employees
the employer has, and where they are situated. It is likely that only the employer
will know that, and accordingly the TICE Regulations require the employer to
comply with a valid request for relevant information made by an employee or
an employees' representative. It is therefore necessary to state first the definition
of 'employees' representatives'.

---

[28] Schedule, para 8(2).   [29] Regulation 24(1), read with reg 23(1) and (2).
[30] See reg 2(1) of the TICE Regulations.
[31] See reg 24(2)–(4). See reg 38 for the procedural requirements relating to a complaint to the
CAC, and for the effect of a declaration or order of the CAC.

Employees' representatives for the purposes of the TICE Regulations

10.22 Employees' representatives for the purposes of the TICE Regulations may be of an independent trade union which is recognised by the employees' employer, but only if (1) the employees are of a description in respect of which an independent trade union is recognised by their employer for the purpose of collective bargaining; (2) the representatives 'normally take part as negotiators in the collective bargaining process'; and (3) the representatives are not 'expected to receive information relevant only to a specific aspect of the terms and conditions or interests of the employees, such as health and safety or collective redundancies'.[32] Employees' representatives may also be:

> any other employee representatives elected or appointed by employees to positions in which they are expected to receive, on behalf of the employees, information—
>
> > (i) which is relevant to the terms and conditions of employment of the employees, or
> > (ii) about the activities of the undertaking which may significantly affect the interests of the employees,

although, again, the representatives must not be 'expected to receive information relevant only to a specific aspect of the terms and conditions or interests of the employees, such as health and safety or collective redundancies'.[33]

10.23 Accordingly, the existence of trade union representatives does not preclude the employees from being represented by elected representatives.

Provision of information relating to the undertaking

10.24 Regulations 7 and 8 of the TICE Regulations concern the giving of information for the purpose of determining whether a UK employer is part of a Community-scale undertaking or Community-scale group of undertakings. Regulation 7(1) entitles an employee or an employees' representative to request information from the management of an establishment or undertaking in the United Kingdom 'for the purpose of determining whether, in the case of an establishment, it is part of a Community-scale undertaking or Community-scale group of undertakings, or, in the case of an undertaking, it is a Community-scale undertaking or is part of a Community-scale group of undertakings'. This obligation (and the rest of regulation 7) applies to a Community-scale undertaking or Community-scale group of undertakings whether or not the central management is situated in the United Kingdom. The recipient of the request must provide the employee or the employees' representative who has made the request with information 'on the average number of employees employed by the undertaking, or as the case may be group of undertakings, in the United

---

[32] Regulation 2(1).   [33] ibid.

Kingdom and in each of the other Member States in the last two years'.[34] It was held by the ECJ in *Betreibsrat der bofrost* Josef H Boquoi Deutschland West GmbH& Co KJ v bofrost* Josef H Boquoi Deutschland West GmbH & Co KG*[35] that

> where information relating to the structure or organisation of a group of undertakings forms part of the information which is essential to the opening of negotiations for the setting-up of a European Works Council or for the transnational information and consultation of employees, an undertaking within the group is required to supply information which it possesses or is able to obtain to the internal workers' representative bodies requesting it.

The ECJ also held in that case that   **10.25**

> to the extent that it is necessary in order to make it possible for the employees concerned or their representatives to gain access to the information which is essential if they are to be able to determine whether or not they are entitled to request the opening of negotiations, communication of documents clarifying and explaining the information which is indispensable for that purpose may also be required, in so far as that communication is necessary.[36]

The central management of a Community-scale group of undertakings may   **10.26**
not be situated in any Member State. Where such management fails to make available to the deemed central management (ie the representative agent or the UK management, as provided for by regulation 5(2)[37]) information which is required by employees' representatives for the opening of negotiations for the establishment of an EWC, the deemed central management (1) must request the information from other undertakings in the group which are situated in the Member States; and (2) has a right to receive that information.[38] The management of each of the other undertakings belonging to the group which are located in the Member States is then under an obligation to supply the deemed central management with the information concerned if it is in its possession or it is in a position to obtain it.[39] The information which it may be necessary to supply

> encompasses information on the average total number of employees and their distribution across the Member States, the establishments of the undertaking and the group undertakings, and on the structure of the undertaking and of the undertakings in the group, as well as the names and addresses of the employee representation which might participate in the setting up of a special negotiating body . . . or in the establishment of a European Works Council, where that

---

[34] Regulation 7(3).   [35] Case C–62/99, [2001] IRLR 403, para 39.
[36] ibid, para 40.   [37] See para 10.09 above.
[38] *Gesamtbetriebsrat der Kühne & Nagel AG & Co KG v Kühne & Nagel AG & Co KG*, Case C–440/00, [2004] IRLR 332, para 64.
[39] ibid.

information is essential to the opening of negotiations for the establishment of such a council.[40]

10.27 Regulation 8(1) of the TICE Regulations gives an employee or employees' representative who has requested information under regulation 7 the right to present a complaint to the CAC that the recipient of the request for the information has failed to provide the information referred to in regulation 7(3)[41] or that the information which has been provided is 'false and incomplete in a material particular'. The complaint must be presented no sooner than after the expiry of the period of one month beginning on the date of the request made under regulation 7.[42]

10.28 If the CAC finds the complaint to have been well founded then it must make an order requiring the recipient to disclose, by a date which must be not less than one week from the date of the order, to the complainant the information in respect of which the CAC found the complaint to be well-founded.[43] The order must also state the date (or, if more than one, the earliest date) on which the recipient failed or refused to disclose information, or disclosed false or incomplete information.[44] If the CAC considers from the information it has obtained in considering the complaint that it is beyond doubt that the undertaking is, or that the establishment is part of, a Community-scale undertaking or that the establishment or undertaking is part of a Community-scale group of undertakings, then it may make a declaration to that effect.[45]

The initiation of negotiations

10.29 If a valid request has been made to a Community-scale undertaking or group of undertakings, then the central management must 'initiate negotiations for the establishment of a European Works Council or an information and consultation procedure'.[46] A 'valid request' for this purpose is one which is made by 'at least 100 employees, or employees' representatives[47] who represent at least that number, in at least two undertakings or establishments in at least two different Member States'.[48] Thus, there must be at least 100 employees who make the request, or the representatives must represent at least 100 employees, and the employees must be in at least two undertakings in Member States.

---

[40] *Gesamtbetriebsrat der Kühne e Nagel AG & Co KG v Kühne & Nagel AG & Co KG*, Case C–440/00 [2004] IRCR 332, para 72.

[41] Concerning which, see para 10.24 above.

[42] Regulation 8(4). See reg 38 for the procedural requirements of the complaint.

[43] Regulation 8(2)(a) and (c). Such an order takes effect as if it were made by the High Court or (in Scotland) the Court of Session: reg 38(3) and (4). An appeal on a question of law may be made to the EAT: reg 38(8), read with reg 2(1).

[44] Regulation 8(2)(b).   [45] Regulation 8(3).   [46] Regulation 9(1).

[47] See para 10.22 above concerning such representatives.   [48] Regulation 9(2)(a).

There may be a single such request, or there may for this purpose be 'a number of separate requests made on the same day or different days by employees, or by employees' representatives'.[49] Each such request must (1) be in writing; (2) be sent to the central management or to the local management; and (3) specify the date on which it was sent.[50] If a decision has been made under regulation 16(3) within the previous two years, then the request will not be valid unless the 'special negotiating body' and central management have agreed otherwise.[51]

The central management may itself initiate negotiations for the establishment **10.30** of an EWC or an information and consultation procedure without there having been such a valid request.[52]

A dispute concerning the validity of a request made under regulation 9 of the **10.31** TICE Regulations may be referred to the CAC under regulation 10.[53]

The conduct of negotiations

Regulations 11 to 15 of the TICE Regulations concern a body which is called **10.32** by the regulations the 'special negotiating body'. This body is 'the body established for the purposes of negotiating with central management an agreement for a European Works Council or an information and consultation procedure'.[54] Regulation 16 specifies the negotiation procedure which is to be followed by the special negotiating body with a view to concluding an agreement under regulation 17. That body may, under regulation 16(3), by a majority which must be of at least two-thirds of the votes cast by its members, decide not to open negotiations with central management, or to terminate such negotiations. If it does so, then the procedure for the negotiation of an agreement under regulation 17 ends from the date of the decision.[55] The central management, information and consultation representatives, and the EWC 'are under a duty to work in a spirit of cooperation with due regard to their reciprocal rights and obligations'.[56]

Enforcement of obligations under the TICE Regulations

Failure in relation to the establishment of an EWC or information and consultation procedure

A complaint of a failure on the part of the central management which has led **10.33** to the non-establishment of an EWC or an information and negotiation procedure, or which has caused it not to be established fully in accordance with an

---

[49] Regulation 9(2)(b).   [50] Regulation 9(3)(a)–(c).
[51] See reg 9(3)(d). See para 10.32 below concerning the 'special negotiating body' and for the effect of reg 16(3).
[52] Regulation 9(5).
[53] See also reg 38 for the procedural requirements relating to a complaint to the CAC.
[54] Regulation 2(1).   [55] TICE Regulations, reg 16(4)(a).   [56] Regulation 19.

agreement under regulation 17, or (as the case may be) in accordance with the provisions of the Schedule to the TICE Regulations, may be made to the EAT.[57] For this purpose, the word 'failure' means an act or omission, and 'a failure by the local management shall be treated as a failure by the central management'.[58] The complaint may be made only by the special negotiating body where it exists, and, if it does not exist, then the complaint may be made only by an employees' representative or, where the special negotiating body previously existed, by a person who was a member of that body.[59]

10.34 If the EAT finds the complaint to be well-founded, it must make a declaration to that effect and may make an order requiring the central management to take such steps as are necessary to establish the EWC or information and consultation procedure in accordance with the terms of the regulation 17 agreement or (as the case may be) to establish the EWC in accordance with the provisions of the Schedule.[60] It is a defence to such a complaint that the request for the establishment of an EWC or information and consultation procedure made under regulation 9 was invalid.[61] The EAT's order must state the steps which the central management must take and the period within which the order must be complied with.[62] The order must also state the date of the relevant failure of the central management.[63]

10.35 Unless the EAT is satisfied that the failure 'resulted from a reason beyond the central management's control or that it has some other reasonable excuse for its failure', the EAT must 'issue a written penalty notice to the central management requiring it to pay a penalty to the Secretary of State in respect of the failure'.[64]

10.36 Regulation 22 of the TICE Regulations governs the penalty notice and its effect. The notice must specify (1) the amount of the penalty which is payable; (2) the date 'before which the penalty must be paid'; and (3) the failure and the period to which the penalty relates.[65] The maximum penalty is £75,000, and, in setting the amount of the penalty, the EAT must 'take into account (a) the gravity of the failure; (b) the period of time over which the failure occurred; (c) the reason for the failure; (d) the number of employees affected by the failure; and (e) the number of employees of the Community-scale undertaking or Community-scale group of undertakings in the Member States'.[66] The penalty may not take effect before the time for appealing against the EAT's decision

---

[57] TICE Regulations, reg 20(1).   [58] Regulation 20(2).
[59] Regulation 20(3). See para 10.32 above concerning the 'special negotiating body', and para 10.22 above for the definition of 'employees' representative'.
[60] Regulation 20(4).   [61] Regulation 20(5).   [62] Regulation 20(6)(a) and (c).
[63] Regulation 20(6)(b).   [64] Regulation 20(7) and (8).   [65] Regulation 22(1).
[66] Regulation 22(2) and (3).

has expired (currently 21 days[67]), or, if such an appeal is made, before the determination of the appeal.[68] The penalty is payable to the Secretary of State and such part of the penalty as remains outstanding may be recovered from the central management as a civil debt.[69]

Sanctions for failure to comply with terms of regulation 17 agreement or the Schedule to the TICE Regulations

Where an EWC or an information and consultation procedure has been estab- **10.37**
lished, a failure to comply with the terms of an agreement reached under regulation 17 or of the Schedule to the TICE Regulations may be the subject of a complaint made to the EAT.[70] For this purpose also, the word 'failure' means an act or omission, and 'a failure by the local management shall be treated as a failure by the central management'.[71] Where the failure concerns an EWC, the complaint may be made either by the central management or by the council.[72] Where the failure concerns an information and consultation procedure, the complaint may be made either by the central management or by any one or more of the information and consultation representatives.[73]

If the EAT finds the complaint to be well-founded, it must make a decision to **10.38**
that effect and may make an order requiring the party in default ('the defaulter') to take such steps as are necessary to comply with the terms of the agreement under regulation 17 or (as the case may be) the provisions of the Schedule.[74] The EAT's order must state the steps which the defaulter must take and the period within which the order must be complied with.[75] The order must also state the date of the relevant failure.[76]

Where the defaulter is the central management, the EAT must issue to the **10.39**
central management a written penalty notice requiring it to pay a penalty to the Secretary of State in respect of the failure unless the EAT is satisfied that the failure 'resulted from a reason beyond the central management's control or that it has some other reasonable excuse for its failure'.[77] Regulation 22 of the TICE Regulations applies to a penalty notice issued under regulation 21 in the same way that it applies to a penalty notice issued under regulation 20.[78]

---

[67] See Civil Procedure Rules 1998, SI 1998/3132, r 52.4, as amended by SI 2005/3515.
[68] Regulation 22(4)–(6).
[69] Regulation 22(5). The sum is paid into the Consolidated Fund: reg 22(7).
[70] See reg 21(1).　　　[71] Regulation 21(2).　　　[72] Regulation 21(3)(a).
[73] Regulation 21(3)(b). See para 10.13 above for the definition of 'information and consultation representative'.
[74] Regulation 21(4).　　　[75] Regulation 21(5)(a) and (c).　　　[76] Regulation 21(5)(b).
[77] Regulation 21(6) and (7).
[78] Regulation 21(8). See para 10.36 above for the effects of reg 22.

Protection of employees who are members, or candidates to be, of relevant bodies

10.40   Employees who are (1) members of special negotiating bodies or EWCs; (2) information and consultation representatives; or (3) candidates in an election to be such a member or representative, are entitled to a reasonable amount of paid time off during working hours in order to perform their functions as such members, representatives, or candidates.[79] They are also protected against being subjected to a detriment in connection with such function or activity,[80] and from being dismissed for having performed any such function or activity or for having made a request to take such time off, or for having proposed to do so.[81] There is in addition protection from victimisation similar to that which applies under the various enactments concerning discrimination.[82]

C. The Information and Consultation of Employees Regulations 2004

Introduction and overview

10.41   The ICE Regulations impose obligations on undertakings (and, in contrast to the TICE Regulations, the word 'undertaking' is defined by the regulations: it means 'a public or private undertaking carrying out an economic activity, whether or not operating for gain'[83]) with (currently) at least 150 employees. The ICE Regulations will as from 6 April 2007 onwards apply to employers who employ 100 or more employees, and from 6 April 2008 they will apply to employers who employ 50 or more employees.[84] As with the TICE Regulations, the obligations imposed by the ICE Regulations are to inform and consult the workforce in relation to the current situation of, and intended or likely changes to, the employer's business.

10.42   Also like the TICE Regulations, the ICE Regulations impose obligations on an employer to whom the regulations apply only where a valid request for the purposes of the regulations has been made. The initial obligation is to seek to agree a procedure for informing and consulting the workforce. If agreement on such a procedure cannot be achieved, then the employer is obliged to inform

---

[79] Regulations 25(1) and 26(1).   [80] See regs 31 and 32.
[81] Regulation 28(1)–(3). Dismissal for the disclosure of confidential information is not protected unless the employee reasonably believed the disclosure to be a 'protected disclosure' within the meaning of s 43A of the ERA 1996: reg 28(4).
[82] See reg 28(1) and (5)–(7) and reg 31(1) and (5)–(7). The case of *Chief Constable of West Yorkshire v Khan* [2001] ICR 1065 is of particular relevance in this context.
[83] ICE Regulations, reg 2.   [84] See para 10.44 below.

and consult the workforce in accordance with some default provisions (called 'the standard information and consultation provisions'[85]). However, unlike the TICE Regulations, the ICE Regulations may not apply where section 188 of TULRA or regulation 13 of TUPE applies. As with the TICE Regulations, the ICE Regulations envisage the employer initiating negotiations.[86] Also as with the TICE Regulations, the parties are under a duty to co-operate: regulation 21 provides:

> The parties are under a duty, when negotiating or implementing a negotiated agreement or when implementing the standard information and consultation provisions, to work in a spirit of co-operation and with due regard for their reciprocal rights and obligations, taking into account the interests of both the undertaking and the employees.

A failure to comply with a material obligation in relation to the negotiation of an agreed procedure or to inform and consult the workforce may be the subject eventually of a penalty, payable to the Secretary of State under regulation 23 of the ICE Regulations, of a maximum of £75,000. **10.43**

Undertakings to which the ICE Regulations apply

The ICE Regulations currently apply to undertakings (defined as stated in paragraph 10.41 above) which employ in the UK at least 150 employees, determined in accordance with regulation 4 of the ICE Regulations.[87] From 6 April 2007 onwards, the ICE Regulations will apply to such undertakings which employ at least 100 employees in the UK, and from 6 April 2008 onwards the ICE Regulations will apply to such undertakings which employ at least 50 employees in the UK.[88] **10.44**

The manner in which the ICE Regulations may affect a business reorganisation

Where the ICE Regulations apply,[89] and there is no agreement under regulation 16 concerning the manner in which the employer is to inform and consult employees which has been negotiated under regulation 14,[90] the employer in **10.45**

---

[85] See regs 2 and 20. See para 10.46 below for the standard information and consultation provisions.

[86] See para 10.63 below.

[87] See reg 3(1) of, and Sch 1 to, the ICE Regulations. See reg 3(2) in relation to companies which are partly based in Northern Ireland.

[88] Regulation 3(1) of, and Sch 1 to, the ICE Regulations.

[89] See the preceding paragraph above and para 10.55 onwards below for the circumstances in which the ICE Regulations apply.

[90] See paras 10.61–10.62 below regarding regs 14 and 16.

question may be under an obligation to comply with the 'standard information and consultation provisions' set out in regulation 20.[91]

The standard information and consultation provisions

10.46 Those provisions require the employer to provide to 'information and consultation representatives' (who will in the envisaged circumstances have to have been elected under regulation 19[92]) information on 'the recent and probable development of the undertaking's activities and economic situation'.[93] Regulation 20(1) also requires an employer to provide information to the information and consultation representatives in relation to, and consult those representatives on, the following matters:

> (b) the situation, structure and probable development of employment within the undertaking and . . . any anticipatory measures envisaged, in particular, where there is a threat to employment within the undertaking; and
>
> (c) subject to paragraph (5), decisions likely to lead to substantial changes in work organisation or in contractual relations, including those referred to in—
>> (i) sections 188 to 192 of the Trade Union and Labour Relations (Consolidation) Act 1992; and
>> (ii) [regulations 13 to 15 of the TUPE Regulations 2006].[94]

10.47 The duties in regulation 20 in respect of the matters stated in regulation 20(1)(c) (ie those matters set out immediately above) cease to apply 'once the employer is under a duty under' the provisions to which regulation 20(1)(c) applies *and* the employer has

> notified the information and consultation representatives in writing that he will be complying with his duty under [the relevant provision] instead of under these Regulations, provided that the notification is given on each occasion on which the employer has become or is about to become subject to the duty.[95]

10.48 The ICE Regulations will therefore apply in any event where section 188 of TULRA does not apply, and that will be the case where an employer proposes to dismiss fewer than 20 employees, as long as the decision in question is 'likely to lead to substantial changes in work organisation or in contractual relations'. It could, for example, sensibly be said that changes to the working practices of

---

[91] See paras 10.64–10.66 below for the circumstances in which reg 20 will apply.
[92] See the definition of 'information and consultation representative' in reg 2(1). See para 10.67 for the manner in which the election takes place.
[93] Regulation 20(1)(a).
[94] ICE Regulations, reg 20(1)(b) and (c), read with ss 17(2)(a) and 23(1) and (2) of the Interpretation Act 1978.
[95] ICE Regulations, reg 20(5).

10 out of a total of 50 employees in one undertaking would constitute a substantial change in 'work organisation or in contractual relations'. A change to the working practices of 10 employees out of a total workforce of 1,000 on the other hand may not be such a 'substantial' change.

Definition of 'consultation' for the purposes of the ICE Regulations

The word 'consultation' is defined by regulation 2(1) of the ICE Regulations **10.49**
to mean

> the exchange of views and establishment of a dialogue between—
> (a) information and consultation representatives and the employer; or
> (b) in the case of a negotiated agreement which provides as mentioned in regulation 16(1)(f)(ii), the employees and the employer.

Confidential information

An employer is not obliged to disclose any information or document for **10.50**
the purposes of the ICE Regulations 'when the nature of the information or document is such that, according to objective criteria, the disclosure of the information or document would seriously harm the functioning of, or would be prejudicial to, the undertaking'.[96] Any dispute as to whether the nature of the information or document is of such a nature may be the subject of an application to the CAC for a ruling and, if the ruling is against the central management, for a declaration and order accordingly.[97]

Department of Trade and Industry's guidance

Guidance has been issued by the DTI (ie the Department of Trade and Industry) **10.51**
on the operation of the ICE Regulations, and in paragraph 55 of the current guidance (issued in January 2006[98]), the following is said:[99]

> It is not possible to specify a lower limit in terms of the number of employees who would have to be affected—this will depend on the circumstances of the individual case. Clearly, the more employees affected, and the greater the proportion of all the employees in the undertaking, the more likely it is to be covered. A situation that was likely to lead on to collective redundancies as defined by statute (that is, 20 or more redundancies at one establishment) would be covered.

Paragraph 55 of the DTI's guidance contains some further valuable guidance as **10.52**
to the times when the ICE Regulations are likely to apply. For example, the

---

[96] Regulation 26(1).
[97] See reg 26(2)–(4). See reg 35 for the procedural requirements relating to a complaint to the CAC, and for the effect of a declaration or order of the CAC.
[98] This guidance is available on the Internet at <http://www.dti.gov.uk/er/consultation/ic_guidance_jan2006.pdf>.
[99] At p 44.

guidance there states that the 'structure' of employment 'can be understood to mean how employees are distributed within the undertaking, for example, geographically at different establishments (eg plants, offices, factories, retail outlets, branches), or organisationally within different divisions or units of the undertaking'. There is clearly some overlap between regulation 20(1)(b) and 20(1)(c). Thus, as the guidance states in relation to the matters to which regulation 20(1)(b) relates:[100]

> The emphasis here is on the overall number of employees within the under-taking—both the present level of employment and future levels. It would therefore include recruitment of new employees and redundancies (both voluntary and compulsory), employee turnover, the possibility of moving to reduced hours working or the need for overtime, and could include changes in retirement policy or early retirement schemes.

10.53   The guidance also states in relation to the matters to which regulation 20(1)(c) relates:[101]

> In DTI's view, 'changes in work organisation' would include:
> * changes in the level, or distribution of employment within the undertaking, including redundancies and relocation of posts;
> * changes in policy on flexible working, part-time working, overtime;
> * a move to reduced hours or overtime working, changes in shift working or other work patterns;
> * introduction of significant new technology or equipment, and any training associated with it.
>
> In DTI's view, 'changes in contractual relations' would include:
> * a change of employer as a result of a transfer of the business, or part of the business;
> * changes in employees' terms and conditions (including hours of work, leave entitlement, rest breaks). This would not necessarily include any and every change in terms and conditions. It should be a substantial change that affected the overall contractual relations between the employer and employees;
> * introduction of, or a change to, compulsory retirement age;
> * changes to an occupational pension scheme but only where there was a con-tractual right to participate in the scheme as that right would form part of the contract;
> * changes in disciplinary or grievance procedures.
>
> In addition, any consideration of the phrase 'changes in contractual relations' must be consistent with the Treaty Base (Article 137) under which the Directive has been adopted, which states that matters such as pay are not covered by that Article. In DTI's view therefore, category (c) would not cover changes in pay or benefits that have a monetary value.

---

[100] Paragraph 55, at p 43.   [101] Paragraph 55, at pp 43–44.

None of this guidance is binding. It is nevertheless helpful. **10.54**

The operation of the ICE Regulations

Request by employees

An employer to whom the ICE Regulations apply must initiate negotiations **10.55** under regulation 14 when a valid request within the meaning of regulation 7 is made. In order to be valid, such a request must be made, either as a single request, or a series of such requests which together are made over a period of six months, by at least 10 per cent of the employees in the undertaking unless that number would be under 15 employees or over 2,500 employees.[102] If 10 per cent of the workforce amounts to less than 15 employees, then the request must be made by at least 15 employees.[103] If 10 per cent of the workforce amounts to more than 2,500 employees, then the request must be made by at least 2,500 employees.[104]

The request must be made in writing and must be sent to 'the registered office, **10.56** head office or principal place of business of the employer', or the CAC.[105] It must also specify the employees making it and the date on which it was sent.[106] If the request is sent to the CAC, the CAC must notify the employer as soon as is reasonably practicable that it has received the request and 'request from the employer such information as it needs to verify the number and names of the employees who have made the request'.[107] The employer must comply with such a request as soon as is reasonably practicable.[108] The CAC must then inform both the employer and the employees who have made the request 'how many employees have made the request on the basis of the information provided by the employees and the employer', ie the precise number for the purposes of regulation 7(2) and (3).[109]

Employee ballot where there is a 'pre-existing agreement'

Where a valid employee request has been made under regulation 7 by fewer **10.57** than 40 per cent of the employees who were employed in the undertaking on the date when the request was made, and where there exists one or more pre-existing agreements which (a) are in writing, (b) cover all of the employees of the undertaking, (c) have been approved by the employees, and (d) 'set out how the employer is to give information to the employees or their representatives and seek their views on such information', then the employer may, instead of initiating negotiations under regulation 14, 'hold a ballot to seek the

---

[102] Regulation 7(2) and (3).   [103] Regulation 7(3).   [104] ibid.
[105] ICE Regulations, reg 7(4)(a) and (b).   [106] Regulation 7(4)(c).
[107] Regulation 7(5)(a) and (b).   [108] Regulation 7(6).   [109] Regulation 7(5)(c).

endorsement of the employees of the undertaking for the employee request in accordance with [regulation 8(3) and (4)]'.[110]

10.58 In *Stewart v Moray Council*,[111] the CAC held that three agreements which applied to the whole of the workforce of the employer 'covered' all of the employees of the employer's undertaking notwithstanding that they provided only for consultation with trade union representatives.[112] The CAC also held that the agreements had been approved by the employees for the purposes of regulation 8 even though they had been approved only by trade union representatives and there had been no endorsement of the agreements by employees who were not members of the trade unions.[113] However, one of the agreements did not satisfy the requirement in regulation 8(1)(d) that it 'set out how the employer is to give information to the employees or their representatives and seek their views on such information'. This was because the only provision which could have been said to give effect to this requirement was a statement that the joint negotiating committee 'will be a forum for discussion and/or consultation on a range of matters not subject to national bargaining'. The CAC held that this was not a sufficiently detailed description of the way in which the employers would inform and consult the employees concerned, not least because the other two agreements had far more detailed provision concerning the process of informing and consulting.[114] Both parties appealed to the EAT against the CAC's decision. The EAT dismissed both the appeal and the cross-appeal, with one minor reservation, which did not affect the outcome.[115]

10.59 Only if (a) at least 40 per cent of the employees who are employed in the undertaking, and (b) the majority of the employees who vote in the ballot, vote in favour of endorsing the request made under regulation 7, does the employer need to initiate negotiations under regulation 14.[116] Any dispute about the operation of the ballot arrangements under regulation 8 can be referred to the CAC.[117]

10.60 Regulation 9 makes similar provision for pre-existing agreements covering groups of undertakings, applying regulation 8 to the circumstances, modified as appropriate.

---

[110] Regulation 8(1) and (2).   [111] [2006] IRLR 168.   [112] ibid, para 19.
[113] ibid, para 21.   [114] See para 23.   [115] See [2006] IRLR 592.
[116] Regulation 8(5)(b) and (c) and reg 8(6).
[117] See regs 8(7)–(9), 10, and 13. See reg 35 for the procedural requirements concerning a complaint to the CAC and the effect of an order of the CAC.

Negotiations to reach an agreement

In order to initiate negotiations to reach an agreement under the ICE **10.61**
Regulations,[118] an employer must as soon as is reasonably practicable make
arrangements in accordance with regulation 14(2) for the election or appointment by all employees of the undertaking of one or more 'negotiating representatives'.[119] Any dispute about the operation of regulation 14(2) may be the
subject of a complaint made to the CAC under regulation 15(1). Such a
complaint must be presented to the CAC within 21 days of the election
or appointment in question.[120] The CAC may then order the process of
appointment or election to be repeated.[121]

Once the employer has complied with regulation 14(2), the employer must **10.62**
inform the employees in writing of the identity of the negotiating representatives and invite those representatives to 'enter into negotiations to reach a
negotiated agreement'.[122] The clear intention of the legislation is therefore that
the agreement is in no way imposed by the employer on the employees. A
negotiated agreement must cover all of the employees of the undertaking.[123]

Valid employer notification

The employer may voluntarily start the negotiation process provided for by **10.63**
regulation 14(1), and, where that occurs, regulations 14 to 17 apply.[124] The
employer does so by issuing a written notification which is 'published in such
a manner as to bring it to the attention of, so far as reasonably practicable, all
the employees of the undertaking'.[125] This is called for the purposes of the ICE
Regulations a 'valid employer notification'.[126]

Circumstances in which the standard information and consultation provisions apply

If, as a result of the making of a valid employee request or the issue of a valid **10.64**
employer notification, an employer is under a duty to initiate negotiations
under regulation 14(1) but does not do so, then the standard information and
consultation provisions in regulation 20 will apply, either at the end of the

---

[118] See para 10.55 onwards above for the circumstances in which an employer is obliged to
initiate such negotiations.
[119] Regulation 14(1)(a).
[120] Regulation 15(1). See further reg 35 concerning the procedural requirements.
[121] See reg 15(2).   [122] Regulation 14(1)(b) and (c).
[123] See reg 16(1); see the rest of reg 16 for the detailed requirements for a negotiated
agreement and reg 17A concerning any requirement of such an agreement relating to a 'listed
change' within the meaning of reg 6(2) of the Occupational and Personal Pension Schemes
(Consultation by Employers and Miscellaneous Amendment) Regulations 2006, SI 2006/514.
[124] Regulation 11(1).   [125] Regulation 11(2).
[126] Only an 'employer notification' is specifically defined, and that is a notification under
reg 11: see reg 2.

period of six months from the date of the issue of the request or notification or, if sooner, when information and consultation representatives are elected under regulation 19.[127]

10.65 The standard information and consultation provisions will also apply if the negotiations to reach a negotiated agreement mentioned in paragraph 10.61 above last for more than six months after the end of the three-month period beginning with the date when the valid employee request was made or the valid employer notification was issued, subject to the possibility of that period being extended as a result of regulation 14(3) to (7).[128] In the latter case, the standard information and consultation provisions will apply if no negotiated agreement is reached within six months of that extended period.[129] In both these situations, the standard information and consultation provisions will apply either at the end of the period of six months from when the time limit expires, or, if sooner, when information and consultation representatives are elected under regulation 19.

10.66 Where the standard provisions apply, the employer and the information and consultation representatives elected under regulation 19 may then reach agreement that provisions other than the standard provisions will apply.[130]

Election of information and consultation representatives

10.67 Regulation 19 applies where the standard information and consultation provisions are to apply, and requires the employer, before those provisions start to apply, to arrange for the holding of a ballot of its employees to elect the appropriate number of information and consultation representatives. That number is one per 50 employees 'or part thereof' (ie one for any group of less than 50 employees who are left after the rest have been divided into groups of 50), subject to a minimum of two and a maximum of 25.[131] An employee or an employees' representative[132] may make a complaint to the CAC that the employer has not arranged for the holding of a ballot in accordance with regulation 19(1), and the CAC must, if it finds the complaint to be well-founded, make an order requiring the employer to arrange, or rearrange, and hold the ballot.[133] The

---

[127] Regulation 18(1)(a).   [128] Regulation 18(1)(b).   [129] ibid.

[130] Regulation 18(2). In order to have effect, the agreement must comply with the provisions set out in reg 18(3).

[131] Regulation 19(3).

[132] The term 'employees' representative' is not defined in the ICE Regulations, but the DTI guidance states that its use 'is intended to allow employees to make complaints through an intermediary such as a trade union or some other third party, if, for example, they do not want to identify themselves': see n 9 on p 9, n 26 on p 21, and n 34 on p 28 of the guidance issued in January 2006, at <http://www.dti.gov.uk/er/consultation/ic_guidance_jan2006.pdf>.

[133] Regulation 19(4) and (5). See reg 35 for the procedural requirements relating to a complaint to the CAC and for the effect of an order of the CAC.

employee or the employees' representative may then make an application to the EAT under regulation 22(6) of the ICE Regulations, and the EAT may then issue a penalty notice to the employer, requiring the employer to pay up to £75,000.[134]

Enforcement of obligations under a negotiated agreement or the standard information and consultation provisions

A complaint may be made, under regulation 22(1) of the ICE Regulations, **10.68** to the CAC of a failure to comply (whether by act or omission) with the terms of a negotiated agreement or, where there is no such agreement, the standard information and consultation provisions.[135] Where information and consultation representatives have been elected or appointed, the complaint may be made by such a representative.[136] Where no such representatives have been elected or appointed, the complaint may be made by an employee or an employees' representative.[137] The complaint must be made within three months of the alleged failure,[138] there being no provision for an extension of time.

In that connection it is of interest that it is suggested in N Squire, J Healy and **10.69** J Broadbent, *Informing and Consulting Employees—The New Law*[139] that it would be 'logical to see [a failure to inform and consult about a specific business decision] as continuing over a period of time rather than occurring on a specific date'. Thus, it is said (cogently):

> 8.19 . . . For example, negotiations about a possible sale of a business are likely to take place over some weeks. Although the obligation to inform and consult under the relevant procedure will probably be triggered at some point during that process before the agreement is actually signed, the obligation to inform and consult once the obligation has been triggered is a continuous one. The three months for bringing a claim under Regulation 22(1) should not be treated as beginning to run at the point at which the obligation would actually have been triggered.
>
> 8.20 Otherwise, if a strict approach is taken to the issue of when the complaint has to be made, relevant applicants could theoretically be barred from bringing a complaint before they are even aware that there has been a failure to consult under the relevant procedure. This could be the case if the relevant discussions (about a possible sale in the example given above) continue over a long period of time.

---

[134] See regs 19(6) and 22(6)–(8). See further para 10.70 below concerning reg 22(6)–(8).
[135] See reg 35 for the procedural requirements relating to a complaint to the CAC and the effect of a declaration or order of the CAC.
[136] Regulation 22(1) and (3).
[137] ibid. See n 131 in the preceding paragraph above concerning employees' representatives.
[138] Regulation 22(2).   [139] (2005) 151, at paras 8.18–8.19.

10.70 Where the CAC finds the complaint well-founded, it must make a declaration to that effect and may make an order requiring the employer to take 'such steps as are necessary to comply with the terms of the negotiated agreement or, as the case may be, the standard information and consultation provisions'.[140] The specific steps must be stated, as must the period within which they must be taken.[141] An application for a penalty notice to be issued by the EAT may then, within three months of the CAC's declaration, be made by the relevant representative or (as the case may be) an employee.[142] The EAT must then issue a penalty notice to the employer requiring the employer to pay a penalty to the Secretary of State in respect of the failure 'unless satisfied, on hearing representations from the employer, that the failure resulted from a reason beyond the employer's control or that he has some other reasonable excuse for his failure'.[143] The penalty is as provided for by regulation 23 of the ICE Regulations, and, as with a penalty of the same sort under the TICE Regulations,[144] the penalty may be of a maximum of £75,000.[145] In setting the amount of the penalty, the EAT must take into account '(a) the gravity of the failure; (b) the period of time over which the failure occurred; (c) the reason for the failure; (d) the number of employees affected by the failure; and (e) the number of employees employed by the undertaking or, where a negotiated agreement covers employees in more than one undertaking, the number of employees employed by both or all of the undertakings'.[146] As with a penalty notice under the TICE Regulations, a penalty notice under the ICE Regulations may not take effect before the time for appealing against the EAT's decision has expired (currently 21 days[147]), or, if such an appeal is made, before the determination of the appeal.[148] The penalty is payable to the Secretary of State and such part of the penalty as remains outstanding may be recovered from the employer as a civil debt.[149]

Protection of representatives

10.71 Employees who are (1) negotiating representatives;[150] or (2) information and consultation representatives are entitled to a reasonable amount of paid time off during working hours in order to perform their functions as such

---

[140] ICE Regulations, reg 22(4).   [141] Regulation 22(5).
[142] See reg 22(6) read with reg 22(3). See para 10.68 above concerning reg 22(3) and the relevant representative.
[143] Regulation 22(7).   [144] Concerning which, see para 10.33 onwards above.
[145] ICE Regulations, reg 23(2).   [146] Regulation 23(3).
[147] See Civil Procedure Rules 1998, SI 1998/3132, r 52.4, as amended by SI 2005/3515.
[148] ICE Regulations, reg 23(4)–(6).
[149] Regulation 23(5). The sum is paid into the Consolidated Fund: reg 23(7).
[150] See para 10.61 above concerning 'negotiating representatives'.

representatives.[151] They are also protected against being subjected to a detriment other than dismissal in connection with such functions, as are employees who are candidates to be either such representatives, or who are employees' representatives.[152] Employees are also protected against any detriment for having taken, or for having proposed or made a request to take, such time off with pay.[153] There is protection from victimisation falling short of dismissal similar to that which applies under the various enactments concerning discrimination.[154] All of the persons who are protected against detriment or victimisation as described above in this paragraph are protected against being dismissed for the same reason.[155]

---

[151] ICE Regulations, regs 27–29.   [152] See regs 32 and 33.

[153] See reg 32(3)(b) and (c).

[154] See reg 32(1) and (5)–(7) and reg 33. The case of *Chief Constable of West Yorkshire v Khan* [2001] ICR 1065 is of particular relevance in this context.

[155] See reg 30. Dismissal for the disclosure of confidential information is not protected unless the employee reasonably believed the disclosure to be a 'protected disclosure' within the meaning of s 43A of the ERA 1996: reg 30(4).

11

COMMON LAW OBLIGATIONS

A. Introduction

The issues considered in this chapter

A description of the law relating to business reorganisations would be **11.01** incomplete without a statement of the common law principles which may apply. The situation in which the common law is perhaps most likely to be of practical importance is where the employer has a policy of giving employees who are dismissed by reason of redundancy more by way of compensation for the loss of that employment than is required by the ERA 1996. The question whether the employer is obliged by the law of contract to give employees such enhanced redundancy payments will then arise. A subsidiary question which may arise where there is such a contractual obligation is whether the employer can lawfully dismiss for a reason other than redundancy an employee whose dismissal for redundancy would otherwise have occurred.

11.02 A second way in which the common law may affect a business reorganisation is in relation to the information given to employees about their rights in the circumstances.

11.03 The possibility of an employee claiming damages for personal injury arising from stress caused by the manner in which the employer treated the employee in the circumstances leading up to the employee's dismissal for redundancy is by no means fanciful. Accordingly, the principles applicable in that situation need to be mentioned. The relationship between the law of discrimination and the common law in that context is troublesome, and therefore also needs to be mentioned.

11.04 Several situations in which the common law may affect reorganisations in the public sector also need to be examined. One is where an employee (typically a senior employee) is employed under a fixed-term contract of employment and the employer agrees with the employee that, if the employee's contract of employment is not renewed at the end of the fixed term, then the employee will receive enhanced pension payments which are payable only where the employee is redundant or the employee's retirement is in the interests of the efficient discharge of the employer's functions. The question that will then arise is whether the employer's agreement to pay such enhanced payments was lawful.

11.05 A related question is whether a public sector employer's certification that an employee is redundant suffices to entitle the employee to enhanced pension payments under a statutory scheme where such payments are payable in the event of redundancy.

11.06 A final question which needs to be addressed is the potential impact on a public sector employer of guidance given by central government, and in particular the document entitled 'Staff Transfers in the Public Sector—Statement of Practice'.[1]

The effect at common law of a business transfer

11.07 Before those questions are considered, however, it is necessary to state the effect at common law of the transfer of the business in which an employee is employed. In *Nokes v Doncaster Amalgamated Collieries Ltd*,[2] the House of Lords held that 'without some statutory novation of the contract [of employment] the transfer of an undertaking from one employer to another automatically determines contracts of service'.[3] There is of course such novation where

---

[1] It is available, at <http://www.civilservice.gov.uk/publications/pdf/stafftransfers.pdf>.

[2] [1940] AC 1014.

[3] See the helpful summary of the effect of *Nokes* in *Secretary of State for Employment v Spence* [1986] ICR 651, 661, per Balcombe LJ, with whom Mustill and Stephen Brown LJJ agreed.

TUPE applies. Assuming that there is no such statutory novation, for example where TUPE does not apply, there will nevertheless be continuity of employment for all purposes between the two employments as a result of section 218(2) of the ERA 1996 if the employee accepts the change in the employer.[4]

B. The Contractual Effect of a Redundancy Policy

Introduction

A redundancy policy may be incorporated in a contract of employment by express reference. If it is so incorporated, then the question may arise whether an employee who is at risk of being dismissed for redundancy can validly be dismissed for some other reason. If it is not so incorporated, then the question may arise whether it has been impliedly incorporated by means of custom and practice. The latter question is addressed first. **11.08**

Custom and practice

The question whether an employee has acquired the right to an enhanced redundancy payment (ie a payment which is above the statutory minimum) where there is no express contractual right to such a payment was considered by the EAT in *Quinn v Calder Industrial Materials Ltd.*[5] There, the parent company of the employer (which was a member of a group of companies) had in 1987 issued a policy document containing guidelines on the making of redundancy payments above the amounts required by the Employment Protection (Consolidation) Act 1978. The terms of the policy were communicated neither to the employees of the members of the group, nor to their trade unions. Whenever staff had to be made redundant from 1986 until the summer of 1994 (and that happened on at least four occasions) they were paid in accordance with the terms of the policy document, although on each occasion the manager who authorised the payments had to obtain authorisation from his own managers before doing so. The employees claimed that the terms of the policy document had been implied into their contracts of employment, in part on the basis of custom and practice. The EAT noted that it had previously held, in *Duke v Reliance Systems,*[6] that: **11.09**

> A policy adopted by management unilaterally cannot become a term of the employees' contracts on the grounds that it is an established custom and practice unless it is at least shown that the policy has been drawn to the attention of the employees or has been followed without exception for a substantial period.

---

[4] See further para 4.29 above.   [5] [1996] IRLR 126.   [6] [1982] IRLR 347, para 9.

11.10 This is a somewhat weaker test than that which is normally thought to apply in relation to the implication of a term by custom and practice, the normal test being whether the term is reasonable, certain, and notorious, either within the locality or the relevant trade. It is of note that, in *Solectron Scotland Ltd v Roper*,[7] the EAT (Elias J presiding) commented that

> 21 . . . A custom or established practice applied with sufficient regularity may eventually become the source of an implied contractual term. That occurs where the point is reached when the courts are able to infer from the regular application of the practice that the parties must be taken to have accepted that the practice has crystallised into contractual rights.
>
> 22 The parties must be shown to be applying the term because there is a sense of legal obligation to do so. That will often be a difficult matter to prove. For example, if a practice is adopted because a party does so as a matter of policy rather than out of a sense of legal obligation, then it will not confer contractual rights: see *Young v Canadian Northern Railway Company* [1931] AC 32 (PC). Again the practice must be 'reasonable, notorious and certain': see *Devonald v Rosser & Sons* [1916] 2 KB 728 at 743, per Farwell LJ. In that case the employers contended that they could close their works where there was a lack of orders without making any payment to the employees. It was said that there was an established practice to that effect. The Court of Appeal rejected the argument. It met none of the criteria for a custom and practice. Farwell LJ said that:
>
>> 'It is neither reasonable nor certain because it is precarious depending on the will of the master.'

11.11 In *Quinn v Calder* the EAT held (in paragraph 7) that the test in *Duke v Reliance Systems* set out at the end of paragraph 11.09 above referred to factors which

> are likely to be among the most important circumstances to be taken into account, but they have to be taken into account along with all the other circumstances of the case. Thus, for example, in our view, the question is not whether the period for which a policy has been followed is 'substantial' in some abstract sense, but whether, in relation to the other circumstances, it is sufficient to support the inference that that policy has achieved the status of a contractual term. Again, with regard to communication, the question seems to us to be not so much whether the policy has been made or become known directly to the employees or through intermediaries, but whether the circumstances in which it was made or has become known support the inference that the employers intended to become contractually bound by it.

11.12 Accordingly, employees are likely to find it difficult to persuade a court or tribunal that their employers have conferred on them a contractual right to enhanced redundancy payments. The same reasoning will apply to any other

---

[7] [2004] IRLR 4.

claim that an employee has acquired a contractual right to something from his employer by reason of custom and practice.

Dismissing for a reason other than redundancy

Assuming that an employee has a contractual right to an enhanced redundancy **11.13** payment, it will not be open to the employer to dismiss the employee for another reason 'without justification'. This is the effect of the ruling of Elias J in *Jenvey v Australian Broadcasting Corporation*,[8] where he said:

> 26. . . . In redundancy situations, as with sickness, the employer may have promised to cater for the particular circumstances by conferring a benefit on the employee according to an established scheme. In my view there are circumstances where it would be contrary to the functioning of the redundancy scheme, and to its purpose, to permit the employer to exercise his contractual powers so as to deny the employee the very benefits which the scheme envisages will be paid. At the very least, it seems to me that where the employer has resolved to dismiss the employee by reason of redundancy, he should not without justification be entitled to defeat the employee's claim to compensation by dismissing him for some other independent reason, or indeed no reason at all. I would formulate the terms as follows:
>
> > 'Once an employer has determined that an employee will be dismissed by reason of redundancy, such that his dismissal for any other reason will defeat the employee's right to contractual benefits which accrue when the dismissal is by reason of redundancy, the employer may not lawfully dismiss the employee for any reason other than redundancy, unless the dismissal is for good cause.'
>
> In my opinion this term can readily be implied whether on the officious bystander or the business efficacy tests of implied contractual incorporation. (In practice, however, it is difficult to see in a redundancy situation what any good cause can be other than lawful summary dismissal.)
>
> 27 This term does not of course oblige the employer to dismiss for redundancy at all. He can change his mind and retain the employee in post. It simply requires that if he does dismiss, any such dismissal must, absent good cause, be for redundancy.

The possible limit of this fetter on the employer's power to dismiss for a reason **11.14** other than redundancy was helpfully stated by Elias J in paragraph 29 of his judgment, where he said:

> The term which I have found should be implied in this case is narrower than that formulated by [counsel for the claimant employee]. On his proposed implied term [namely 'to the effect that in the event of a redundancy situation arising, the contract would not be operated so as to remove the claimant's entitlement to

---

[8] [2003] ICR 79.

contactual redundancy benefits, save with good cause'], even if there had been no decision by the defendant to dismiss the particular claimant by reason of redundancy by the time his contract was in fact terminated, it would still have been unlawful for the claimant to have been dismissed once the redundancy situation had arisen, save for cause. [Counsel for the claimant] draws a direct analogy with the sickness cases to which I have referred. In those cases, as we have seen, the claimant may be protected from dismissal even when he is in the course of accruing his right to a long term sickness benefit. I would reserve my position on whether that wider term is to be implied in law. As I have said, it is in my view difficult to say that an individual accrues a redundancy payment in the way in which he does sickness entitlement, and the mere recognition that redundancies will be necessary may be too soon for any implied limitation on the power to dismiss to arise. Moreover, even if the employer could not lawfully dismiss (save for cause) whilst the selection of employees to be made was under active consideration, it may not necessarily follow that the damages would be the redundancy compensation. The employer will often be able to say that he might in good faith not have dismissed the employee by reason of redundancy at all because, for example, there are other volunteers, or it would have been cheaper to dismiss others. Accordingly, the employer may be able to rely upon the principle that the contract breaker should be treated as though he would have exercised his rights under the contract in a way most favourable to himself: see *Lavarack v Woods of Colchester Ltd* [1967] 1 QB 278. However, I reach no concluded view on this issue, which must await consideration on another day.

C. Obligations in Relation to Information

11.15 An employer will only rarely be liable at common law to employees in connection with the giving of, or failure to give, information to the employees in connection with a business reorganisation. The transferor was so liable on the facts of *Hagen v ICI Chemicals and Polymers Ltd*,[9] but the facts of the case were unusual, not least because, if the employees had not been persuaded to agree to the transfer of their employment, then the transfer would not have occurred.[10]

11.16 That case nevertheless made it clear that an employer may be liable for a negligent mis-statement made to an employee in connection with a TUPE transfer, as long as it causes the employee loss. The same must be true of any other statement made to an employee in connection with any other kind of business reorganisation.

11.17 However, as Elias J held, a statement would have to constitute 'wanton negligence bordering on recklessness or gross indifference' or 'demonstrate a

---

[9] [2002] IRLR 31, HC.

[10] See paras 47–49 of the judgment of Elias J. The effect in the circumstances of that unusual factor is stated in para 50 of that judgment.

real and unacceptable disregard for the interests of the employee' before it could properly be said to constitute a breach of the implied term of trust and confidence.[11]

Further, a mere statement of opinion that it would be in the employee's best **11.18** interests for example to transfer to the employment of a TUPE transferee would be highly unlikely to (and did not in *Hagen*[12]) give rise to a breach of any duty of care. As Elias J said in *Hagen*:[13]

> When giving advice of this nature, which is not objectively capable of being analysed as right or wrong, the only question is whether the management could reasonably give that advice in the light of the circumstances as they reasonably perceived them to be.[14]

D. Damages for Personal Injury Caused by Stress

The general principles

An employee may claim that personal injury has been caused by the stress of **11.19** knowing that he or she may be, or is to be, made redundant. Assuming that such stress was caused at least in part by the circumstances existing before the dismissal, so that the stress was not caused solely by the dismissal itself (in which case the stress could not give rise to a valid claim for damages for personal injury[15]), a claim for damages for personal injury could be made.

However, such a claim would be unlikely to be successful. Naturally, the **11.20** strength of the claim would depend on the circumstances. Nevertheless, given that the approach of the Court of Appeal in *Hatton v Sutherland*[16] concerning an employer's duty of care was specifically affirmed (albeit with some qualification) by the Court of Appeal in *Hartman v South Essex Mental Health and Community Care NHS Trust*[17] despite the successful appeal to the House of Lords in one of the cases which was joined in *Hatton* (*Barber v Somerset County Council*[18]), and given that there will be reasonable and proper cause for putting an employee under the stress of knowing that he or she may be made redundant, such a claim would be unlikely to succeed unless there were something

---

[11] See paras 311 and 55, respectively.   [12] See paras 96–103 and 257.
[13] Para 257.
[14] It is of interest that Elias J went on to say in the same paragraph: 'Whilst I accept that there may on occasion have been some over-enthusiasm in transmitting that message, I do not believe that it rendered the advice negligent.'
[15] See *Johnson v Unisys Ltd* [2001] UKHL 13; [2003] 1 AC 518, as interpreted in *Eastwood v Magnox Electric plc* [2004] UKHL 35; [2005] 1 AC 503.
[16] [2002] EWCA Civ 76; [2002] ICR 613.   [17] [2005] EWCA Civ 6; [2005] ICR 782.
[18] [2004] UKHL 13; [2004] ICR 457.

more than the norm in the circumstances. This would be so even if the employee were known by the employer to be vulnerable to either psychiatric injury or stress-induced illnesses.

The impact of the law of discrimination

11.21 An employee may claim that his or her dismissal was tainted by unlawful discrimination and that that discrimination caused personal injury. Such a claim is, according to the Court of Appeal's decision in *Sheriff v Klyne Tugs (Lowestoft) Ltd*[19] (applying *Henderson v Henderson*[20] to the circumstances), capable of being made only in the discrimination proceedings. In *Sheriff,* a claim for damages for personal injury arising from negligence was struck out because it could have been made in the employment tribunal proceedings on the basis that it was a claim 'which the parties, exercising reasonable diligence, might have brought forward at the time'.[21]

11.22 It is at least arguable that the Court of Appeal's ruling in *Sheriff* is inconsistent with what was said by the House of Lords in *Eastwood v Magnox Electric plc.*[22] There, in paragraph 30, Lord Nicholls, with whom Lord Hoffman, Lord Rodger, and Lord Brown agreed, said this:

> If identifying the boundary between the common law rights and remedies and the statutory rights and remedies is comparatively straightforward, the same cannot be said of the practical consequences of this unusual boundary. Particularly in cases concerning financial loss flowing from psychiatric illnesses, some of the practical consequences are far from straightforward or desirable. The first and most obvious drawback is that in such cases the division of remedial jurisdiction between the court and an employment tribunal will lead to duplication of proceedings. In practice there will be cases where the employment tribunal and the court each traverse much of the same ground in deciding the factual issues before them, with attendant waste of resources and costs.

However, whether *Sheriff* is properly to be regarded as being inconsistent with *Eastwood* has yet to be decided.

11.23 In the meantime, it is of note that the Court of Appeal has relatively recently, in *London Borough of Enfield v Sivanandan*,[23] confirmed the continuing validity of *Sheriff*. It is of interest that *Eastwood* may not have been relied on by the

---

[19] [1999] ICR 1170.   [20] [1843] 3 Hare 100.
[21] See [1999] ICR 1170, 1180, para 23; the quoted words are from the extract from *Henderson* which is set out in that paragraph.
[22] [2004] UKHL 35; [2005] 1 AC 503.
[23] [2005] EWCA Civ 10; The Times, 25 January 2005.

claimant in *Sivanandan* in connection with this issue.[24] It is also of note that, in *Friend v Civil Aviation Authority*,[25] the Court of Appeal declined to apply *Henderson v Henderson* to a claim for damages for (among other things) breach of the implied term of trust and confidence where the employee had already claimed unfair dismissal and succeeded on liability, but lost on compensation since it was held that he had contributed 100 per cent to his dismissal.

Friend was not cited in *Sivanandan*. However, *Sheriff* was not cited in *Friend*. **11.24** Nevertheless, the decision in *Sivanandan* that the claim was an abuse of process was obiter.[26] *Sivanandan* therefore should not be regarded as a complete bar (or in some circumstances any bar) to a claim which concerns the same facts as those which were the subject of litigation in employment tribunal proceedings.

E. Some Public Law Considerations

An employer such as a local authority may enter into an agreement with one or **11.25** more of its employees that they will receive enhanced redundancy payments in the event of redundancy. If there is a detailed statutory regime governing the amounts which may be paid in the event of redundancy, as there was in *Allsop v North Tyneside Metropolitan Borough Council*,[27] then it is likely that an agreement entered into to pay more than such amounts would be unlawful.

However, this would not preclude a local authority from agreeing to make **11.26** relatively generous payments in compensation for the loss of particular contractual entitlements. Such an agreement would be likely to be invalid only if it was irrationally generous to the employee or employees in question.[28] Even if it were invalid, the effect would be that the original rights persisted.[29]

Similarly, it is likely that a local authority could properly fetter its discretion **11.27** in relation to the number of years of additional pension rights which it will grant an employee when the employee's fixed-term contract of employment ends (there being a discretion under the Local Government Pension Scheme Regulations 1997[30] to grant additional pension rights). Support for this proposition can be found in *R v Hammersmith London Borough Council, ex parte Beddowes*,[31] where Fox LJ said:

---

[24] *Eastwood* was relied on by the claimant in *Sivanandan*, but apparently only in connection with a different issue: *Eastwood* was referred to only in paras 76–78 of the judgment of the Court of Appeal in *Sivanandan*, which concerned a different issue.

[25] [2002] ICR 525.

[26] See paras 125–142 of the judgment of Wall LJ, with whom Buxton and Peter Gibson LJJ agreed.

[27] [1992] ICR 639, CA.   [28] *Newbold v Leicester City Council* [1999] ICR 1182, CA.

[29] ibid.   [30] SI 1997/1612.   [31] [1987] QB 1050, 1064.

> If a statutory power is lawfully exercised so as to create legal rights and obligations between the council and third parties, the result will be that the council for the time being is bound, even though that hinders or prevents the exercise of other statutory powers.[32]

11.28　In *Whitewater Leisure Management Ltd v Franklin*,[33] it was argued on the basis of *Allsop* that a local authority's 'redundancy scheme for payment over and above the statutory redundancy payment as calculated under the Employment Rights Act was ultra vires, and thus unenforceable by way of a claim for breach of contract against the new employer' (to whom the employee's contract of employment was transferred under TUPE). The submission was that

> a blanket policy on the part of [the authority] to pay the enhanced redundancy payment to employees who were dismissed by reason of redundancy was not a proper exercise of that authority's discretion. The operation of such a blanket policy takes away the proper exercise of discretion.

11.29　It was in addition submitted that 'the authority's discretion to make the increased redundancy payment can only arise as and when a person is dismissed by reason of redundancy' and that the policy was as a result ultra vires. The EAT regarded these arguments as 'wholly misconceived'.

11.30　In any event, an invalid agreement to terminate a contract of employment on a certain date may nevertheless have some effect. That occurred in *Eastbourne Borough Council v Foster*,[34] where the employee was employed by a local authority as its director of environmental services. When the authority decided to reorganise its operations and abolish the environmental services department, the authority agreed with the employee that he would be placed on 'garden leave' from 10 February 1999 until 31 August 1999, although during that time he would be available to give assistance to anyone who, acting on behalf of the authority, wanted it from him. That agreement was held by the Court of Appeal to have been ultra vires and therefore void, but the court also decided that 'the relationship and status of employment continued'.[35] The court went on to hold that the relationship of employment came to an end on 31 August 1999, although it remitted to the court below the question of the effect of the continued employment to that date.

11.31　Further, the imposition by Parliament of a cap on the amount of a gratuity to be paid in the event of retirement would not necessarily make unlawful retrospectively an agreement which was entered into before Parliament intervened,

---

[32] See too at 1065, per Fox LJ and 1076, per Sir Denys Buckley.
[33] EAT/964/98. The case is not available on the EAT website, but it is available at <www.bailii.org>.
[34] [2002] ICR 234, CA.　　[35] See para 35, per Rix LJ.

even though the effect of the agreement was that the gratuity would be paid after the new cap came into force.[36]

F. Pensions: The Sufficiency of a Public Body's Certificate

A further issue to which reference needs to be made in this chapter is the **11.32** sufficiency or otherwise of a certificate given by a public body under the terms of a statute or statutory instrument governing a pension scheme that a certain state of affairs (usually including redundancy) exists. The question will then arise whether that certificate is conclusive or whether it is open to the body which is responsible for the administration of the pension scheme (and therefore a court) to go behind that certificate and decide that the state of affairs does not exist, or did not exist at the material time.

In *Teachers' Pensions Agency v Hill*,[37] Sullivan J held that an employer's **11.33** notification for the purposes of the Teachers' Superannuation (Consolidation) Regulations 1988[38] (which have now been superseded by the Teachers' Pensions Regulations 1997[39]) was only a necessary, but not a sufficient, condition for the employee to become entitled to an early retirement pension which could properly be granted only where the employer had terminated his employment by reason of redundancy or in the interests of the efficient discharge of the employer's functions. As Sullivan J said:

> No doubt the employer's view as to whether, and if so why, a person's employment had been terminated is persuasive and helpful, in that in the great majority of cases the agency will be able to accept the notification at its face value rather than have to conduct its own inquiries, but there is no obvious reason why it should be conclusive, particularly if a question of law is involved.

This makes sense in relation to the termination of an employee's contract by **11.34** reason of redundancy. It is, however, a little difficult to see how for example the Teachers' Pensions Agency could discern whether or not the termination of a teacher's employment was in the interests of the efficient discharge of the employer's functions. That is therefore likely to be determinable mainly by reference to the employer's perception of the situation, although a decision which was plainly made in bad faith would clearly be unlawful and therefore not determinative.

---

[36] *Nicholls v Greenwich London Borough Council* [2003] ICR 1020, CA.
[37] [1999] ICR 435, 443–444.   [38] SI 1988/1652.   [39] SI 1997/3001.

G. The Impact of Government Policy Statements on Public Bodies

11.35   Finally, it is necessary to consider the effect of a statement made by central government because of the issue by the Government in 2000 of a document entitled 'Staff Transfers in the Public Sector—Statement of Practice'.[40] It includes the following statement:[41]

- contracting-out exercises with the private sector and voluntary organisations and transfers between different parts of the public sector, will be conducted on the basis that staff will transfer and TUPE should apply, unless there are genuinely exceptional reasons not to do so;

- this includes second and subsequent round contracts that result in a new contractor and where a function is brought back into a public sector organisation where, in both cases, when the contract was first awarded staff transferred from the public sector;

- in circumstances where TUPE does not apply in strict legal terms to certain types of transfer between different parts of the public sector, the principles of TUPE should be followed (where possible using legislation to effect the transfer) and the staff involved should be treated no less favourably than had the Regulations applied; and

- there should be appropriate arrangements to protect occupational pensions, redundancy and severance terms of staff in all these types of transfer.

11.36   This cannot have the effect that TUPE applies where it would not otherwise apply. It also cannot require a public authority such as a local authority to act in the manner described. However, even though it is non-statutory guidance, the public body in question would be obliged at least to take it into account properly, although it would not need to apply it slavishly. This is the effect of the line of cases including *R v Police Complaints Board, ex parte Madden*.[42] There, a slavish following of guidance issued by the Secretary of State, to which the Complaints Board was obliged by statute to 'have regard', was quashed. The guidance referred to the approach taken by the Director of Public Prosecutions in relation to disciplinary charges, and it was held that the Board had acted unlawfully and in any event had fettered its discretion by allowing itself to be bound by the approach of the Director of Public Prosecutions in relation to disciplinary charges. Similarly, in *De Falco v Crawley Borough Council*,[43] the Court of Appeal ruled that guidance to which the respondent local authority was under a duty to 'have regard' was of no direct statutory force or effect, and that the authority was not bound to follow it in any particular case.[44]

---

[40] It is available, at <http://www.civilservice.gov.uk/publications/pdf/stafftransfers.pdf>.
[41] At p 3.   [42] [1983] 2 All ER 353.   [43] [1980] QB 460.
[44] ibid, 482 and 478.

In any event, the Government's Statement of Practice is likely to tip the balance **11.37** in favour of the application of TUPE only rarely. Where TUPE does not apply, the Statement of Practice may as a matter of practice cause a public sector employer to act as if it did. The circumstances in which that might happen are outside the scope of this book.

INDEX